INHERITING THE TRADE

*A Northern Family Confronts Its Legacy
as the Largest Slave-Trading Dynasty in U.S. History*

THOMAS NORMAN DEWOLF

BEACON PRESS, BOSTON

Beacon Press
25 Beacon Street
Boston, Massachusetts 02108-2892
www.beacon.org

Beacon Press books
are published under the auspices of
the Unitarian Universalist Association of Congregations.

12 11 10 09 8 7 6 5 4 3 2 1

This book is printed on acid-free paper that meets the uncoated
paper ANSI/NISO specifications for permanence as revised in 1992.

Text design and composition by Wilsted & Taylor Publishing Services

Library of Congress Cataloging-in-Publication Data

DeWolf, Thomas Norman
   Inheriting the trade : a northern family confronts its legacy as the
largest slave-trading dynasty in U.S. history / Thomas Norman DeWolf.
      p. cm.
   Includes bibliographical references.
   ISBN 978-0-8070-7282-0
   1. Slave traders—New England—Biography. 2. DeWolf, Charles, b. 1695
—Family. 3. DeWolf, Thomas Norman, 1954—Family. 4. New England—
Biography. 5. Slave trade—New England—History. 6. Slave trade—Africa,
West—History. 7. Slave trade—Cuba—History. 8. DeWolf, Thomas
Norman, 1954—Travel—New England. 9. DeWolf, Thomas Norman,
1954—Travel—Africa, West. 10. DeWolf, Thomas Norman, 1954—
Travel—Cuba. I. Title.

   F3.D48 2008
   306.3'620974—dc22   2007019708

For my grandchildren,
Seth and Allison

And for your grandchildren

May you embrace the things you fear
in order to awaken your heart

CONTENTS

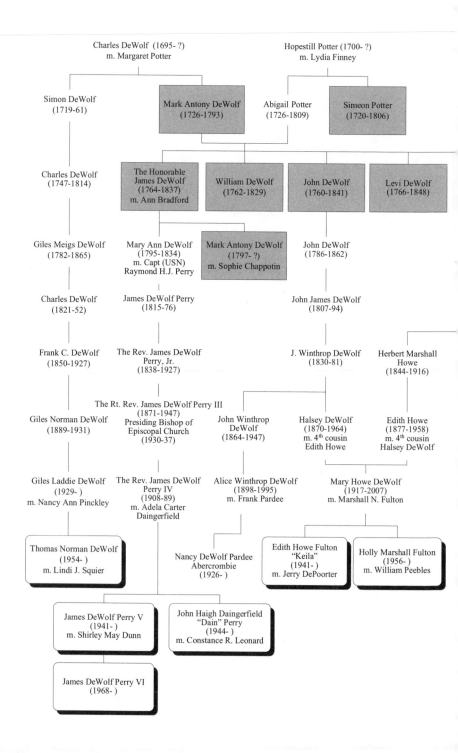

Abbreviated DeWolf Family Tree
(limited to those directly connected to *Inheriting the Trade*)

Shaded boxes indicate family members involved in the slave trade
or related business dealings.
Rounded boxes indicate Family of Ten.

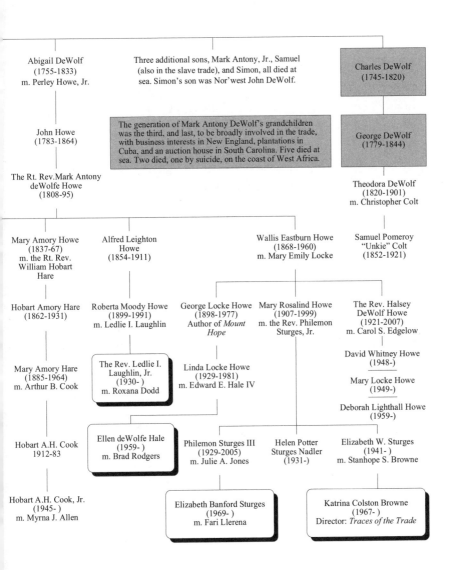

Your high independence only reveals the immeasurable distance between us. The blessings in which you, this day, rejoice, are not enjoyed in common. The rich inheritance of justice, liberty, prosperity and independence, bequeathed by your fathers, is shared by you, not by me. The sunlight that brought light and healing to you, has brought stripes and death to me. This Fourth of July is yours, not mine.

—FREDERICK DOUGLASS, JULY 4, 1852

PREFACE

Everyone has secrets—shameful episodes in our past that we try to keep buried. Heaven forbid that anyone should find out. What would people say? This book is about one family's secret: my family's. It is also about an American secret of which too few are fully aware.

When I was a child, I was taught with pride about our Founding Fathers. I reveled in hearing the patriotic stories about George Washington and Thomas Jefferson. I imagined myself carrying on their legacy and basked in their glory. I share the human inclination to believe that the noble acts of our ancestors are reflected in who we are today. If new information tarnishes those stories, our pride tends to diminish. What I've learned in the last few years challenges the stories I grew up with.

During the summer of 2001, I traveled to New England, West Africa, and Cuba with Katrina Browne and eight other distant cousins to retrace the steps of our ancestors—the DeWolfs—who were active in the slave trade. Katrina had decided to make a documentary feature film, *Traces of the Trade: A Story from the Deep North,* and the memoir you now hold is my story about not only that journey but about what comes after.

I learned new truths about myself, my ancestors, and the founding of the United States, and that it's impossible to think constructively, and honestly, about race without simultaneously examining issues involving gender, class, and privilege. I learned that slavery wasn't limited to the South: black people were enslaved in the North for over two hundred years, the vast majority of all U.S. slave *trading* was done by northerners, and, astonishingly, half of all those voyages originated in Rhode Island. Compromises made by my childhood heroes ensured that slavery would continue as the driving force in our nation's economy. Throughout this country's history, white people have benefited as a direct result of the riches in land, money, and prestige that were gained because of slavery.

A question that white people sometimes ask each other about black people in regard to slavery is "Why can't they just get over it?" During our journey, several African Americans provided a terse and accurate response: "Because it's not over."

Even after the Civil War, blacks were prevented from becoming equal citizens through Jim Crow laws, racial violence, lynching, and various other forms of terror and discrimination. Though civil and voting rights laws were adopted in the 1960s, the pecking order that has been in place for hundreds of years—with major disparities between blacks and whites in terms of education, housing, employment, health care, and treatment within and by the criminal justice system—continues.

It's easy to agree that slavery prior to the Civil War was wrong. It's much more difficult for whites to reflect on the systemic racism that lingers today. In my experience, one of the major impediments to discussing the legacy of slavery is that the subject is so overwhelming. My hope is that focusing on one family's history will help readers get a better grasp on it, so that we can all begin an honest dialogue about race in the United States.

Our nation was founded on the ideals of equality and freedom, but these "unalienable rights" have never been secured once and for all for all people. It is a perpetual struggle, an ongoing journey. The journey you are about to embark upon began when nine people responded to an invitation. It altered my life. I invite you to join us.

CHAPTER 1

GROWING UP WHITE

"Here we are," says Katrina Browne, leaning forward in her chair with a welcoming smile. She appears calm for someone haunted by ghosts.

Her eyes flit from face to face and her smile gives way to a tiny laugh. Today is July 1, 2001. Nine of us, four men and five women, sit in a circle of chairs on the back porch of a white clapboard house near Bristol, Rhode Island. The house is surrounded by trees and bushes so thick I can't tell how close the nearest neighbors live. I feel detached from the rest of the world. The only sounds intruding upon the silence are those we make, and those of the birds. I can smell the ocean from here.

These people are my distant cousins. I met most of them for the first time earlier this morning at church and have met Katrina once before. She looks cool in her short hair and sleeveless blouse despite the summer heat. A trickle of sweat slithers down inside my long-sleeved shirt, tickling my right side. I discreetly brush my bicep against my ribcage to stem the current and then wipe droplets from my forehead with my fingers.

Katrina's calm vanishes as she begins to speak about why we

are here: how she learned from her grandmother about her slave-trading ancestors, and decided to make a documentary film that will expose the horror of our family's past. I don't know if it's the subject matter, the camera, speaking in front of us, or simply the culmination of more than three years of work and anticipation on her part, but Katrina now appears fragile and troubled. She speaks in a hushed voice for many minutes, pausing, stopping, looking down at her fidgeting hands, then up at some of us.

Finally, she sits in silence. A voice interrupts from the side. "Can you do it again?" Jude Ray, the film's codirector, says she needs to be more concise and make her voice stronger.

Liz Dory, the director of photography, shoulders the professional-grade video camera focused in close-up on Katrina's face. Jeff Livesey, the sound man, holds the boom microphone above her head. We have Liz to thank for our seating in direct sunlight. A large umbrella was removed because the shadows fouled up her shots. It's supposed to get up to about ninety today, but it feels much hotter. Jude, Liz, and Jeff stand with the confident air of people who've been on many film sets.

"Umm, I . . ." Tears well up in Katrina's eyes. The corners of her mouth begin to turn up in a smile, but drop as she looks down again. The glowing red light on the camera indicates that Liz continues to record.

One of the men in the group rises, spreads his arms, and smiles. "How about a group hug?" This is Dain Perry. Dressed in khaki shorts, a light shirt, and broad-brimmed straw hat to shade his head, he appears to be in his mid-fifties. I exhale the breath I've been holding, glad that Dain has broken the tension. Dark patches of sweat dot his shirt as well. We all stand and embrace, resting our arms around each others' shoulders or waists for several silent moments. Though Dain's gesture seems intended to support Katrina, this feels like the first time we've all actually connected.

When we sit back down, the tears fall from Katrina's eyes. She explains that when she was in her late twenties she read a booklet about her family history written by her grandmother. She hesitates and looks down again. "It's hard and scary to know that one is connected to evil people. There was so much family pride."

Now she felt far from proud. She could not say out loud to anyone that she was descended from slave traders. "And, um..." She looks again from face to face. She wipes her tears, takes a deep breath, and smiles. Her voice becomes stronger.

She explains that the intense part was not just the shock of discovering her slave-trading ancestry, but the realization that on some level she knew already but had buried it. "I prided myself on being self-aware and self-reflective in thinking about issues of race and society and yet I had managed to completely repress the fact that I was descended from slave traders."

Her voice becomes more animated as she explains that in reading the booklet, "I just knew instantly that I already knew. But I have no idea when I first found out, how I found out, who told me, how I reacted, and yet this is a pretty big deal. So I started asking questions about our family and about this buried history of New England." She explains that she started out on a solo journey but realized it needed to be a family process. She is honored that we've chosen to join her.

"A lot of people who aren't here are totally supportive," says Elly, another cousin who flew from the west coast to be here. Elly works for the Environmental Protection Agency in Seattle, monitoring Superfund Sites. Like me, she's never met any of these people before. Her long, dark hair is held back in a ponytail.

Elly's right. Many family members Katrina contacted, as well as friends and colleagues, of hers and ours, applaud her efforts. There are also people who oppose the project. Some live in Bristol, and indeed, some are family members.

The oldest of the women present—about sixty, not quite twice Katrina's age—introduces herself with careful and deliberate words.

I sense a burden even heavier than the one Katrina bears. With no hint of a smile, she looks off into the distance and then down at the deck as she begins to speak. "Well, my name today is Keila De-Poorter. I say 'today' because when I was young I was christened Edith Howe Fulton. I'm Holly's oldest sister." She smiles at the woman sitting next to her. "She's the youngest in the family and I'm the oldest. Changing my name, which I did back in 1975, was part of my effort to move away from family. I was named after my grandmother Edith Howe, and I adored her. But carrying that name felt like this heavy thing for me when I was young. It had a lot of nonverbal expectation."

Like Katrina, Keila continues to shift her gaze back and forth from the patio deck to us as she speaks. "I grew up here in Bristol. My grandparents had a dairy farm across the street from where we lived and I don't ever remember not just being in love with animals. I lived from one summer to the next. We lived in Providence in the wintertime, which I suffered through to go back to Bristol, to go back to the farm. That's where my heart was, on the land, with the animals.

"When I was ten years old I would get up at four-thirty in the morning to help with morning milking. I loved working with the farmers. They felt so real to me. They weren't playing this strange game that my family played that I just could not identify with." Elizabeth, the youngest of the women, nods and smiles. "There were times when I used to think, 'I wish I was an animal, I don't like being a human being. I don't like seeing what grown-ups do.' "

I sit to Keila's right with crossed legs, my hands folded in my lap.

"My life has felt like a struggle because I love my family so much." She says she's always felt "pushed–pulled," a phrase I've never heard before but know exactly what she means. Looking down, Keila tilts her head and a smile begins to form as she tells us that one of the unwritten rules in her family was something called the No Talk Rule.

Holly lifts her hands from her knees and with an exaggerated expression mouths the words, "It's big..."

Keila chuckles and nods her head in agreement with her sister. "It's very big. You don't talk about unpleasant things. There's a line in one of our family books that one of our ancestors said, that we should never talk about sex. What were the others?" She looks to Holly.

"Religion."

"Religion," Keila repeats.

"I think politics," says Holly.

"Right," says Keila. "And the last one was 'and the Negroes.'"

I look from face to face as people nod and chuckle uncomfortably. What am I doing here? Though I am distantly related, I'm the only one here who isn't descended from slave traders, not directly anyway. I feel another trickle of sweat, on my left side this time.

———•—•———

This place is foreign to me. I live in Bend, Oregon, about as far from Bristol as you can get, and not just geographically. How have I ended up with this group of virtual strangers, speaking about such unpleasant things?

Twenty years ago, David Howe, a friend of mine, told me he suspected we might be related because his father's middle name is DeWolf. He was right. My wife, Lindi, and I first met David's father in 1986. Halsey DeWolf Howe and his wife, Carol, invited us to spend the night with them on our way through Massachusetts on our honeymoon. After dinner, Halsey explained my connection to David.

"Your father and David are sixth cousins, as you can see here." He pointed to a name at the top of the genealogy chart he'd created to delineate my relationship to David. "Charles DeWolf is the common ancestor. He was born in 1695 and probably died in Guadeloupe in the West Indies. Our line descends from one of his sons, Mark Antony DeWolf. You descend from his older brother, Simon."

Halsey grew up in Bristol, as have generations of Mark Antony DeWolf's descendants. They used to gather at one of the old DeWolf mansions, Linden Place, for a family reunion each year to watch the Fourth of July parade. Halsey regaled me all evening with stories of a time and place long past, filled with eccentric characters. He began with James DeWolf, the man most responsible for the family's fame and fortune.

"Captain Jim was a true scoundrel in every sense of the word. He was a slave trader, rum runner, and privateer." Visions of the Disneyland ride Pirates of the Caribbean entered my mind. James DeWolf became a United States senator and amassed a fortune from his adventurous exploits.

Linden Place was built by James's nephew George DeWolf. George's daughter, Theodora, married Christopher Colt, the brother of Samuel Colt, who invented the revolver. There were once several mansions in Bristol owned by the family, but only Linden Place remains standing today.

Mark Antony's grandson "Nor'west" John DeWolf sailed from Bristol around South America and north along the coast of the Oregon Territory in 1805 to Vancouver Island and Alaska on a fur-trading mission. He sold his ship and traversed the fifty-five hundred miles overland across Siberia from east to west. He then sailed back home to Bristol.[1] He wed Mary Melville and became uncle to young Herman, whose imagination was stirred by the seafaring tales of his uncle "Nor'west" John. Melville had his own adventures at sea before eventually writing *Moby Dick*, where "Captain D'Wolf" appears in chapter 45. (D'Wolf was an alternate spelling of DeWolf.)

William DeWolf Hopper, who played Paul Drake on the *Perry Mason* television series, boasted ties to Bristol through his father and grandmother. (William's mother was the notorious gossip columnist Hedda Hopper.) Theodora and Christopher Colt's grandson furnished the other notable theatrical connection when he married the famous actress Ethel Barrymore, who once lived at Linden Place. Listening to Halsey, I felt like a child sitting enthralled at the feet of a master storyteller. Throughout that night, and for months after, I focused not on the more unsavory acts of my newly discovered relatives, but on the fact that I was related to Hoppers, Colts, Barrymores, and Melvilles. I became obsessed with genealogy and making connections with distant cousins, dead or alive, famous or not.

———•——

In December 2000, David received a letter from Katrina, who is the daughter of his cousin Libby, and shared it with me.

Dear kith and kin,

I'm writing with information and invitations related to the documentary film project I have embarked upon about our mutual DeWolf ancestors and the slave trade.

Two and a half years ago I decided to produce a documentary about the DeWolfs, the role of New England in slavery, and the legacy of all this in the present. For all the progress that has been made in race relations and racial equality, the disparity in social opportunity and life prospects is still huge and the lack of trust still profound between blacks and whites.

So I want to begin with our family and try to better understand the whole can of worms: privilege, shelteredness, productive feelings of guilt, unproductive feelings of guilt, fear, etc.

I would like to invite fellow descendants to do the journey with me—literally, as well as existentially. I will be organizing a 3-part journey: 1) a gathering in Rhode Island; 2) then a trip to Cuba and West Africa; which 3) will culminate back in Rhode Island again.

I invite you to think about the possibility of participating in these gatherings and voyages.

I had never heard of Katrina Browne and didn't know how we were related, but was amazed by her letter. At David's suggestion, I called Katrina. In February 2001, Lindi and I drove from Bend to her apartment in Berkeley, where she had attended seminary, to discuss her project. Though she hadn't sent me the letter, she asked me to participate in the journey because she thought I could bring a unique perspective: that of a family member whose direct ancestors were not slave traders.

Once I agreed to go, doubts began to surface. Katrina sought to confront the legacy of slavery and its impact on relations between black and white Americans today. The fact was that my interaction with black people was limited. I grew up in Pomona, California, which had a sizable African American population, but the last time I interacted regularly with black people was in the late 1960s at Palomares Junior High School. Though we shared classes, acted together in school plays, went to dances, and played sports together, my most powerful memories were of fear. This was shortly after the Watts Riots in Los Angeles and race relations were tense. I was never attacked by any black classmates, though I was threatened several times. I always backed down, quite willing to appear weak if it helped me avoid a bloody nose.

There were plenty of fights between blacks and whites at school, both during school hours and after school, and at the park up the street. I remember the afternoon when everyone knew Larry and Greg were going to fight. Their battle had been brewing for weeks. Larry was surrounded by black kids urging him on just like Greg was encouraged by white kids. A huge crowd gathered outside by the lockers after school.

Greg and Larry came from opposite directions. Greg barely removed his jacket before Larry punched him hard in the face and knocked him over a bench. Greg sprung up to fight back but was no match for the quicker black boy. The fight lasted mere moments be-

fore police intervened. It was as if they had been watching from behind the lockers, as if they knew in advance. Larry soon sat hand-
cuffed in the back of a police car. He stared straight ahead, his jaw
rigid, head held high.

As the crowd dispersed, I watched Greg walk away with his
friends, a rag held to his bloody face. I couldn't understand why the
police only arrested Larry. I didn't ask.

By 1969, Martin Luther King's call for nonviolent protest and
reconciliation between the races was a distant memory as far as I
was concerned. I recall police in full riot gear patrolling the halls of
my school almost every day. My parents worried for our safety, so
my father began picking up my sister and me after school. Ninth
grade became my last in public schools. I had tried to make friends
with black classmates, but three years at Palomares taught me that
for the most part, two separate planets circled within the larger
school solar system: blacks hung out with other blacks and whites
with whites.

My parents enrolled us at Western Christian High School, a
private parochial school, where there were no black students, and
we moved several miles from Pomona to Glendora, where there
were fewer black people. Racial tension, and its accompanying fear,
disappeared from my life like spilled water on the hot California
sidewalk.

———————

In spite of a few unpleasant incidents, I recall my childhood with
great fondness. I watched *Leave It to Beaver* on television, and lived
a sheltered *Leave It to Beaver* life. I spent long summer days at the
beach, played games with my friends, and cheered for the Dodgers.
We attended First Christian Church in Pomona every Sunday. My
parents were married there in 1951 and still attend today. My closest friends in junior high and high school were kids at First Chris-

tian, many of whom were also fellow members of Boy Scout Troop 102, which was sponsored by our church.

Two of those friends, Mitchell and Michael, were twins and biracial. Their mother was Italian and their father was black. Race didn't seem to enter the equation with them. Though their skin was darker than mine, we were simply friends. I never understood why many of my black classmates at school were so angry, not to mention the black people I saw on the news. I remember wondering why race relations couldn't be easy, like I assumed my relationships with Mitch and Mike were. As I think about it now, I realize I was too young and naive, and perhaps self-absorbed, to ever ask Mitch and Mike how they felt about it.

In September 1972, I moved a thousand miles north from my parents' home to the dorms at Northwest Christian College in Eugene, Oregon. I saw very few black students on my college campus, and the majority weren't African American—they were African. Battles at NCC were over interpretation of Bible verses, not race relations. I got married in 1974 and my wife gave birth to our two daughters.

I spent six years—instead of the normal four—in undergraduate studies at both NCC and the University of Oregon, which stand adjacent to each other. After graduating from both in 1978, I moved to Bend, in Central Oregon, where I owned and managed a movie theater and restaurant and where I met David Howe. I divorced and remarried. I was elected to the city council in 1992, and to the county commission—as a Republican—in 1998, the job I would hold until 2005. I saw few black people anywhere in Oregon. I thought less and less about the tension I once felt between blacks and whites. It was no longer part of my world.

I was excited to join Katrina to further investigate my family ancestry and to travel to Africa and Cuba. I looked forward to becoming more global in my thinking and awareness, but I was simultaneously anxious. This was going to be an expensive journey where I'd confront issues that I recognized more and more I'd rather not deal with. My anxiety was prescient. My exposure to issues of race would change dramatically in 2001—and in unimagined ways for which my life hadn't prepared me.

CHAPTER 2

"FRAIL LIMB'D, WELL FED, AND SPEAKS GOOD ENGLISH"

Deborah Howe, David's sister, picked me up when I flew into Boston's Logan Airport yesterday and drove me the sixty-five miles south to where I would meet my fellow travelers. Deb drove around Bristol, Rhode Island, showing me some key sites in connection with our DeWolf ancestry. Eventually, she pulled up and parked in front of a new townhouse not far from Bristol Harbor, the home of Nancy Abercrombie, another distant cousin, where I am a guest this week.

My roommate at Nancy's, and for the entire journey, is Ledlie Laughlin. The three of us walked to the Lobster Pot restaurant overlooking the harbor for dinner last night. Like Halsey Howe, Ledlie is a retired Episcopal priest. He began his career in 1956 at a parish in Jersey City, where most of the congregants were African American. After six years he was called to the Cathedral in Newark, where his congregation was mostly white. His next parish was St. Luke's in Greenwich Village, with a largely gay congregation. He spent twenty years there before moving to Florence, Italy, where the pews of St. James were filled each week by many American women who went to Florence to study history or art and ended up with Italian husbands. Ledlie joked that they needed an English-speaking place of solace in the midst of challenges presented by the city and their mothers-in-law.

Nancy and Ledlie last saw each other in 1950 or 1951, before Ledlie went to college to become a priest. "I remember thinking that you had the look of God in your eyes," Nancy recalled.

———•·•———

I walked alone this morning from Nancy's home to St. Michael's. The ten-minute stroll offered what I anticipated would be my only moments of solitude today. Arriving before eight-thirty, I paused across the street to take in the impressive gothic church built of large, brown stone blocks. Closest to the corner, a square bell tower looms high over the street. Large clocks face out from each side. Spires extend above each of its four corners. Below the tower, a small cross crowns the steep roof. Three stained-glass windows rise above the entry.

From the anonymous safety of my corner curb, I watched a woman in front of the church attach a camera to a tripod and saw two balding men walk up the street and stop at the bottom of the church steps. After watching them chat for a few minutes with a woman holding a clipboard, I said, under my breath, "Okay, here we go," and, crossing the street over the red, white, and blue center line, extended my hand to the taller of the two and said, "I'm going to guess you're part of Katrina's project. I'm Tom DeWolf."

"We are," he said. "I'm Jim Perry. This is my brother Dain."

Moments after I shook hands with Dain, Ledlie arrived. I said to the other men, "How come I'm the only one wearing a tie? Do you know something I don't?"

"Just trying to stay cool," said Dain. The temperature has been quickly rising.

Holly and Keila soon walked up and introduced themselves, followed by Elizabeth and Elly. We stood chatting on the wide sidewalk at the foot of the church steps until a familiar woman in a bright-orange blouse crossed the street toward us.

"Boy, I figured if anyone was going to be late..." said Dain, laughing.

"Hi," said Katrina, feigning sheepishness as she first hugged Jim and then the rest of us.

The service was scheduled for nine o'clock. We sat together on hard wooden pews. Stained-glass windows lining both sides of the sanctuary are dedicated to people significant to St. Michael's, many related, at great distance, to me. A bas-relief sculpture of a man is attached to the wall behind the pulpit, on the left. I would later learn that this man is Katrina's great-great-grandfather.

I once found both comfort and strength within walls like these. Influenced by a dynamic youth minister, I attended Northwest Christian College intending to enter the ministry. As we waited for the service to begin, I noticed the enormous stained-glass window behind the altar at the front of the church, which depicts a man with a huge spear in his hands, poised to skewer someone. Elizabeth and Holly, sitting on either side of me, both grew up in Bristol, so I asked them to explain the image. Neither had any idea. They had attended this church their whole lives, and I was surprised that they had never asked about this ghastly depiction of a man with angel's wings pinning another winged man to the ground with his foot, poised to shish-kabob him through the back.

I glanced around the sanctuary and noticed that everyone was white. Bristol isn't so different from Bend—not many black people. Two hundred years ago, these pews were filled by ancestors of some of these same people; they were churchgoing folks who were involved in the slave trade.

When the service began and the congregation sang, I joined in. "Lord Jesus Christ, only Son of the Father, Lord God, Lamb of God, you take away the sin of the world; have mercy on us." I shifted my weight from one foot to the other, fiddled with my tie. I knew I should sing; I was in church, and cameras were aimed at me. But I stopped singing, and listened as the organ played and the other congregants raised their voices in the next hymn without me. "Rise up, ye saints of God! His kingdom tarries long; Lord, bring the day of truth and love and end the night of wrong."

I stopped attending church more than twenty years ago. Instances of hypocrisy chipped away at my faith until it evaporated. I remember the night in June 1978 when I graduated from NCC. I knew I wouldn't enter the ministry and soon stopped attending church altogether. Perhaps I was angry at God. I've witnessed enough false piety among Christ's followers to know that I was certainly angry at some of them. When I spoke with an old friend from First Christian in Pomona, I explained that I wasn't sure I believed in the church anymore, and wasn't even certain if I believed in God. He asked what I was going to find to fill the hole inside me. As I reflect on it now, leaving the church left no hole. The church felt more like a backpack to me: useful for a certain period of time, when I was camping in the wilderness, so to speak. But I finished my long hike and took the backpack off, releasing a weight I no longer needed to bear.

I was jarred from my thoughts by the scripture reading from Galatians. "For freedom Christ has set us free. Stand firm, therefore, and do not submit again to a yoke of slavery, for you were called to freedom..."

"Do not submit again to a yoke of slavery..." How ironic to hear this just before the Fourth of July holiday and on the first day of filming *Traces of the Trade*. I have no doubt that these same words from Paul to the Galatians were also read here in the 1700s and 1800s when DeWolfs were slavers and members of this Church. What were they thinking as they heard these words?

During Holy Eucharist, known as Communion in the congregation in which I was raised, I was consumed by thoughts about the church and its people, not only their role in the slave trade hundreds of years ago but their involvement or noninvolvement in injustice that exists today. Camera or no camera, I remained seated as others passed by to partake of the loaf and cup. Elizabeth and Elly remained behind as well. I didn't ask why.

After church, I stood outside on the grass, sipping icy cold lemonade and making small talk with my new cousins. It felt like the temperature had risen a good ten degrees in the past two hours. A woman about twenty years older than me introduced herself. Helen Nadler is Katrina's aunt. It was at her home that my cousins and I would soon gather. She said she had been looking forward to meeting me because she was born in Bend. Helen is Halsey's niece, the daughter of his sister and brother-in-law, who moved to Oregon some seventy years ago to open Trinity Episcopal Church less than a mile from my house. We laughed and hugged. What an amazing connection.

After a short drive, we arrived at Helen's and walked around back where the rest of the world, except the smell of the ocean, disappeared. We settled into our circle of chairs and Katrina began. "Here we are..."

Elly dabs her forehead and cheeks with a handkerchief. "I am Ellen deWolfe Hale. I'm related by my middle name and by my blood to this family. My grandfather, George Howe, is my connection to the DeWolfs. I read a little bit of the book called *The Gentle Americans*, in which this was mentioned. So I kind of knew about it. I didn't feel like it was necessarily a mark on me. And yet when your letter came," she looks at Katrina, "you pointed out the extent of what they did much more clearly. I thought, 'Wow, I do need to see this.' I like weighty moral issues and I...," she pauses to laugh. "I guess we probably all do. I have no expectation that we're going to solve anything."

I later learn the spelling of Elly's middle name. Her "deWolfe" differs from mine. A variety of spellings have come down through the generations. According to Halsey—who is considered the family historian by everyone in the Howe line—this one came from his brother George, Elly's grandfather. He felt the small "d" and the "e" on the end added tone.

The next speaker is Jim Perry. He and his younger brother, Dain, both sport graying beards. Jim was a foreign service officer in Vietnam, Belgium, and Laos, then before retiring to Arizona he managed and consulted with charitable organizations. Jim's smile does not come as easy or as quick as Dain's, and because of his soft voice, I lean forward to hear him better.

"My name is James DeWolf Perry. I'm the fifth in direct line of succession to have that name. I've been aware all my life of pieces of our connection with the slave trade because James DeWolf was the head of the family, at least the business head of the family and the leading slave trader. The story people seem to enjoy most about him is that when he was a young sea captain he was indicted for murder because one day he took a slave out of the hold of his ship who he believed had smallpox and tied her to a chair and threw her overboard and allegedly then lamented the loss of the chair.

"The way I heard it always was that James DeWolf was involved a little bit in the slave trade and in a lot of other businesses. What I now understand is all those other businesses were in support of the slave trade." He adds that his son, James VI, is also part of the group but won't arrive until Wednesday.

My roommate for the week follows Jim. The broad brim of his white hat keeps the sun off his neck and face and makes him appear as dapper as his name sounds. "My name is Ledlie Laughlin. I'm connected through my mother, who was a Howe. She was very conscious of the family—very conscious of having a grandfather who was an Episcopal bishop, and she always felt that she ought to be more religious. She laid it on her four children and I accepted it. Early on I knew that there was some background in slavery. I also made a connection between the Bishop and slavery and the fact that he was trying to do something about his family. I accepted the role of trying to do good and to be of service. I've had a wonderfully adventurous life as a result."

The "Bishop" mentioned by Ledlie is Mark Antony DeWolfe Howe (1808–1895), who was elected bishop of the new Episcopal Diocese of Central Pennsylvania in 1871, making him the spiritual leader of all Episcopalians in the central and northeastern parts of the state. Except for the Perrys and me, everyone in our group of ten is descended from the Bishop, who is revered in the Howe line of the family. He fathered eighteen children and has a legion of descendants.

"My father came from a very wealthy family," says Ledlie. "I was conscious of growing up with wealth and a responsibility for it. I sought to get away, and one of the ways I found was through the church in a poor black community in Jersey City. That opened up my life in lots of ways; bringing a kind of warmth and easiness that wasn't in my background. I've never quite come to grips with the community I grew up in and have run to other places to find life."

Ledlie's wife, Roxana, is a direct descendant of the abolitionist preacher Henry Ward Beecher—brother of Harriet Beecher Stowe, the author of *Uncle Tom's Cabin*—and of the Civil War general Samuel Chapman Armstrong who, in 1867, founded the Hampton Institute in Virginia to provide a teacher's education for ex-slaves. "Now you know why I married her!" Ledlie tells me later. Unlike some of the others around the circle, Ledlie doesn't display any discomfort. Retired at seventy years of age, he seems to have found whatever he ran away to find.

Sunglasses rest in the long hair tied up on Elizabeth's head. Like Katrina, she battles the heat by wearing a sleeveless blouse. "I'm Elizabeth Banford Sturges and it's really something else to be here," she says with a laugh. "I've spent a lot of time trying to get away from my family. I didn't know until Katrina and I spoke pretty recently the extent that the DeWolfs *were* the slave trade basically." She laughs again, but sounds uncomfortable. "And it feels huge." She looks at Ledlie. "You said you sought life elsewhere. I've done that a lot. Throughout my life I've felt incredible isolation and loneliness within my family, my culture, my ethnicity, and my class. I spent a lot of time as a kid alone, getting messages that I was different from other people around me in the town where I grew up, in Bristol. Something in me always struggled against that, because I like people and I like being with people.

"One of the things I've been thinking about a lot lately has to do with this idea of privilege. The privilege that I do have couldn't be clearer to me, especially in terms of comfort. I mean, I get to sit here." She looks around Helen's yard. "I get to be in beautiful places of my choice that actually belong to my family." Since she grew up here, where she says there weren't any black people, Elizabeth didn't begin interacting with people of African descent until she was a teenager, and when she did she was afraid they wouldn't like her. She has struggled to come to terms with her background. She's since put herself into a situation where she's not isolated, where she's not just around people of her own background. Elizabeth is an artist, lives in New York City, and teaches art in the public schools, where it sometimes feels so hopeless.

With her long dress, pearl earrings and necklace, and a pearl barrette holding her dark-blond hair in place, Holly looks the most well dressed for church of our group.

"My name is Holly Marshall Fulton. I don't remember when I found out that my ancestors were involved with slave trading. But what really stands out that's hard was when I started doing diversity training and I was working with black people. I was walking down the hall with one of my training partners, a black woman. I wanted to tell her about this and I couldn't do it. I stopped talking because I got so choked up inside. I told her that night at dinner. It was so difficult to talk about this with somebody who was black. That was about six years ago."

Holly received an e-mail from Katrina in November 1999 and remembered thinking how good it would be to finally talk about these difficult issues. It's not something that happens easily in her family. Then she laughs and turns to face Keila, saying, "And I'm happy to be here with my sister."

Keila and Holly both live near Denver, Colorado, far from the rest of their family. Keila now wears a smile as big as the Rocky Mountains, yet she still seems more pensive than Holly. A neurological condition restricts her movement and makes it difficult for her to walk. Both sisters told me how upset certain relatives are about this project. Some would prefer to leave the family bones buried.

Keila muses, "We were supposed to be respectable and looked up to; to set a good example. We weren't supposed to be how I felt in life. I just wanted to be dog-shit real." Her eyes open wider. "That's what felt alive to me. The No Talk Rule that I feel so strongly in our family I see in our whole social structure. I played into the game of pretending that I didn't know because I didn't know what to do with it. Y'all are my partners now and I'm very happy and grateful to be here."

Keila says she's a massage therapist, which makes sense. Anyone this in touch with her feelings could naturally be in touch with the external as well. I look at her with a conspiratorial smile, rub my shoulder, and say, "I've got this little ache and want to make sure we stay very close the next couple of months."

"You're on!" she says with her bigger-than-life smile.

My turn. "Captain James DeWolf is my first cousin six times removed. His father, Mark Antony, had a brother Simon who was a carpenter in Connecticut. I'm descended from his line. I don't know a whole lot about my own family's background. My grandfather died when my dad was only two."

I pause. "I'm in a little turmoil. Some of you know Deborah Howe, who picked me up at the airport yesterday." Several people nod. "Deb and I talked all day long about privilege and the things that came with this family. I understand there are plenty of people who totally blew their portion of the fortune yet retained their social status. My side being mostly farmers and ranchers, I didn't have a connection to any of that.

"I also live in a place that's about 95 percent white and I haven't dealt with these issues since junior high."

I look around the circle and say, "I'm Tom DeWolf. What's weird is hearing all this DeWolf history and no one so far has said their last name is DeWolf."

Laughter fills the air again, which feels hotter than ever.

"That's why we wanted you," says Dain, a financial planner and insurance salesman in Boston. During the 1970s, he worked for a nonprofit agency that promoted reform in the criminal justice system. "I'm Dain Perry and I am one of the few in the group that does not have Howe or DeWolf in my name. I was named after my maternal grandfather."

Dain gestures a lot as he speaks. He looks as though he would be comfortable speaking in front of crowds. Though he was born in Boston, his family moved to South Carolina when Dain was three. His father was the priest at an Episcopal church in Charleston for ten years. While living there, the Perrys had black servants. "I grew up with blacks riding in the back of the bus and my thinking not too much of it." At that time he thought that's where they were supposed to be. "I went from that to a boarding school in Connecticut that had more black students than any other in the country. By the end of the first year my best friend was black and it didn't feel like a transformation at all. It felt natural."

Dain has done a great deal of work in inner-city African American communities, worked in prisons, where he developed strong relationships with blacks, and mentored African Americans, which always seemed a very normal thing to him. "Ledlie and I were talking earlier about how an awful lot of us need to be of service and to give back. We were wondering if there might be something in the genes. Jim's and my father was a priest. Our grandfather was a bishop. His father was a priest. There's got to be a message there."

"Maybe there's something good," says Ledlie, "but I don't know. I doubt it."

"Another family business," observes Elly.

"Yeah, right," says Ledlie.

When Dain and Jim refer to the Bishop, they're talking about a different man from the one Ledlie spoke about. Their grandfather, James DeWolf Perry III (1871–1947), was elected bishop of Rhode Island at the young age of thirty-nine. He was later elected presiding bishop of the entire Episcopal Church of the United States in 1930, and his portrait appeared on the cover of *Time* magazine in October 1934.

The more I learn, the more I hear about Episcopal priests in this family. Other than me, I don't know of anyone in my family who contemplated entering the ministry.

We move onto blankets spread over the grass in the shade of Helen's trees. It's still hot, but much more comfortable than being in the sun. Helen's home faces a narrow road with no sidewalks. Birds sing. A gentle breeze blows. This must be a peaceful place to live. I sip fruit juice, eat a turkey sandwich, and lie back. I listen while the others tell stories. Elizabeth has lived in both Italy and China. Katrina grew up six blocks from the Liberty Bell in Philadelphia and also lived in Belgium for a while as a child. Holly used to babysit Elizabeth. Jim and Dain talk about growing up in South Carolina, about living and traveling overseas.

The more I hear, the more isolated I feel. Some of my newfound relatives come from quite privileged backgrounds with international travel, servants, and boarding schools. I've only read about these things in books.

———•••———

I ride with Ledlie back into Bristol, to a parking lot two blocks from St. Michael's. Bristol's historical society occupies the city's former jail. Exterior walls are constructed of uneven rough stones. Inside, a large table with chairs around it rests in the middle of a long open room. A doorway at the far end leads to the old cells with bars still intact. Katrina has arranged for us to meet with a panel of African American people to talk about oppression and slavery in this old jail.

Our guests sit together on one side of the table with us white family members—and, admittedly, I feel very white right now—on the other. Juanita Brown, one of the producers on the film, is the only person of African descent who will accompany us throughout the journey. She and Katrina worked together to plan everywhere we'll go and everyone we'll meet. She lived in Ghana as a student and traveler for a year, four years ago. My comfort level increases knowing that someone with her knowledge of people, places, and cultural norms is part of our group. She's a petite woman whose hair is cropped very close to her skull. Though short in stature, Juanita sits tall and self-assured.

Juanita looks from white face to white face. "I want to thank everyone for being here. This journey began a long time ago, for each of us and for those who came before us. Though we think about this journey as being about the exploration of slavery, it's also about the exploration of liberation."

Juanita explains that the six who have joined us will share their thoughts on what they believe are key things for us to consider as we embark upon our journey. She turns to a woman who begins by explaining that her husband, Hoby, who isn't here, is descended from the DeWolfs. Myrna Cook's own multiracial background includes ancestors of African descent, as well as American Indian, Dutch, and French. She's a direct descendant of the brother of Richard Allen, who was born into slavery in 1760 and died in 1831 as a free man, and was the founder and first bishop of the African Methodist Episcopal Church.

She has a friendly smile and speaks with a clear, confident voice. "A lot of white people in America don't know their European history and their lineage. Whites in America have always been the gatekeepers of democracy and black people have taken the back seat until the sixties. The gatekeepers need to know exactly what happened in history and bring it to light so we can all heal ourselves. My husband's family is very proud of their lineage: the bishops and deacons. I've seen the portraits, very similar to the portraits that are here."

I glance around the room at the many large paintings of famous Bristolians lining the walls and look back at Myrna. She says, "They aren't here today, but I am. You have our support and we'll be there for you."

Juanita signals to the man in wire-rimmed glasses sitting to her left, the most reserved of our guests. Keith Stokes is from Newport, Rhode Island, where he's director of the regional chamber of commerce. He serves on the boards of several national, state, and local historic preservation organizations. Perhaps it is my imagination, but he seems uncomfortable, though when he speaks his words are unwavering. "This journey will be a challenge. Race relations are difficult to talk about. People of color have an especially difficult time talking about it."

I notice the man sitting on the other side of Juanita. His brow furrows and he stares down at the table.

Keith informs us that between 1500 and 1800, fourteen million people came to the New World. Of that total, eleven and a half million were African and were forced immigrants through the slave trade. "This is the foundation of the creation of North America. Your goal should be to keep an open mind and to be ready for difficult discussions and realize that this is about all people who created America: blacks, whites, Jews, and others."

Wayne Winborne is the man who frowned at Keith's statement. He works for Prudential Insurance in race relations. "I disagree with Keith. I believe white people don't talk about race relations, or that they don't talk *honestly* about race relations, or that they don't talk honestly about race relations with people of color."

I wonder if anyone, black or white, really talks about race relations. I've never spoken much with anyone about race relations, and it's Katrina's intention to change that with this journey, as challenging as it might seem to me.

While others have leaned forward while speaking, John Woods sits back in his seat and doesn't make strong gestures. He speaks slowly, drawing words out for emphasis. He smiles and chuckles easily while he talks. He explains that his grandmother was born in Bristol. "At that time my family was crossing the line, as they say, trying to be white. They lived in Bristol as white people."

He leans forward as he emphasizes the last two words. "They were trying to ignore any black heritage in the family. They wanted to dilute what they felt was inferior black blood. In my research on my grandmother, I found out that I was a descendant of the DeWolfs."

This comes as a surprise. I'd like to know more, but John hasn't been able to figure out if he's descended from DeWolfs, DeWolf slaves, or both. Juanita motions to the woman sitting at the far end of the table, who sits with her arms folded across her chest. Jo-Anne Henry looks like a powerful, no-nonsense woman and puts me on edge. She's small, but as she begins to speak, her voice has a power that draws me in like no one else so far. She's animated when she speaks, gesturing with her hands.

Jo-Anne met Katrina about five years ago. She's a social worker and a lawyer and coordinates a child abuse prevention project in Boston. She says that both her mother's and father's families are descended from slaves. From her mother, one line of slaves can be traced back to George Washington, while on her father's side, she's descended from slaves in Trinidad and Guyana.

She hopes that this won't only be a journey of learning about our family history, but an opportunity to ask, "So, then what?" What do we do with this knowledge? What leads to change in our individual lives after we get back? What does that set in motion for our kids and their kids?

Jo-Anne states that another reason she's present today is that she firmly believes that each white-skinned person in this country benefits from this legacy of the institution of slavery. She notes, "That's extremely hard for people to understand, especially if they aren't aware of any history. I differ with Keith. In my twenty years of talking about race, I find that it's most hard for Americans of European descent to have honest conversations about how race affects them. I very much hope that this journey will help other white people in America see a possible connection, a literal day-to-day benefit of having white skin in the United States."

Juanita turns to a large black man whose expressionless face gives away nothing. Carl Senna sits with arms crossed and his head tilted slightly back. His linebacker's torso fills a white T-shirt that displays a wanted poster for a runaway slave named York, "a very black looking fellow, frail limb'd, well fed, and speaks good English." York had run away from Mark Antony DeWolf. The notice, dated March 30, 1763, in Providence, Rhode Island, offers a four-dollar reward for York's return.

After introducing himself, Carl says to Juanita, "You wanted me to say something about this T-shirt?"

Juanita says she does. Carl looks around the room from white face to black, male to female. "My kids and I have a lot of memorabilia and somehow I ended up with this poster. When I told my wife and some other people that I was coming down here, they said, 'Oh, why don't you make a T-shirt for laughs?'"

Juanita asks Carl to explain the financial implications of that four-dollar reward.

"We estimated that four dollars in that period would have come out to about a million, twelve hundred dollars today. So if Mr. Mark Antony DeWolf was still alive, and we could find York walking around here, bring York back and sell him..." Carl laughs. "York's been on the loose for two hundred and thirty-seven years!"

Most everyone laughs. I laugh. Keith isn't laughing. Nor is Jo-Anne. She's seething.

"That is definitely one of the least funny things," she says. The laughter stops instantly.

"Oh, really, I'm sorry. No, I just thought it was a little humorous if, you know, presumably if York was still alive..." Carl's attempt to explain doesn't work with Jo-Anne. No one moves. I look from Carl to Jo-Anne and back again.

After an uncomfortably long pause, Jo-Anne says, "I'll be very interested to see whether, at the end of this journey, that's something people are able to laugh about."

"I'm sorry," Carl says again.

"I didn't say what I said to point fingers," says Jo-Anne, "but I do think it's an interesting barometer. These are the things that happen every day. This is part of white privilege, the things that you're able to laugh about and the things that somebody says in passing that are like a knife."

"I didn't mean to offend...," says Carl.

"I know that," she says.

I'm confused. Jo-Anne seems to be holding the white people at the table accountable for laughing when most of the black people also laughed at something a black man said.

Juanita explains that she laughed at the absurdity of Carl's comment.

Jo-Anne looks over at us white people, who have been silent throughout this conversation, and says, "I know you have something to say. I absolutely would never presume to know what anybody here was thinking and why anybody laughed. Was there a moment of discomfort, or was it just funny?"

"This is really awkward," I say. "We've never met before. I don't know what makes you laugh. What I saw was a bill being handed to this guy who's been dead for two hundred years. It never occurred to me the way that it occurred to you. I never made the connection that a human being would actually get turned over to someone else."

"I appreciate you saying that," she says.

Myrna feels society's focus is misplaced. "Children don't talk about the things of spirit or life," she observes. "It's about money and time. I'm fifty years old. I rode with my mother to downtown Washington, D.C., when it was still segregated. We could not sit at the lunch counter. My mother could not shop in stores she could afford to shop in. I remember being five or six years old and going to the train station by riding on the streetcar in the back. I saw signs that said 'colored' and 'white' and I couldn't use the water fountain. I understand what you're saying," she says to Jo-Anne, "but we have to open up and change the way things happen."

"When I saw that shirt, I was really shocked," says Ledlie. "When you read a poster like that, with your great-great-great-great-grandfather's name on it, saying, 'I want this slave,' boy, I'll tell you, that's . . . that's real." He pauses a moment and sighs deeply before continuing. "As an American citizen, I am responsible for our society. I share that with everybody. But I feel that somehow this family connection gives me not a special guilt, but some kind of special accountability. I'm obliged to do something, regardless of whether I'm guilty or not."

"I'm so glad you said that," says Jo-Anne, "because that is the question. It's being realistic about the benefit. It's not just looking at the history and these family ancestors and what they did, which is very difficult to look at honestly to begin with. It's asking, 'in my life today, how does this affect me; positively or negatively?' Race matters in this country. 'How do I benefit from having white skin or from having this family ancestor?' "

She looks from Ledlie to the rest of us. "If I watch this film, and at the end of the journey it's sort of like, 'Wow, that was hard. We had some great conversations. We went to Cuba. We went to Africa. Okay, on with life.' If there's no conversation about responsibility and what needs to happen next, I would be absolutely devastated."

Our first day of filming concludes. Within a few minutes I stand to the side alone while the crew packs up and others begin to depart for dinner. I didn't say much today. I found myself deferring to our black guests and carefully choosing my few words in ways I never would around a group of white people. I feel guilty, like I did something wrong, and I'm not sure why. Are ten white people about to go traipsing around the world in order to sit around talking about slavery and feeling bad about ourselves? What's that going to accomplish? At one point this afternoon, Wayne spoke about how blaming others is one way we relieve ourselves of guilt. He pointed out that the oppressors were just human and it's too easy to label them as "evil." He described them as decent people sitting around a table like this one, making decisions.

This all feels so complicated. If I harbored any delusion that solutions would become readily apparent, today's conversation nailed that coffin securely shut.

I stare into the eyes of a woman in an ancient portrait hanging on the wall. Her high collar appears to choke her, which may explain the stern expression on her face. Her eyes bore back into mine. "Who are you?" I whisper. "What was it with you people?"

CHAPTER 3

"So let all thine enemies perish, O Lord!"

Glimpses into the past are everywhere in Bristol. St. Michael's Episcopal Church, founded in 1718, and Linden Place, built in 1810, loom high above Hope Street, as does Colt Memorial High School, built of marble and bronze in 1906. I've walked along streets and past homes that are older than the state of Oregon. Standing on the dock, looking out over the harbor from the end of what is known as De-Wolf Wharf on Thames Street, it is easy to imagine the long, colorful history of this place.

Bristol is the only town in America that has celebrated the Fourth of July every year since 1785. Instead of yellow lines to separate traffic lanes, on the streets marking the parade route the lanes are divided by red, white, and blue. This little town of 20,000 swells to 100,000 on the Fourth. Homes are decorated with festive bunting and flags. I've never seen so much red, white, and blue.

Rhode Island, at roughly forty miles long and thirty miles wide, is the smallest state in the Union. Of its 1,545 square miles, 500 are covered by water. Massachusetts lies to the north and east and Connecticut to the west. To the south, the Atlantic Ocean forms the wet and salty final border, passageway to much of the state's sustenance throughout history, which explains the ship's anchor on the state flag.

Bristol rests close to the Massachusetts border in Rhode Island's smallest county, surrounded by water. It encompasses twin peninsulas that resemble a lobster's claw. The town is connected to the rest of the United States by land only on the north, where it borders the town of Warren.

As one leaves downtown to drive along Poppasquash Road past Colt State Park, sidewalks disappear, the home sites are larger, and the trees and bushes grow thicker. Coggeshall Farm Museum, with its eighteenth-century farmhouse, stone springhouse, barns, blacksmith shop, chickens, goats, and oxen, provides a peephole to Rhode Island in the late 1700s.[1]

In 1620, the Pilgrims landed thirty-five miles away at Plymouth. Massasoit, the sachem, or chief, of the Wampanoag—a branch of the Algonquin Nation—ruled the area now called Bristol.[2] Wampanoag people had lived in this region for twelve thousand years. Massasoit's village rested at the foot of Mount Hope, which rises two hundred feet above sea level overlooking Mount Hope Bay. He was born here around 1580.

Between 1616 and 1619, the Wampanoag had been ravaged by a disease unknown on the North American continent prior to the arrival of Europeans. It is astonishing to realize that, in some regions, as many as 90 percent of the inhabitants died.[3] Such a high proportion of Wampanoag people had perished, the Pilgrims found cleared and abandoned fields awaiting them.

The Pilgrims who sailed aboard the *Mayflower* were members of the English Separatist Church who fled their home to escape religious persecution. Some years later these same immigrants enacted laws mandating that any Indians who refused to accept the Puritans' religion would be put to death for blasphemy. Europeans affected American Indians in another pernicious way as well. Explorers captured and enslaved them in the colonies or sold them into slavery in the Caribbean islands and Europe. Between thirty and fifty thousand Indians, and perhaps more, were exported from the colonies between 1670 and 1715.[4]

On March 22, 1621, Massasoit led a small group of braves to Plymouth, where the *Mayflower* remained anchored in the harbor. As his interpreter, he brought Squanto, another Wampanoag who had been kidnapped and then sold in Spain seven years earlier. After escaping to London, Squanto learned English before returning home. Massasoit signed a peace treaty that day which he honored until his death forty years later.

I suspect that in grade school most of us heard the story that the Wampanoag people probably saved the Pilgrims from starving to death. They shared food and taught them to fish. They gave the Pilgrims seed corn and taught them how to plant and cultivate it.

A three-day feast of thanksgiving in the autumn of 1621 celebrated these acts of kindness. Plymouth Colony's governor, William Bradford, sent men hunting after wild ducks and geese to supplement the bountiful harvest of that first year in this new land. The colonists and Wampanoags observed a second thanksgiving feast two years later.

What wasn't taught in any classroom of my youth is what happened soon after that auspicious beginning. Over the next forty years, Massasoit exchanged unpopulated lands for weapons, rum, and horses, which they hadn't encountered before the coming of the Europeans. They also didn't understand the concept of owning land. Samoset, from the Pemaquid Nation, accompanied Massasoit to Plymouth in 1621. Four years later, colonists asked Samoset to give them twelve thousand acres of Pemaquid land. "Samoset knew that land came from the Great Spirit, was as endless as the sky, and belonged to no man. To humor these strangers in their strange ways, however, he went through a ceremony of transferring the land and made his mark on a paper for them. It was the first deed of Indian land to English colonists."[5]

Massasoit was also friendly with the Puritans, who arrived in Boston ten years after the Pilgrims landed at Plymouth. He gave land to Roger Williams when Williams fled Salem in 1636. He sold Miles Standish forty-nine square miles of land. He sold Hog Island, which sits in the mouth of Bristol Harbor, to a man named Richard Smith. It was never enough, as settlers soon came by the thousands. Before long, the colonists didn't bother with formalities like negotiations for purchase or deeds granted by Indian nations.

Massasoit did his best to maintain peace between his people and the colonists, but many of the Wampanoag began to hate the European invaders long before Massasoit died in 1661. His oldest son, Wamsotta, succeeded him and reigned for one year before he also died. Queen Weetamoe, his widow, suspected the Pilgrims had poisoned him.

Wamsotta's brother, Metacom, was twenty-four years old when he became sachem in 1662, and would become known by the Europeans as King Philip. He wanted revenge for his brother's death. The greed of the colonists, in the face of his father's generosity, resulted in the Wampanoag people no longer sharing their land, but losing it. By 1671, so many English settlers lived in the Connecticut, Rhode Island, Plymouth, and Massachusetts Bay colonies that indigenous people were outnumbered two to one. Metacom foresaw the ruin of his people and formed alliances with other tribes, including the Narragansett, to defend against the colonists.

William Bradford, who had served as Plymouth Colony's governor for all but six years since 1620, had died in office in 1657. With the passing of the generation that had forged an uneasy alliance four decades earlier, the bonds which united the two peoples unraveled. Increasing tension erupted into open hostility in 1675.

Initially, the colonial armies were unsuccessful. Metacom and his allies attacked dozens of settlements, destroying some. Indian forces moved easily over the terrain, organized themselves efficiently, and primarily attacked outlying towns and farms.

But over the years, colonists had succeeded in converting some Indian people to Christianity. Many of these "praying Indians" were herded into internment camps to prevent them from aiding Metacom. Some became soldiers for the colonists and taught them how to locate Metacom's warriors and fight as they fought. Both sides were ruthless in their execution of the war, and mercy was rarely shown.

Just as Indian tribes had joined forces, several New England colonies united in the spreading war. On December 19, 1675, a contingent of the colonial army found a Narragansett fort surrounded by a stagnant and frozen swamp and a jungle of cedar trees. Inside huddled three thousand men, women, and children crowded into five hundred wigwams. A blizzard raged as the attack began. More than two hundred members of the militia died. Hundreds of Narragansett fighters perished, and hundreds of women, children, and invalids burned to death at the hands of colonists.

Increase and Cotton Mather, father and son, were considered the very voice of God in early Puritan New England. Cotton later exulted about the victory in the Great Swamp Massacre: "We have heard of two and twenty Indian captains slain, all of them brought down to Hell in one day. When they came to see the ashes of their friends, mingled with the ashes of their fort, and the Bodies of so many of their Country terribly Barbikew'd, where the English had been doing a good day's work, they Howl'd, they Roar'd, they Stamp'd, they Tore their hair..."

His father, Increase, exclaimed, "So let all thine enemies perish, O Lord!"[6]

In 1676, Metacom's forces attacked Providence, burning eighty houses. He spared the remaining twenty due to the pleas of Roger Williams, the aging friend of his father. Colonel Benjamin Church recruited an army from Queen Awashonks of Sakonnet. On July 20, 1676, they captured or killed 173 of Metacom's people. His wife and son were taken prisoner and sold into slavery.

Metacom's spirit must have been crushed by years of broken promises by the colonists his father had befriended, by the death or capture of so many of his people, and by his own retreat in a war he was losing. Yet the harshest reality Metacom faced was the knowledge that many of his own people were deserting him to side with the European invaders. He killed one of his own braves for suggesting peace with the colonists.

On August 12, Colonel Church, eighteen colonists, and twenty-two Indians who had sided with them surrounded Metacom near his base of operations at Mount Hope, located in modern-day Bristol. Alderman, the brother of the brave that Metacom had slain, shot Metacom through the heart. Anawon, Metacom's field commander, escaped with a small group of Wampanoag but was captured a few weeks later and executed.

King Philip's War remains the costliest war, per capita, in American history. Of roughly one hundred New England towns, one-third were attacked and abandoned. Approximately 7 percent of New England's population died—a death rate more than double that of the Civil War and seven times that of the Revolutionary War. Just less than 1 percent of the adult male population of the United States was lost during World War II. Almost 8 percent of Plymouth Colony's men died in King Philip's War.

As costly as the war was to the colonists, the result was virtual extermination of traditional indigenous life throughout New England. Three or more Indian people died for every colonist. Between 60 and 80 percent of the Indian population was lost.[7] The only indigenous communities that remained were those that stayed neutral, fought on the side of the colonists, or were considered Christian. They fell under the total authority of the colonies; most adopted Christianity in order to survive. Many were sold into slavery abroad or forced into slavery in the colonies.

I imagine the European immigrants considered the people they encountered upon their arrival here as savages, as less than human.

Whereas reliance upon their good graces initially helped the colonists survive in the New World, controlling or destroying them, or selling them into slavery, became keys to colonial prosperity. This set the stage for the much more ubiquitous and long-lasting African slavery system, and it's another chapter in American history that I never learned in school.

Metacom was dismembered and his body parts hung from trees. His head was placed atop a pole at Plymouth, where it remained on public display for over twenty years. Alderman kept Metacom's hand in a pail of rum and showed it "to such gentlemen as would bestow gratuities on him."[8]

Two of the colonial soldiers who fought in King Philip's War at the Great Swamp Massacre were brothers Edward and Stephen De-Wolf, sons of Balthazar, the first DeWolf to arrive in colonial America. Edward DeWolf is my grandfather, ten generations back.

I was amazed that such a significant war in our nation's history seems largely forgotten today, or at least downplayed, but it no doubt clashes with the innocent and idyllic image of that first peaceful Thanksgiving celebration. I've always been taught that America was founded on the ideals of equality, freedom, and liberty. It's been difficult to admit that I've often been too eager to believe the legends and overlook the sometimes brutal reality.

After King Philip's War, Bristol was settled in 1680 as part of Plymouth Colony, which was absorbed into Massachusetts Bay Colony in 1691, the same year Cotton Mather began his crusade against witches in Salem. Massachusetts ceded Bristol to the Rhode Island colony in 1747. The town was laid out in a large grid. Along Hope Street, each of the open-ended cross streets afforded a view of the harbor.

The first colonists to settle in Bristol were quite poor, growing crops and wearing homemade clothes. The first town meeting-house, built in 1684 on the west edge of the town common, hosted

Congregational church services. Black and Indian slaves
balcony.

Though Mark Antony DeWolf first sailed to Africa in 1769, it
wasn't until after the Revolutionary War that Bristolians, and the
DeWolf family in particular, attained great wealth and influence
through shipping, privateering, and the trading of rum for African people. The town soon hosted the rich and the famous. On
March 15, 1781, General George Washington passed through Bristol. Schoolchildren memorized a poem for the occasion:

> In fourteen hundred ninety-two Columbus sailed
> the ocean blue.
> In seventeen hundred eighty-one I saw General
> Washington.[9]

————•◦•————

Plimoth Plantation is a tourist destination re-creating both the Pilgrim village and a Wampanoag home site from the 1620s.[10] Because
I grew up hearing the story from only the Pilgrim perspective, I
spent most of my first visit in November 2004 at the Wampanoag
home site. I watched a woman clothed in animal skins cook food in
two iron pots hanging over a large outdoor fire. A man nearby, covered in even more layers of fur, explained his process of burning
and carving the inside of a log to construct a canoe. I listened to a
young man tell stories inside a dome-shaped house covered with
bark while a small, warm fire warded off the November chill.

Back outside, I listened to another Wampanoag man explain how
to tan hides and show how his leggings and moccasins were made.
A woman asked him what his ancestors did to survive. He replied
that men were involved in "life-taking" activities, including killing
game, fishing, and cutting down trees to make canoes. They brought
back food to the women, who then prepared it for everyone to eat.

When she asked about the role of women, he explained that they were life-givers. They bore children and harvested food. They used cattails and branches from bushes to make bags and baskets. Women harvested things that would grow back the following year; they didn't kill them.

I asked, "How often are you here?"

"Five days a week, all year round."

"What is it like having people like us asking you questions?"

He smiled. "If you weren't here, I wouldn't be here."

"My ancestor was here with your ancestors," I said. "He was rewarded for taking part in King Philip's War."

"That was a bad thing and you probably aren't very proud of it."

"No, I'm not."

"As long as you aren't like him..."

"Are you hopeful?" I asked.

"What do you mean?"

"For the future; are you hopeful for the future?"

"Yes," he said, "as long as we are together talking, working, and learning, I am hopeful." Then he smiled at me. "Now it is time for more music."

He began to play a song called "Dancing Sticks." Resting one foot on a log on the edge of the fire, he tapped together two foot-long sticks, burned and carved very smooth, drawing different rhythms and tones from within them while a female companion closed her eyes and sang. He taught us where to join in during the chorus, and we sang together.

CHAPTER 4

THE GREAT FOLKS

Early Monday morning, on my second full day in Bristol, I begin reading an article Katrina gave each of us entitled "White Privilege: Unpacking the Invisible Knapsack" by Peggy McIntosh.[1] She writes, "I have come to see white privilege as an invisible package of unearned assets which I can count on cashing in each day, but about which I was 'meant' to remain oblivious. White privilege is like an invisible weightless knapsack of special provisions, maps, passports, codebooks, visas, clothes, tools, and blank checks."

McIntosh's interest in the subject began with her frustration with men who were unwilling to admit their privilege in comparison with women. She then recognized that she benefited from overprivilege based on her race. She listed several privileges she experiences in her daily life solely because she is white. I see many that apply to me. "I can, if I wish, arrange to be in the company of people of my race most of the time." That's easy to do in Bend. "I can avoid spending time with people whom I was trained to mistrust and who have learned to mistrust my kind or me." Again, this pertains to me. I keep reading.

"I can go shopping alone most of the time, pretty well assured that I will not be followed or harassed." True.

"I do not have to educate my children to be aware of systemic racism for their own daily physical protection." Again, yes.

"I can do well in a challenging situation without being called a credit to my race." I've heard that one before. I think Archie Bunker used to say it on *All in the Family* on TV.

"I am never asked to speak for all the people of my racial group." That's interesting. No white person is ever asked to speak for all white people. But as I reflect about it, I can remember thinking that if a black person said something, I figured all black people probably felt pretty much the same way.

McIntosh lists dozens of different ways she was privileged because of her white skin. Intellectually, I understand most of them. I'm surprised by several and realize I've had the privilege of not needing to reflect on them before. I've never been followed around in a store because the owner thinks I might steal something or ever even contemplated the fact that most of the people I see on television or in newspapers look like me. I never realized that when history teachers presented our national heritage, they always talked about the white people who were involved in its creation. I never thought about black people not being able to find a hairdresser who could cut their hair. I fidget while I read because I begin to see how my white skin has given me privilege that I've had the luxury of taking for granted.

McIntosh hits home when she writes about the importance of relinquishing the myth of meritocracy. "If these things are true, this is not such a free country; one's life is not what one makes it; many doors open for certain people through no virtues of their own." She describes unearned advantages males receive due to their gender, and essentially calls for a redesign of our social structure. Of course, the people in position to effect such change are the people in power: primarily white men, and the question of whether, or why, this demographic group would choose to change is a profound one.

———◦•—

I leave Nancy's to walk to the former DeWolf warehouse on Thames Street. A two-story and a three-story building were constructed side by side of wood and brick. At some point, they were connected in the middle. One roof rises above the other. They're painted the color of red bricks and trimmed in white. Attached to this double building in back, toward the harbor, stands the old stone warehouse. The whole thing is about to be renovated. With three separate, yet connected buildings and different construction materials and styles, it looks like a remodeling nightmare.

Elizabeth walks over. I ask her if she's read the "Invisible Knapsack" article.

"Not yet. I decided that before I read her list, I wanted to think about my life and write down my own privileges."

I ask if she's willing to share her thoughts, and she retrieves a small notebook from her bag, opens it, and begins reading. "Men are not threatened by me. I'm seen as dumb, nice, and blond."

"Ouch. That's fairly negative."

"I'm just being honest. I can enjoy privileges such as riding a bus without having change because I'm not seen as a threat. I do not get stopped, watched, harassed, or beaten by police. I have the ability to walk into corporate environments without being questioned. I know how to dress, talk, act, and use the body language of the ruling class and the powers that be. It's all been ingrained since childhood. The corollary to that is that I not only know how, but it is comfortable and easy, which is a plus. I am on the inside track instantly."

We're called to join the others.

Local historic preservationist Bonnie Warren will accompany us as we traipse around the wharf. A white woman who appears to be in her sixties, Bonnie carries a wide-brimmed orange hat in her hand. We stand in the alley that leads from Thames street to the waterfront between the old stone DeWolf warehouse and a recently renovated brick building to the south.

"If the walls could talk...," she says. "You're standing on the most important maritime site in New England that relates to the history of the eighteenth to the mid-nineteenth century. This is now called the DeWolf Wharf and it is being renovated as Thames Street Landing. But the history goes back to the seventeenth century."

She points to the remodeled brick building. William DeWolf, James's brother, purchased it in 1795. It became a DeWolf distillery. Molasses was imported from Cuba and then made into rum, which became the staple of the Triangle Trade. I can see the place on the exterior wall where the distillery's original brick pattern ends and the newer one begins.

During excavation, a series of rum vats was uncovered. "I tried to get somebody to stop the construction so they could preserve the history," says Bonnie, "but next thing we knew they were all covered by a large cement slab."

"In New England?" I ask. "I thought you people were all about preserving history."

"It is hard to believe such a thing could happen today, particularly here. But it did. The barrels are entombed right there."

She then explains that Charles DeWolf moved his family from Connecticut to Guadeloupe in the Caribbean Islands. His son Mark Antony was hired as a clerk by Captain Simeon Potter in 1744. They sailed to Bristol, Potter's home town, where Mark Antony met, and soon married, Potter's sister, Abigail, at St. Michael's, which sits diagonally opposite from where Potter's house once stood.

Simeon Potter captained a privateer during King George's War

(1744–48). He invested his share of the plunder in shipping and land and became wealthy. He was the first captain from Bristol to invest in transporting Africans to the Caribbean and the southern colonies. Six years younger than Potter, Mark Antony worked for Simeon in various capacities. He became a sea captain and made his first slave-trading voyage in 1769. With fifteen children to support, however, Mark Antony lived and died a poor man.

After being introduced to privateering and the slave trade by their Uncle Simeon, several of Mark Antony's children did substantially better than their father in amassing their own fortunes. After the Revolutionary War, during which his house near St. Michael's was burned by the British, Potter built a new home on Bristol Harbor, just north of, and adjacent to, where we now stand. William, one of the sons of Mark Antony and Abigail, was thirty-three when he bought this property. His brother James became his partner six months later. James was thirty-one.[2]

Six of Mark Antony's sons, and one grandson, sailed in the trade (others participated in various supporting roles). The DeWolfs financed eighty-eight voyages, which transported approximately ten thousand Africans. Alone, or in partnership with others, the DeWolf family was accountable for almost 60 percent of all African voyages sailing from Bristol, making them the largest slave-trading dynasty in early America. The closest competition was two firms in Newport that each sent out twenty-two vessels.[3]

Control of the family business rested with family members. Bonnie said, "You didn't get into this unless you were a son, a son-in-law, a daughter, a daughter-in-law, or married to a cousin. It's all in the family." However, Bonnie also describes a study documenting business transactions between the DeWolfs and four hundred different people in Bristol, which had a total population of sixteen hundred at the time.

We walk to the back of the building and pause while Bonnie inserts a key into the padlock on the large door. We're about to enter the warehouse where James DeWolf reportedly kept slaves shackled to the walls. I remember my conversation with Halsey and my image of Pirates of the Caribbean. But Disneyland has nothing to do with this. Some of these ancestors *were* pirates in the Caribbean. The thick door creaks as Bonnie hefts it open. I jump as a seagull screeches overhead. That's perfect. Alfred Hitchcock is much more appropriate for this scene than Walt Disney. I'm walking onto the set of a horror film as I cross the threshold into the old, stone building.

At a hundred and forty feet in depth, the warehouse was originally built with hand-hewn beams, as large as sixteen inches square, with wooden pegs securing the tusk tenon joints. There are no nails. This place was built to handle incredible weight. Now, a few metal braces supplement the original gnarled tree-trunk posts that shore up the heavy beams along the ceiling. Katrina says some of the stones in the exterior walls of the warehouse are thought to have come from West Africa, used as ballast on slaving ships. Wires and pipes run along the walls and low ceiling. Many dangle. Ducking and dodging obstacles, we move further inside. A ten-inch-long metal hook protrudes down from one beam. Whole sections of broken or missing ceiling expose dark recesses here and there. At any moment, I expect to see rats crawling across a thick rope.

Climbing a set of bare wooden stairs, we emerge in a large room on the second floor. Dain reaches out and slowly turns an enormous wheel—with a diameter four feet greater than his height—held in place by hefty columns on either side. Bonnie points out the openings cut into the floor, with doors held by big iron hinges. When goods were brought in from the dock on the lower level these doors were opened and with a very simple pull of the tremendous hoisting wheel, men were able to bring heavy goods to this level. Standing today in the decaying dark and gloom, it's hard to imagine the enormous stacks of trade goods and cartons Bonnie describes; the noise and clanging and people.

We make our way up another narrow set of enclosed stairs between the two connected buildings. On one side there is brick, on the other clapboard. We enter what Bonnie calls the counting room. "This would be the equivalent today of the business office. James DeWolf sat in this room, located directly above his store, and could watch his ships coming and going from his dock."

Bonnie shifts gears. "A bit of history is helpful here. The man who made the most money in New England in the War of 1812 was James DeWolf."

During the war DeWolf was a privateer, essentially a legalized pirate authorized by the government to seize enemy ships and share the booty with the government. Privateering was a wartime practice accepted by both Great Britain and the United States, and it probably allowed the young nation to keep its independence from Britain.[4] James was very good at it. The DeWolf family actually owned more ships in 1812 than the United States Navy.[5]

Though many people in Bristol, including members of our family, believe slaves were held in this building, Bonnie explains that the slave trade—which was federally outlawed in 1808—was over by the time the warehouse was added in 1818. There were still trading activities with Cuba and the South, but in terms of direct voyages between Africa and Bristol, James DeWolf was cautious. He got out of the slave trade and into textiles, since he recognized the future was in manufacturing.

"I thought the DeWolfs continued trading in people long after it was illegal," says Elizabeth.

Slave trading had been illegal in Rhode Island since 1787, but many in the trade, including the DeWolfs, ignored the law.[6] Slaving continued even after 1808, but not in Bristol—not directly anyway. George DeWolf reportedly traded in African people until 1820.[7] Moreover, the DeWolfs were still involved in slavery by virtue of their continued ownership of Cuban plantations and the shipping and trading of slave-produced goods. When James died in

1837, he left three plantations—one sugar and two coffee—to his four sons. An old document Katrina found indicates that ownership of Cuban plantations stayed in the family until at least the 1850s. Most of the warehouse's contents listed in the inventory of James DeWolf's will were related to coffee, not sugar or rum.

"James is savvy enough to know how to make money, how to change, how to roll with the times. James DeWolf is brilliant. He knew how to get political favors to help his business. And he was, in his own way, extremely generous. It's a very complicated story, but this is what men did here, the merchant princes of this period," Bonnie explains, noting how many people depended on James De-Wolf and the slave trade. There were shipbuilders, iron workers who forged shackles, and coopers who made barrels for rum. Ships needed sails, rope, and crew members. Others sold food and other goods and services to the shippers. James's younger brother Levi, who quit the trade in disgust after one voyage, became a farmer. But farmers supplied the ships with Bristol's famous onions and other foods, partly for the voyage and partly for trade goods. People were invested in the slave trade in another way as well. In the stock market today people buy shares in a new company. Back then, many bought shares in slave ships.

"You can see in ships' records the name of the captain, the owners, and then thirty, forty different names of everybody who bought a sixteenth, a tenth, or whatever proportion it was," Bonnie says. "And when a voyage failed, you lost your shirt, literally. Everything you had."

Dain—the financial planner—asks what kind of return investors expected.

"You anticipated an average of twenty-five percent return on your money on a slave vessel," she says. "It was a high risk and a high return because if you hit it well, you made a great deal of money."

I shake my head in disbelief. I had no clue how pervasive this business was. In the slave trade, it seems that it was not just one person, or one family, who was involved but the entire town.

When the Newport insurance companies stopped insuring slave vessels, James DeWolf founded his own firm. James and his brothers owned the ships, plantations in Cuba, the rum distillery, the warehouse, and the insurance company, and they also owned the bank. During the final four years the trade was legal in the United States, James's nephew Henry operated an auction house in Charleston, South Carolina, where cargoes of Africans could be sold.[8] The final piece of the completed puzzle was getting into politics.

James DeWolf lobbied Congress to create a new customs district for Bristol, which was approved in 1801. Three years later he successfully petitioned President Thomas Jefferson—whom he supported in his run for the presidency, which was quite rare among men of substance in New England—to have Charles Collins appointed as collector. Collins became responsible for inspecting all the cargoes that went in and out of Bristol. If you wanted to do something illegal, Collins was the man who could make it easier.

Charles Collins was married to Lydia Bradford, the sister of James DeWolf's wife, Ann Bradford. The Bradford sisters were daughters of George Washington's close friend Lieutenant Governor William Bradford, and descendants of the William Bradford who arrived on the *Mayflower* and served as governor of Plymouth Colony in the 1600s.[9] According to James DeWolf's will, Collins was half owner of the sugar estate in Cuba. Collins maintained the position of collector until 1820, when President Monroe fired him, and trading in slaves became a federal offense punishable by hanging.

"If you have one family that owns all the necessary businesses, products, and ships, and lots of people in town are investing in that family, who's not involved?" I ask. "Was there anyone around who was not involved in some way either directly or indirectly through the purchases or investments they made?"

"I think in general the whole town was supporting what was going on here," Bonnie confirms.

It dawns on me that the DeWolf family operated like one of those huge modern conglomerates that is vertically integrated, controlling virtually every aspect of their business. People throughout Bristol supported that business, apparently willing to overlook certain unsavory things, undoubtedly for economic reasons.

------·•·------

The following day, a few of us stand inside a small room at the historical society. Inside a gray metal filing cabinet in the corner are file after file of two-hundred-year-old letters and other records that document the business dealings of the DeWolf family. We soon don protective white gloves to handle the fragile papers. They've been brought from upstairs and now lie on the same table around which—two days ago—we sat discussing the T-shirt Carl Senna had made. The woman with the high collar continues to oversee our proceedings from within her golden frame on the wall. The words before us are difficult to decipher; written as they were when an ƒ and an s looked alike, and the ink is often faded. Still, I'm able to make out certain phrases.

" …divide the Negroes to sell them…"

"I do not think it advisable for you to come out here. The Smallpox is raging on many of the plantations. A great proportion of those Negroes is down with it, and that alone forbids any attempt to divide them."

Dain reads a letter written in 1826 from the Republican Party to John DeWolf, asking him to extend financial assistance to Thomas Jefferson. Jefferson died on July 4 that year.

Elly and I have a few letters spread out before us. She says one appears to be a correspondence between two DeWolf brothers, James and John. She reads aloud with more than a little sarcasm in her voice. "Dear brother: Money, money, money, money, money, money, money, money..."

Katrina holds a letter dated July 4, 1795: "...bought nine prime slaves, one woman and eight men. Paid for them tobacco, rum, hats, bread, mackerel..."

It's sickening and just plain creepy reading this. I can't imagine the mixture of anger and sadness an African American person would feel looking at these documents.

Holly stares at the whip and a pair of manacles lying in the middle of the table. Her chin quivers. In a quiet voice she says, "I'm having a hard time looking at these."

"They are from The Mount," says Katrina, "which was James DeWolf's estate."

"It is really disturbing to me," says Holly. "Just looking at the whip and thinking about what we're doing, and what it's done."

I understand Katrina's intention that we deeply explore the legacy of slavery, but having these items on the table while we're being filmed viewing documents bothers me as well. Yesterday, Elizabeth confided in me, "In a little while I have to go over to the neighbors to borrow a whip and manacles. Most people say, 'Gee, can I borrow a cup of sugar' and I get to ask for a chain and a whip. I don't really want to do that." The ancestors of Elizabeth's neighbors were apparently close friends with her great-grandfather, Wallis Howe.

The conversation turns to James DeWolf's personal slaves. Two children, purchased during a slaving voyage, were given by James as Christmas gifts to his wife in 1803.[10]

"They were around into old age," says Jim. "Did any of you grow up hearing that rhyme?"

"Something about Adjua and Pauledore?" asks Elizabeth. "Something about the kitchen floor?"

"From what I understand, it was like a nursery rhyme that was taught and it's been passed on," says Katrina. In fact, late in life when Adjua and Pauledore sat in the sun on the slanting entry to their cellar, James and Ann's grandchildren created the poem to tease them.[11]

Adjua and Pauledore
Sitting on the cellar door;
Pauledore and Adjua;
Sitting in the cellar way!
Down fell the cellar door,
Bump went Pauledore;
Up flew the cellar way,
Off blew Adjua!

"The other thing about Adjua and Pauledore," says Katrina, "was that the family wrote about them very affectionately and how well they were treated and how much they loved the DeWolfs." According to family lore, an abolitionist approached James DeWolf to convince him to free Adjua and Pauledore so they could return to the newly created republic of Liberia—established by abolitionists for ex-slaves from the United States. The story is that James refused and that Adjua and Pauledore were relieved. I wonder if this is true or just another myth created by white families who wanted to believe, or have others believe, that enslaved people were well treated and happy. It's not so different from the mythology northerners have accused southerners of creating.

"We talk about Africans having their history erased so they weren't able to think about liberating themselves," says Elizabeth. "The same thing has happened to us. I didn't know this history. Because I didn't know this I couldn't think about it. The reality of slavery, the early European settlers here and how they killed the Native Americans, was completely glossed over. I didn't learn any of it. It was made nice so that nobody had to deal with anything uncomfortable."

Elizabeth worked at Linden Place in different capacities while growing up here. "Nobody wanted to ever talk about this and it made everybody very uncomfortable. What these people are used to doing is presenting this pretty picture of who the DeWolfs were and taking people through Linden Place and pointing out the nice portraits and the beautiful chandeliers, and everyone goes, 'Oh, how lovely. What a beautiful home. I wish it was mine. I'd like to have this as my living room.' That's the extent of it."

I wonder if I would have done things any differently if I'd been responsible for Linden Place. It's easy to have this conversation in 2001 with like-minded people making a movie about the slave trade. I'm not so sure how fair we're being to Linden Place or to Bristol.

"I want to say something about the name," says Holly, "because it's huge—the name DeWolf. 'Don't soil the name.' That's the message I'm getting. The bottom line is don't soil it."

"And probably all of Bristol feels that," says Ledlie. "I imagine that it's sullying Bristol."

"Well, if there was a sign coming into town that said, 'You are entering Bristol, the historic center of U.S. slave trading,' things would be very different," says Dain.

As I look around the room at my cousins, and these papers lying out on the table before us that document all the aspects of the De-Wolf family's Triangle Trade business dealings from Bristol to West Africa, Cuba, and the American South, I wonder how many letters and ledgers and family papers lie in dusty boxes and trunks and filing cabinets in old closets and attics all across our country. I wonder how many have been destroyed by embarrassed descendants who don't want to soil their own family names.

———•◦•———

Back home at Nancy's after she and Ledlie have both turned in for the evening, I turn on the television and plug in a videotape Holly loaned me. It's the ten-minute trailer that Katrina created to help people understand what *Traces of the Trade* is about and to help convince foundations and others to invest in the project. As I sit in Nancy's darkened living room, with the image on the screen providing the only illumination, I watch as a small box covered with a white lace doily is passed from one pair of hands to another, and then another. I hear Katrina's voice.

"What do we inherit from seven generations ago? A face, a laugh, a ring, a Bible, table manners, a name? What do we inherit without even realizing it? What family secrets hide in the unspoken and unseen? New England, where my mother's family is from, has its share of unacknowledged ghosts. My cousin calls it the Deep North."

A camera pulls back from an indiscernible black-and-white pattern to reveal the hold of a slave ship, African people crammed tightly together. Katrina says, "I discovered I was descended from the largest slave-trading family in early America." Her face appears for the first time.

"How does this two-hundred-year-old story connect to who I am today? How has it shaped my conscious and unconscious sense of myself? I've started researching the past so I might find its traces in the present."

She tells the story of involvement in the Triangle Trade by the DeWolf family, Rhode Island, and all of New England. "A family business. A family secret. New England business. A New England secret."

She explains that after the slave trade ended, DeWolf descendants' knowledge of their role evolved into a vague, distorted, and even romanticized picture. They became a large, influential family of philanthropists, ministers, bishops, writers, professors, artists, and architects—upright Yankees and leading citizens. The DeWolfs of Bristol became affectionately known as "The Great Folks."

Deborah Howe appears, sitting on a couch. She says, "To think that somebody whose blood runs in me was manacling somebody or whipping somebody is kind of a chilling thought."

Elizabeth sits in front of some watercolor paintings, her dark-blond hair undone and hanging below her shoulders. With her left hand she brushes it back behind her ear. She explains that the way racism has affected her is that she's afraid black people will hate her. She laughs out loud, but it is a disconcerted laugh, one that seems to acknowledge her own surprise at her words. It is not a happy smile on her face when she says, "It's really hard."

The Fourth of July parade from some thirty years ago marches up Hope Street, with parents and children gathered in front of Linden Place to watch. Men with short hair stand around in suits and ties. Cigarettes are smoked. Men dressed as Revolutionary War soldiers walk by. Balloons float from strings.

A small girl in a red-and-white striped dress hangs from the wrought-iron fence, watching the parade. A boy in blue, a white anchor embroidered on his shirt, held by his mother, claps his hands. Katrina's voiceover says, "Family pride. How ordinary, how unsurprising, how troubling."

The parade marches by. "Town pride. Ordinary, unsurprising, troubling."

The little girl in the red-and-white dress goes down the front walk of Linden Place, heading toward the street. She holds a small American flag with both hands. The frame freezes. Katrina says, "Me, age three, inheriting."

I watch the credits roll by in the dark. The Great Folks. Amazing.

After crawling into bed, I stare at the ceiling in the dark as the clock strikes midnight. This is heavier than I expected. The impact of race is so much greater and more deeply ingrained in our collective psyche than I ever realized. I wonder what an African American person would think about the trailer. It feels like I'm beginning to scratch the surface of how black people and white people may view the world in very different ways. If I were black, I think I'd be angry—not only at what took place over the past few hundred years, but at white people who don't have a clue what's going on today.

CHAPTER 5

"I TREMBLE FOR MY COUNTRY..."

Yesterday we stood on the lawn at Linden Place, like so many generations before us, to watch the 216th annual Fourth of July parade. James DeWolf Perry VI, Jim's son, arrived, so our entire Family of Ten is now here. I watched the first part of the parade leaning on the wrought-iron fence that separates the mansion grounds from Hope Street. The Linden Place lawn sits a couple feet above the sidewalk. It felt a little uncomfortable standing up above, looking down on everyone below.

After watching fireworks explode over Bristol Harbor last night, I went back and stood alone on the sidewalk, outside the fence, looking up at the mansion rising stark and eerie against the black sky. Lights illuminated the white exterior from below. Standing on the outside and looking in, I felt different, separate. The entire day was peculiar as a result of what I've experienced my first few days here.

———•◦•———

Nancy, Ledlie, and I drive a short distance from Nancy's home to the old DeWolf cemetery, where James DeWolf is buried. Poison ivy grows freely. Walking along a path between the markers and monuments all around us, we come upon the headstone of Adjua, one of the two Africans James DeWolf gave to his wife. According to her headstone, Adjua was seventy-four when she died in 1868. I would love to learn more about her: how long she was enslaved (slavery wasn't banned in Rhode Island until 1843) and what life was like for her in Bristol.[1] She and Pauledore arrived when slave trading was legal. She died three years after the end of the Civil War. There must be something to the old family stories of how beloved Adjua and Pauledore were. Carved into the stone is the name ADJUA D'WOLF. She's buried in the family cemetery. No one but James DeWolf's immediate family and descendants are buried here. We can't find a headstone for Pauledore.

I'd called Halsey Howe for help locating James DeWolf's grave. Having been repeatedly vandalized, it isn't marked. Continuing along the path to the back of the cemetery, we encounter a large mound of dirt, under which he lies—fifteen feet tall with a circumference of about forty-five feet—with a huge tree growing from the top. Exposed roots snake down, holding the old slaver in their gnarly grasp. Other, smaller trees with exposed roots grow here as well, with poison ivy growing up wild through rotting leaves.

I walk around Captain Jim's earthen mausoleum, careful to avoid the oily three-leaf clusters at my feet, and find the moss-covered opening to what I presume to be his crypt. There is no headstone or marker of any kind with his name, nothing to indicate that a former Rhode Island legislator and United States senator rests here. Thousands of lives were affected because of this man and his legacy. His place in history isn't recognized at his grave, but it has been carved into the soul of America.

I walk the rest of the way around and find another crypt, hollowed out and empty. Beer cans, bottles, and broken glass litter the clearing, with foliage so thick above me that it blocks out the sky. A dark and eerie gloom engulfs me as midday approaches. Elizabeth later tells me this is a popular hangout for parties.

Many generations of DeWolfs from other family lines are interred at Juniper Hill Cemetery across town. Its largest monument was erected to honor James DeWolf's parents, Mark Antony DeWolf and his wife, Abigail. Carved into the marble below their names is a verse from the Bible—Luke, chapter 1, verse 6: "They were both righteous before God walking in all the commandments and ordinances of the Lord, blameless."

After dropping Nancy off at home, Ledlie and I meet the others downtown for the short drive to the Old State House in Providence. We'll spend the day in the very room in which debates were held over two hundred years ago about slavery and Rhode Island's part in it. The benches resemble hard old wooden church pews, only more painful, if that is possible. The backs rise at a ninety-degree angle from the seats and are painted white, with brown hardwood railings on top that dig into my shoulder blades if I lean back. There will be no comfort here. The light-green walls of the well-maintained chamber have tall windows bordered with ornate trim. Fancy carved beams break up the ceiling into ten-foot-square sections, and intricate patterns are also carved at the tops of the columns that hold them up. The light fixtures are sets of four small white globes that hang down about four feet below the ceiling. An American flag and a Rhode Island state flag stand behind the dais. The room has been reserved for our use today.

Even though it's another very warm day, the air conditioning remains off and windows are closed to keep noise to a minimum. The lighting necessary for filming intensifies the heat. It's a good thing we are family, because in addition to sharing what's in our minds and hearts I suspect we're about to become familiar with each other's bodily aromas as well.

We are joined by two guests. Ron Bailey, an African American, hails from a small town outside Savannah, Georgia. He earned a

Ph.D. in black studies from Stanford and currently serves as vice president for academic affairs at Knoxville College in Tennessee. Dr. Bailey, a large man with graying hair, a goatee, and wire-rimmed glasses, wears a dark suit and tie.

Joanne Pope Melish is of European descent. Her green blouse almost matches the walls in the courtroom. She holds a Ph.D. in American studies from Brown University. Dr. Melish teaches in the history department at the University of Kentucky and has written a book called *Disowning Slavery*. Her brown hair is brushed behind her ears.

Growing up in Waterbury, Connecticut, in the fifties, Joanne knew nothing about slavery in New England. Slavery was a southern scourge. Virtuous northerners went south to enlighten the unevolved southerners. It was during Joanne's college days in Rhode Island that it began to dawn on her that there was a very distinctive, and hidden, racism in New England. People were enthusiastic about the abstract idea of equality, but "don't move into my neighborhood, don't sit next to me" was the prevailing reality. She witnessed what she calls "constructed amnesia" about the domestic institution of slavery and the slave trade in New England, and found it particularly striking in Rhode Island.

Joanne explains that one of the slave-trading families in Providence was that of John Brown—not the fiery abolitionist who raided the federal arsenal at Harper's Ferry, Virginia, in 1859, but a pro-slavery leader in late-eighteenth-century New England. John Brown of Providence was from the Rhode Island family for which Brown University is named. These Browns were involved in shipping, whaling, chocolate, iron, tobacco, and candles, all industries undergirded by slavery. John Brown believed that slaves were better off in America than in Africa. James DeWolf worked for John Brown—who was twenty-eight years his senior—as a teenager on a privateer, and later on one of Brown's slave ships. They were both politicians as well as business tycoons. Brown served in both the U.S. House and Senate.

John's brother Moses was his chief antagonist. After the four Brown brothers invested in a disastrous slave-trading voyage in 1765 in which more than half of the Africans who were purchased died, Moses became a Quaker and a staunch abolitionist. However, Moses represents all that is complicated about slavery and constructed amnesia in America. Though Moses opposed slavery, created the Anti-Slavery Society in Rhode Island, and brought charges against both James DeWolf and his own brother John, he stayed invested in family businesses that relied on slavery to thrive. He owned a textile business while fighting for abolition. The cloth created in his mill, the very tapestry of America, was woven with cotton picked by slaves on southern plantations.[2]

Moses Brown lobbied for a federal law to outlaw the slave trade. The U.S. Congress passed—and on March 2, 1807, President Jefferson signed—just such a bill. It became effective January 1, 1808. However, between 1808 and 1820 a vigorous, clandestine slave trade continued to operate out of Bristol, due in no small part to the work of collector Charles Collins. There was virtually no prosecution during those years. And, of course, the institution of slavery lasted in the United States until the Civil War.

Ron Bailey discusses the dynamics of the struggle for independence from Great Britain and the political and economic role that slavery and the slave trade played. "It was John Adams who said, 'I don't know why we should blush to confess that molasses was an essential ingredient in our independence.'"

Molasses, of course, was the essential ingredient in rum, the staple of the Triangle Trade for Rhode Islanders. Political dynamics were inextricably tied to economics. One key concern of the founding fathers was economic survival once political independence was achieved.

Joanne expands on Bonnie Warren's point that involvement in the slave trade was not limited to the wealthy. "Many slave ships go down in storms. Others succumb to revolt. Some ships simply have a galloping disease on board, and all of the slaves die. It's an enormous risk. Even though it's insured, wealthy investors realize that they don't want to underwrite that entire risk themselves. So they get other partners to invest with them. It turns out that shares of slave ships would be sold to middle-class people like me."

Joanne points out that the economic and moral involvement of New England society in the slave trade was spread broadly across classes. "It means people like me were thinking that it was reasonable to make a bit of a profit on black bodies. They were ordinary people, whose descendants, like you, are everywhere."

Ron explains how central the textile industry and other commercial activities were to the history of this country. Widespread use of Eli Whitney's cotton gin revolutionized textile manufacturing. In 1814 the textile industry in Massachusetts was very small. Within a few decades, 100,000 people were employed in large-scale textile plants. Machine building was perfected. The manufacture of train engines and interchangeable parts had to be improved because trains were used to transport cotton and interchangeable parts kept the textile machines operating.

"Yet the contributions of African Americans get left out of the picture," he stresses. "Ninety percent of the cotton was produced by slave labor up until the 1860s, but this fact escapes the discussion and distorts the real history."

Joanne observes that in order to make room for cotton culture, tens of thousands of Creek, Choctaw, and Cherokee were displaced and moved west, with thousands of them dying in the process. People know about the Trail of Tears, but they don't connect it to cotton culture and, in turn, to the slave trade and slavery. They're all connected.

These revelations are overwhelming and my anger grows. So

much of this is about material greed. Dain is obviously thinking along the same line because he notes the conversation thus far is about economics. He wonders if there was a moral and spiritual component.

"One's ideology is not unconnected to one's material interest," remarks Joanne. "Mr. Jefferson says, 'I tremble for my country when I realize that God is just,' and he doesn't free his slaves."

In the original draft of the Declaration of Independence, Thomas Jefferson included in his list of "unremitting injuries and usurpations" committed by "his present majesty" (King George III) that "he has waged cruel war against human nature itself, violating its most sacred rights of life & liberty in the persons of a distant people who never offended him, captivating & carrying them into slavery in another hemisphere, or to incur miserable death in their transportation thither."[3]

Yet Jefferson owned slaves when he wrote these words. He owned slaves until his death. "He names it, and he doesn't free his slaves," underscores Joanne.

The more we hear, the more frustrated we become. Keila asks the obvious question in all of our minds. "Is this being taught in either high schools or colleges?"

"Some schools have a quarter of black history," says Joanne. "There are political people who believe that if you tell a tarnished story, you will make people bad patriots; that you will disinvest them in their country."

"The exact opposite happens," says Elizabeth, my school-teaching cousin from New York City. "By *not* teaching the full story, you're creating bad patriots. People aren't stupid. Those who are being oppressed and who are disenfranchised in this society completely understand that. They know when they're being left out of what goes on in school, so they don't go to school and this whole thing continues."

Ron agrees. "Regardless of what we feel about the story, that's the story. So let's tell the story and let the chips fall where they may. It might end up with me not liking you or your granddaddy, but it might end up with both of us realizing there is a connection between my family, the DeWolfs, the Browns, and cotton and slavery, which might just be the basis for an honest dialogue about the uneven distribution of political and economic power in the U.S. or in the world today."

Joanne says students typically understand American history to be the story of great white men, with a cursory glance at peripheral characters. Ron points out how empowering it can be for black students to see slavery as one of the central engines driving the progress of western civilization. Slavery created tremendous wealth for people who went on to found Brown University, build Symphony Hall in Boston, and pursue other philanthropic activities.

The following morning we're back at Linden Place again. We won't be filming inside. Either their board or their lawyers won't grant Katrina permission. So, standing outside the mansion, we meet a smallish white man with glasses and a baseball cap. Kevin Jordan, who teaches historic preservation at Roger Williams University here in Bristol, looks to be in his mid-fifties. The cane he limps along with is courtesy of an injury he sustained falling off a roof last May. We walk through the front gate and around to the back of the mansion.

Built in 1810 for George DeWolf, this is the only one of the four original DeWolf mansions in Bristol—all designed by Russell Warren, an important Rhode Island architect—still standing. It's a Federal-style building, and each of the top two stories is shorter than the one below.

George was James DeWolf's nephew, the oldest son of Charles, James's oldest sibling. One of the letters we read at the historical society referred to George's abominable behavior and despicable treatment of slaves in Cuba. George was the family member who continued in the slave trade after 1808. The profits from a single year of the outlawed trade allowed him to build this house that surpassed the grandeur of those of his uncles, right in the middle of town. After the War of 1812 he was elected commanding general of the 4th Brigade of Rhode Island. Like his Uncle James, he served in the Rhode Island legislature.

There is no way to tell how much George made in the illegal trade between 1808 and 1820, when it became a hanging crime. All records of the illegal commerce were apparently falsified or destroyed. But in 1818 enough molasses was imported to distill 100,000 gallons of rum, a suspiciously large amount that far exceeded what could be sold domestically.[4]

After 1820, with the end of the slave trade, a recession began in Bristol. The economy shifted to other industries, and Bristol suffered. In 1825, when the annual crop on his plantation in Cuba failed, George was unable to deliver cargoes of sugar as promised. The news shook Bristol. What happened next shows just how pervasive and interrelated business dealings were. Borrowers whose notes had been called in by nervous banks demanded payment of the debts owed to them by George. Investments and losses had always been spread among so many people that no one believed the whole system could crumble. But the riches that had poured into Bristol over many years from privateering and the slave trade disappeared into a fog of speculative investments. People couldn't pay their own debts because they couldn't collect on money they were owed. The house of cards fell and George DeWolf was at the center of it all.[5]

He disappeared with his wife and children in the middle of the night, and they sailed to their plantation in Cuba. The townspeople swarmed the mansion and plundered all its valuables. Linden Place was sold to cover a portion of George's debts and was purchased by James DeWolf. He sold it to his son William Henry for a tidy profit.

Kevin explains that in the late 1840s, William Henry went off to Cuba with his mistress and left his wife, Sarah, at Linden Place. When she died in 1865 the mansion was put up for auction. A man from Connecticut named Edward Colt bought it for his mother. She turned out to be Theodora DeWolf Colt, one of the children who'd slipped away in the middle of the night with her father, George, four decades earlier. As Halsey told me years ago, she had married the brother of Samuel Colt, the inventor of the revolver.

Theodora's youngest son, Samuel Pomeroy Colt, became the most prominent of the Colts. He worked at the National Rubber Company, which was owned by Augustus Bourn, the former governor of Rhode Island. When Bourn was appointed consul general to Italy by President Harrison, Colt was appointed as Bourn's agent with power of attorney at National Rubber. Within six months, Colt had the company in bankruptcy. Six months after that he emerged as sole owner.

"He basically stole it from Bourn," says Kevin. "When he came back, Bourn sued him. It went to court but was finally thrown out by the attorney general of Rhode Island, who happened to be Samuel Pomeroy Colt."

I shake my head in disgust. Several of my cousins groan.

"Colt then combined that with another rubber company in Woonsocket and started United States Rubber Company, which is the forerunner of the Uniroyal Corporation. Sam P. Colt was one of the robber barons Teddy Roosevelt used to scream about."

Colt combined five Bristol banks with several in Providence to create Industrial National Bank, a forerunner to Fleet Bank. It was his son, Russell Colt, who married actress Ethel Barrymore. When Samuel P. Colt died in 1921, he left Linden Place equally to his children and grandchildren until only one remained. It was left in trust until then at Industrial National Bank. Two of Colt's grandchildren survived into the 1980s until, finally, only one remained to inherit Linden Place. She was in her late seventies, lived in Arizona, and put the mansion up for sale. In the late 1980s, a nonprofit organization was formed to purchase and operate Linden Place as a museum.

Elizabeth explains that she grew up in Bristol and worked at Linden Place. She asks Kevin about the reactions he's received when he's brought this history up with people here.

"Linden Place is funny," he replies. "There are a lot of people who call him 'Unkie Colt' like he's this glamorous figure. He's an S.O.B. When they had a strike he went to Italy and Portugal and imported workers to break the strike. During another strike he hired only women and figured they'd be docile. When *they* went on strike he hired only married women and figured the men would control them. In the 1890s it was illegal to bring workers to this country as indentured servants. He did it. Like most wealthy people, he gave a little bit back. He gave money to build the stone chapel at St. Michael's and his four-hundred-acre farm became Colt State Park."

It wasn't exactly a gift. The state purchased Colt's farm and turned it into the gem of the Rhode Island state parks system. The western side borders Narragansett Bay. This choice acreage, with its spectacular view of the bay, was once home to well-tended cattle, draft horses, and elegant parties populated by Rhode Island's social elite. It now contains miles of bicycle, jogging, and walking trails and groves of trees, open lawns, stone walls, ponds, and playgrounds.

"He gave a school," says Kevin. "He'd throw a Fourth of July party. But that's typical of what all of the robber barons did and are doing today. He was also a son of a bitch. He had a Portuguese worker who showed up to work one day in new clothes, only to have Colt make him change into his old clothes so he wouldn't look so good."

Dain wonders how the Bristol community will respond to Katrina's film.

"Most will say it has nothing to do with them," says Kevin. "You've got to remember Bristol is sixty to seventy percent either Portuguese or descendants of Portuguese immigrants, and most will say it's not their history. They claim they were just fisher-men. The truth is the first Portuguese came to Bristol because the Azores is north of Goree. As crewmen died on the ships that were going down the African coast they'd stop and pick up more crew-men. Many of the Portuguese got here not as fishermen, but as crews of slavers."

The Azores, a group of Portuguese islands, lies eighteen hundred miles north of Goree Island. Once a center for the transatlantic slave trade, Goree Island lies less than two miles off the shore of Dakar, the capital of Senegal.

"You can't understand Bristol without understanding its role in the slave trade," says Kevin. "You can't understand America with-out understanding what the slave trade did for it. It's equivalent to saying, 'if there hadn't been a Hitler there wouldn't have been a German Holocaust.' Except that Hitler never personally killed any-one. Six million Jews were killed by someone, and it wasn't Hitler. At Dachau, the whole town said, 'We didn't know it was there,' but they picked up the clothes, they brought in the food; everyone in town lived off it. So you can blame Hitler if you want. Clearly he set an ideology. You can blame Colt or General George DeWolf, but they were sharing an ideology. It's part and parcel of the whole cul-ture. Until slavery is seen in that light, we're ignoring the whole framework."

"That's the parallel," says James. "We're singling out certain people. They committed terrible acts but they're not strikingly dif-ferent from the rest of their communities, their cultures, and their peers. These people were probably not all that much different from all of us. If we were there at that time, some of us may well have been involved in the slave trade."

I guess he could be right. We can't use today's glasses to judge people who have been dead for centuries. When I asked James yes-terday what he does for a living, he smiled and said, "I collect de-grees." He seemed to be joking, but he's hard for me to read. Clearly the intellectual of the Family of Ten, James DeWolf Perry VI was born in Belgium when his father worked at the embassy in Brussels. From seventh grade on, he attended Roxbury Latin, a private prep school in Boston. He majored in government as an undergraduate at Harvard, went to law school at Columbia, and is now in the Ph.D. program in political science at Harvard. He also teaches there. I'm impressed, but I don't have a clear sense of James yet.

After thanking Kevin and walking back to Linden Place, we drive to the north end of town, then to Poppasquash, and on to the south end of Colt State Park, near where Elizabeth grew up. Poppasquash is six miles long and two miles wide. From the deck of the Lobster Pot restaurant the other night, Ledlie, Nancy, and I saw Poppasquash across Bristol Harbor, just north of Hog Island. We pull off the road where a wooden sign reading "Coggeshall Farm Museum" swings from a hand-hewn post and beam.

Though it took only fifteen minutes to get here, it feels as if we have stepped into a different world. Chickens and sheep move about freely. Old wooden structures, blacksmiths' bellows, crosscut saws, scythes, and other hand-operated equipment allow me to easily imagine African people toiling away on Rhode Island farms two hundred years ago. After milling about, checking out the buildings and the animals, we gather on blankets in the middle of the grass to talk further with Joanne Pope Melish.

I can't comprehend how so much history in the North just vanished. According to Joanne, by 1715 one-fifth of the slaves in this country were in the North. That percentage shrank as southern slavery took off. After the growth of the cotton industry, the vast majority of the slaves were in the South. The peak of Rhode Island slavery was around 1750, when 11 percent of the population was black and enslaved. Of all the New England states, Rhode Island had the highest percentage of its population enslaved as domestic workers.

Beginning in the early 1800s, one tactic white northerners used to help distance themselves from the slavery experience was to vilify black people. Joanne explains how white people made fun of the Africans' speech, looks, dress, and activities. Consciously or unconsciously, the result was to create and expand separation. Whites hoped to get blacks to move back to Africa, a place most of them had never lived and knew nothing about.

She passes around an old cartoon as an example of the kind of literature that began to appear in newspapers and magazines. "Here's a black woman in an exaggerated hat because she's living above her station. She's got two black men with their arms around her because, of course, she's lascivious and unchaste. There's a black man you can't see very well who's drunk on the floor. And look at the language: '12th annebersary ob Affricum bobalition,' because, of course, that's the way black people speak."

The story of an enslaved South and a free North is willful and constructed amnesia: whites, who, a few generations removed, had no recollection or knowledge of northern slavery, reasoned that blacks were disproportionately poor and illiterate due to an innate inferiority. Separation between the races increased, and whites felt superior. This explains much about northern racism.

Joanne asks Elizabeth if she knew she was descended from a major slave trader.

"I didn't know it was major," she answers. "I knew it was a slave trader."

"Was it an open discussion in your family?" Joanne asks.

"No, not at all," says Elizabeth.

James says that's been his experience as well. Family and the past were very important, but his family was very selective about what they focused on. Elly says that, to be fair, what she heard from her mother would have been what her mother experienced in life. She didn't know any slave traders. Who knows much of anything about family members more than one or two generations back?

"If you forget that history," says Katrina, "then when current events are about racial injustice, you're not implicated. You can point the finger elsewhere. It explains a whole northern, white, liberal thing. We know we're not supposed to be prejudiced and we're supposed to consider everyone to be equal. But that's the end of the story and you put it out of your mind because you're a good person. Your region and your family have always been good. If there's a problem it must be somebody else's problem."

"Does it strike you that there's an unusual absence in your lives of engagement with people who are not like you?" asks Joanne.

"Not at all...," says Dain with a laugh. I can't tell if he's being sarcastic or serious.

Joanne explains one argument that has been made since the Civil War: northern racism is evidenced by an engagement with issues of social justice on the one hand, but an almost deliberate disengagement with actual black people on the other. They support civil rights but haven't ever had a meaningful conversation with a black person.

"Yet," says Dain. "I don't know the numbers on this, but my impression is that a huge number of people from New England went down to civil rights marches in the South."

"Bull's-eye!" says Joanne. "Oh yes, because they're going to straighten out the South! We marched south in the Civil War. During Reconstruction we sent schoolteachers south to improve the literacy rate among black people. Aren't you proving my point? White northerners have been terribly concerned about social justice and black empowerment somewhere else, not here. God forbid you empower them next door. Empower them in Alabama."

I choose this moment to toss in a thought as the California boy. I don't think New England is the Lone Ranger here. I struggle to explain that I did not know how to talk to black people about my fear when I was young. There was no basis or education for that kind of dialogue. I also didn't know about any of the family history, let alone about slavery in the North. There's no amnesia, there's no guilt—for me, it didn't exist. Katrina asks what I would think if I were my ancestor Simon. Even though I'm not guilty, how I would deal with the fact that my brother was a slave trader?

I pause for a moment. "It was almost two hundred years ago. It was a different time, it was a different culture. I don't want to defend anything that happened in this family or in New England or in America but I don't want to vilify these people either because I don't know. I wasn't walking in their shoes."

Although I'm not aware of it at the moment, in Ghana I will have an epiphany that will profoundly alter my beliefs.

Over the past week, Katrina met individually with each of us in order to capture some personal background along with our hopes and fears regarding this journey. Ledlie said, "My fears about going to Ghana are that it won't mean a lot to me. I will see where the slaves were imprisoned and it won't come alive for me. My other fear is that it will come alive for me."

His words haunt me.

CHAPTER 6

AKWAABA

Our week together in Bristol came to an end and Holly drove me to the airport in Boston for my flight home. She told me about a conversation she had with her stepfather. She'd given him a brochure about *Traces of the Trade* and newspaper articles about Katrina and the film from the *Providence Journal* and the *Boston Globe*. Before picking me up at Nancy's that morning, she asked for his reactions. "His first response was 'Well, I just want to say my family came after the Civil War.' He chuckled, and had a smile on his face."

Holly glanced at me and then turned back to the road ahead. "Then he said, 'I just think this is fearsome.' He didn't say it with negative energy, he just said it quietly and then he paused and said, 'I'm afraid. But then again, I'm not going to be around five years from now.' And if I grew up when he did, in his milieu, and I was his age, I'd probably have the same reaction."

"I'm not his age and I have that reaction," I said.

———•••———

After a two-week break, I fly across the country again. Meeting my fellow travelers on Wednesday morning, July 25, I expect a long and tedious day at JFK International in New York, but checking in proves to be anything but. Each passenger can check up to seventy pounds, so we weigh bags, then combine and shrink-wrap them together in the most efficient way possible. Every pound over seventy costs $8.50; every bag over two each is $120; our pile of film and sound equipment is enormous. Nerves become frayed, mine included.

There are thirteen of us to coordinate: nine family members—Jim Perry will travel separately and meet us in Ghana—and our production team of Jude Ray, Juanita Brown, Jeff Livesey, and Liz Dory.

Katrina gathers us together, inviting us to reflect about the first leg of the journey through the Triangle Trade that was taken in the past. What must crew members have felt, leaving family and friends in Bristol behind as they began the long voyage to the coast of Africa? Steam-powered vessels weren't in use yet, so it would take weeks, or perhaps months, to reach their destination. I imagine an antiquated ship sailing on the open sea filled with dozens of hogsheads of rum and tobacco to be used in trade. The ship and crew also would have been well outfitted with food and other provisions. Then there were the other supplies: the manacles, chains, and whips for the Africans they intended to bring back. I glance around the terminal at African American people waiting for the same flight as us and feel depressed about the images in my head.

Our DC-10 is completely full. I look around at all the dark-skinned faces and imagine most of our fellow passengers are heading for the Panafest celebration. Many African Americans visit Ghana during Panafest to reconnect with their ancestral roots. The segments of our journey have been scheduled to coincide with Independence Day in Rhode Island, Panafest in Ghana, and Carnival in Cuba.

—•—

It's light outside when I awake. We fly far above green foliage, brown land, and villages below. Roads are also brown. Ghana is slightly smaller than Oregon, but its population dwarfs my state twenty million to three. The city of Accra alone is home to three million people.

Kotoka International Airport is one surprise after another. The first is that we don't walk off the plane through a jet bridge into the terminal. Instead, rolling stairs lead onto the apron and toward the terminal. I read the word *akwaaba* at the top of the entrance to the terminal building as I walk inside with Holly.

The terminal is a madhouse. Bags are piled everywhere. More are added to the heap from arriving planes. People walk over and around bags and cut between carts and other people to find their belongings. Two hours pass before we succeed in gathering our luggage and equipment into one massive mound. Africanus Aveh, our line producer in Ghana, will help supervise and coordinate various aspects of filming here. He talks with the authorities about getting us through customs. Africanus stands about six feet tall. His size, his calm, and even his glasses, goatee, and smile give off an air of authority. Then, without warning, we are told to pick up all our bags and go. We zip through customs, without even one bag being inspected.

Outside the terminal, we wait as everything is loaded onto two small buses. Young Ghanaians ask us for money and gifts. Elizabeth receives a marriage proposal. I hand my business card to one teenager who asks for it. Everyone is extremely friendly. There are hundreds and hundreds of people of all ages, but we are the only white people I see.

The Family of Ten boards a white bus with the words "Calvary Methodist Church—Accra" in blue letters on the side and "The Lord Provides" across the front. The crew rides in a second bus. Along the side of the road, throngs of young people sell CDs, clothing, toilet paper, artwork, and varieties of food. They approach our bus whenever we stop, which is often, due to the thick traffic. To-morrow we will drive from Accra to Cape Coast, which is 145 kilo-meters away. Perhaps it won't be this congested once we leave the city.

We pull into a walled enclosure that resembles a school, the W. E. B. Du Bois Center. Inside the fence, abundant tall trees shade the grounds, which are mostly dirt and concrete. The humidity is stifling. One large, white single-story building and two other smaller buildings stand nearby.

While the crew sets up, a few local people gather around us. One teenage boy extends his hand in greeting. As we shake hands, he says, "I am Hector the Selector." He nods toward the young man standing next to him. "This is my friend Kofi."

"You mean like Kofi Annan from the United Nations?" I ask.

"Every Friday-born male is called Kofi," says Hector. "You want me to teach you some words in my language?"

"Sure," I say. There are dozens of different linguistic and cul-tural groups in Ghana. Akan is the most widely spoken native lan-guage, though English is the common language throughout Ghana. Hector's language is Akan. I ask him about the word painted on the side of the terminal building at the airport.

"*Akwaaba* means 'welcome,'" he says. When I thank him, he tells me the word for "thank you" in Akan is *madasi*. "*Atese* means 'how are you?' *Mempe* is what you say when you don't like or need something. *Mempe* will come in handy for you as many people will want you to buy things."

"I see. *Madasi*, Hector." We continue to chat while waiting for filming to begin. He asks where I'm from, and then what Oregon is like.

"Are you married?" he asks.

"Yes, I am."

"You must buy a necklace from me for a gift for your beauti-ful wife."

"Well, I'll need to think about that. We just arrived and . . ."

"I wish you God's many blessings. I trust you. Do you trust me? I have very nice jewelry for your wife. She will love it."

How awkward. The temperature jumps a few degrees. Hector has suddenly shifted from helpful teacher to high-pressure salesman. What was that word he just taught me? I've got to pay closer attention. My protective drawbridge begins to rise as I tell Hector I'm thirsty and look around for the cooler to get a bottle of water. He smiles. Relief comes when Katrina announces that we're starting.

By chance, we have arrived as a group of high school students begins to practice a play they've prepared for Panafest. They perform a brief history of slavery on a concrete outdoor stage. One shouts, "My Africa! Africa, of proud warriors! My blood is charged with your blood. Your beautiful black blood, spread abroad, over the field, the blood of your sweat, the sweat of your labor, the labor of your slavery, the slavery of your children." The play lasts only a few minutes and ends with all the actors singing "We Shall Overcome."

When they conclude, we applaud and invite them to join us in a semicircle of white plastic chairs. Katrina stands before the gathered assembly of over thirty people. Seated next to her is Robert Addo-Fenning, professor of history at the University of Ghana, the man we've arranged to meet. As with the clothes of so many people I've seen today, the blue, purple, and white colors of his shirt are bright and striking.

Katrina introduces herself. She thanks everyone for joining us and tells them who we are and why we're here. Professor Addo-Fenning remains seated and begins to describe society in this part of the world before contact with Europeans. "In 1471, the Portuguese were the first Europeans to establish contact. At the time they arrived, the people of this area were in a process of developing into states."

Though our surroundings are just as relaxed as in Rhode Island

—even more so—our conversation here feels different, more formal. We felt welcome to address professors Bailey, Melish, and Jordan by their first names. Not wanting to be presumptuous about what is appropriate in this culture, we address our guest as Professor Addo-Fenning.

He holds notes, but rarely refers to them. Smiling as he talks, he emphasizes his words with broad gestures, yet his demeanor is quite peaceful. He explains how the concept of land ownership was unknown before the Europeans arrived. People traditionally used the land and left it for future generations (which sounds similar to the attitude of the indigenous North Americans before Columbus). They believed departed ancestors were still in contact with, and influenced the day-to-day activities of, the living. Before the colonial powers divided the continent of Africa into countries, this region was composed of numerous small communities, with well-defined structures and leadership.

Elly, whose upper body and head are wrapped in a large scarf to protect her skin from the hot sun, asks the professor how he thinks West African society might have continued to evolve if the Europeans hadn't come.

It's impossible to know, of course. The professor explains that the Europeans replicated a trade network that was already directed north across the Sahara toward the Middle East and beyond. That system had been in place since the eighth century A.D. The Europeans created a new network that directed trade southward into European ships.

Ledlie says, "In the United States, when we talk about the slave trade, the comment is often made, 'Well we didn't start it. The tribal leaders in Africa started it.' Would you comment on this?"

"That is not true," responds Addo-Fenning. "That is absolutely false. First of all, slavery is not peculiar to Africa. Every civilization—from Mesopotamia to China, India, ancient Greece, Rome—has known slavery. Africa also practiced slavery. The commodities going across the Sahara included slaves. When the Europeans first made contact, they asked for gold and ivory." They later began trading for African people.

The professor explains that Africa reacted to demands from the West. When the West wanted gold, they traded gold. Then, when Westerners desired labor, Africans supported the slave trade. During industrialization they required raw materials, so the Africans remained at home, producing palm oil, cotton, and other commodities. It was all economically driven.

Slavery in various forms existed in many parts of Africa prior to the arrival of the Europeans. Most of the enslaved were captured during war. Others were criminals or owed debts. Some were given to the new in-laws as part of a dowry. Slavery as practiced in Africa was often, but not always, more benign than that which would soon be established in the New World. Some could earn their freedom. Others married free people. However, enslaved people were also brutalized and sometimes killed in ceremonies of sacrifice. The fact that slavery, in whatever form, already existed, meant that there were African agents ready and willing to deal with Europeans when they arrived with rum, whiskey, tobacco, and textiles.[1]

"Then these African agents would go into the interior and provoke ethnic conflict," Addo-Fenning continues. "The actual procurement was done by Africans. When the Europeans realized that it's wrong and stopped trading, slave trading stopped. Europeans assumed the posture of a civilizing mission. They knew the higher order. They knew the difference between what was right and what was wrong. They introduced God to us. What conclusion do you come to? It's like you're coming to civilize this little boy. You introduce him to something and he gets hooked on it. You blame him for getting hooked on it when you introduced him to it in the first place."

I feel ambivalent about the argument that European greed was worse than African greed. It sounds like those in power, both Europeans and Africans, expanded and solidified their power at the expense of weaker people. Granted, Europeans had more power and exercised it. But without the willing support of tribal leaders, I wonder if the slave trade would have become the behemoth it did.

I'm surprised to hear that people in Ghana don't know much about the slave trade because it isn't taught. Addo-Fenning explains that very few came back across the ocean to tell their story. Africans who sold others into slavery rarely had any idea what happened to their victims.

One of the students asks, "How cordial was the relationship between the black people and the white people?"

"Until colonial rule, the Europeans recognized that they were guests of the rulers of this country," says the professor. "When they arrived, they required permission to build a fort. They obtained that permission from the King of Elmina. They paid rent. They lived under the sovereignty of the people. They had to stand well because when a chief got angry he could forbid any of his subjects to trade with the white people, and that was it. They were cooped up in their forts and castles, with mosquitoes and malaria in the region, dependant on the goodwill of these African rulers. Only with the coming of colonial rule did we lose our sovereignty. Before that we called the shots."

A voice from several seats to the right of me says, "Thank you for your presentation. I appreciate the information. I respectfully disagree when you say that Africa lost its sovereignty at the time of colonialism."

I look around to where the voice comes from. From his accent, it is clear that he is African American. A man in his mid-twenties introduces himself as Kwame Shabazz. He's studying at Harvard and working on his Ph.D. in Ghana.

He continues, "It's my understanding that the King refused to let the Europeans build their fort at Elmina, and the Europeans forced the matter. From the very beginning the Europeans had the physical force, the military force, from that very first relationship. The African king said no, but the European was able to force his desires on the African people."

Shabazz goes on to argue that there was a lopsided relationship between Europe and Africa. The Europeans always had the advantage. They determined the terms of the trade. Throughout the world Europeans have sought to dominate, exploit, rape, plunder, and control others. "As African people, we need to understand the negative relationship we have and will continue to have with people of European descent."

Addo-Fenning appears calm. I'm not. The tension inside me just ratcheted up several notches. The professor acknowledges the unequal power. After all, when one side has bows and arrows and the other uses repeater rifles, it's no match. But Addo-Fenning defends his position that Africa retained sovereignty until being colonized.

"My friend Kofi is a graduate student here at the University of Ghana," Shabazz replies, patting the arm of the man sitting next to him, a man I met earlier. Kofi Peprah has been hired as an advisor for the film here in Ghana. "Kofi has documented how Europeans control the gold-mining industry here and how the gold that comes up out of Africa goes to the benefit of Europeans. Nigeria is the sixth-largest producer of oil in the world. Yet Nigeria imports petroleum products. Maybe it makes us feel better to say we control our land, but the truth of the matter is we don't control anything. The Europeans control what comes out of our land, what happens to it, and who makes the finished product. It's misleading, unproductive, unrealistic, and not even logical to say we control the land. How can we say that?"

"To the extent that we have the option to say no," says Addo-Fenning. He is firm. "If Nigeria decided not to sell oil or did not allow the Europeans to mine oil, would the Europeans come in aircrafts and bomb the Nigerians? It is a decision that is made by an African government. The choice is yours, isn't it?"

"No," says Shabazz, "because the Europeans control the options you have." He is just as firm as the professor and more animated than ever. He gives several examples of how governments and others in power determine the limited choices people end up having. Though I'm unnerved by his assertiveness, Kwame's arguments are powerful. His presence has certainly intensified the conversation, which continues for several more minutes.

Dain asks the other students for their reaction to all that's been discussed. One says, "My question is to the group who is here. Some blacks in America are calling for reparations for slavery. Now that you have realized the role played by your ancestors in these heinous crimes, what is your position on the idea?"

Dain says, "I don't think that reparations would work. It would tear black people and white people even further apart than they are now. I don't think it can politically be successful."

It is soon clear that the students are referring to damage to Africa, not just African Americans.

James says that reparations don't make sense for the consequences in Africa of slavery. Africans weren't forced to participate in the slave trade. In James's opinion, the record is clear that Africans welcomed, willingly participated in, and profited from the slave trade. In the colonial era, there was a far different pattern of behavior by those in power. James believes that reparations for the damage resulting from colonialism must be considered.

Dain turns to the students. "What do you think?"

"You need to say you are sorry." I turn to look at the young man to my left, who is speaking. "We know that you benefited from us by slaves working—whatever they did on the plantation for you. If you say you are sorry, now help us, because we are in so many conditions that hurt very bad."

I don't know how to respond. I agree that much should be done to improve things in Africa; this continent has been decimated. Much remains to be done in terms of equality back home as well, and I'm just starting to think through what options would be effective. What Dain said makes sense to me, but the more I hear, the more I wonder whether we might be wrong. Little do I know at this point how much our journey will alter my thinking.

"We are a new generation," says another student. "We are starting to discuss and understand how this came about. The people engaged in it are dead and gone. We need to sit down, both the black and the white, and agree, and get together again as human beings."

The day's light fades. As we break and wait for dinner to arrive, Hector renews, in earnest, his pressure on me to purchase a necklace from him. I tell him I don't have any Ghanaian currency (cedis). "I'll be trading American money for cedis tomorrow," I tell him. We both know I won't see him tomorrow, or ever again, probably. I'll be many miles away.

"You can pay me in American dollars," he says. "You are just saying these things because you don't want to tell me no."

That's true, but I don't say so. I don't know what to say. What's that word he taught me for not wanting something? I've got it here in my notes somewhere. I've never had a conversation quite like this before. He's really in my face and yet he's friendly as can be. I don't want to lie and I don't want to hurt his feelings. Is this Hector's act that he has honed in order to get more money from guilty visitors like me? I assume so. I look around for Juanita to see if she can help me understand this, but she's consumed in her own conversations. She'd probably just laugh at my discomfort and tell me to work through it on my own. I avoid it. I continue to talk with him, but I dance around the subject of money. I run my fingers through my hair. I look around and hope one of my cousins will join in. I smile and look interested in what Hector says, but my first in-depth communication with a Ghanaian has been disconcerting.

The dinner Juanita arranged for us arrives. Finally, a Styrofoam container of spicy chicken and rice provides a legitimate reason to excuse myself. Hector disappears and I'm relieved. My first day in Africa ends in confusion. I'm mixed up about being here, being white in a place where there are no other white people, about trust when my first extended conversation with a Ghanaian felt like we were jockeying for position, about fear of what may come next. It's only been a few hours and we have a full week's schedule ahead. What's it going to be like with other Ghanaians, and with African Americans, particularly at Panafest events and at the slave forts? I look at my hands, covered with fleecy-white skin. I feel guilty, but I'm not even sure why. I'm tired and my doubts bounce around my head. I make no further effort to answer them.

We climb into our Methodist bus for the short drive to the Mensvic Palace Hotel. It looks as though the construction workers put the finishing touches on it this afternoon. Everything about this hotel looks new compared to the other buildings we've been inside at the airport and the Du Bois Center. The light-brown pavers of the entryway are not yet stained by tires or oil. The bushes lining the entry are neatly trimmed. An American flag flies from a pole in front. The brown brick building is three stories tall, with balconies extending from many of the rooms. I look up to see a large satellite dish on the roof. The twin beds in the room Ledlie and I share are firm, as are the pillows. We both fall quickly asleep.

In the morning we climb into our buses for the drive to Cape Coast. I grew up near Los Angeles and I've never seen traffic like this. Two lanes, just one in each direction, lead to and from Accra. It is mostly paved, but where the asphalt is gone, there is hard dirt. On both shoulders there is more hard-packed dirt, wide enough for a couple more lanes. This becomes important. No signs or signals direct traffic, and there are no police. Traffic moves the same direction as in the United States, but on the shoulders two additional lines of vehicles move in the opposite direction as the legitimate lanes. People drive in the dirt on the outside of the road in an attempt to move faster. The result is four lanes of traffic, each one side by side with vehicles moving the opposite direction. If we were moving more than five miles per hour, this would be dangerous.

People sell things everywhere along the road. Poverty surrounds and engulfs us. We are moving so slowly that we are able to have brief conversations with several people. Horns honk and dust rises. People, mostly young men, yell to us from the street, trying to sell us things or to ask for money.

After a few hours, we pull off the road and stop at the Forex Bureau to exchange American money for Ghanaian cedis. The largest note in Ghana, five thousand cedis, is worth less than a dollar.

Juanita walks out of the exchange store with a full backpack and two extra bags of money. Three hundred dollars just became a stack of cedis five inches thick: 2,130,000 cedis. I'm a millionaire. It's bizarre and depressing at the same time.

Our bus crawls past Jesus Children School, God's Love Café, Fast Food Café and Funerals, Saviour Electricals.

Today's schedule is ruined. Though Cape Coast is only 145 kilometers away—about 90 miles—the traffic is so slow we'll arrive three hours later than planned. I read concern in the creases in Katrina's forehead. We'll have to rush to set up when we arrive. I overhear her say that she wants to be sensitive about filming at Panafest and doesn't want to offend or interrupt people, or get in the way. Jeff assures her that they'll be discerning about filming.

I look back out the window as we pass the Invite Jesus Into Your Life Fashion Centre. The upper floor of an old dilapidated building is painted orange. The long wall is all windows with no glass. White letters read "Infant Jesus School." In almost everyone and everything we pass, I see evidence of tremendous hardship: buildings in disrepair, open sewers, and people who appear destitute. I can't help but think about how blessed I am. I've been protected from seeing or experiencing this kind of poverty all my life. I suddenly feel very naive.

I turn my attention to Katrina's continuing conversation regarding today's logistics. Throughout the journey we will have two film crews because there are so many people and events to cover. Though we were with Liz and Jeff for the most part in Rhode Island, another crew filmed as well. In both Ghana and Cuba, locals will make up the additional crew, which provides the added benefit of greater knowledge about local dynamics and respect for local people and traditions. Kofi Peprah, the advisor for the film whom I met yesterday at the Du Bois Center, and Ebenezer Quaye, the sound man on our Ghanaian crew, join the discussion with Katrina and Jeff. Both say to go ahead and shoot this afternoon; that there will be other film crews at Panafest as well, both black and white.

Kofi sits beside me and asks, "Is the reason you haven't traveled in your life because you're so comfortable in the U.S. and you don't want to see the rest of the world?"

It is a challenging question. I had explained earlier to Kofi that I've traveled around the United States, but other than brief excursions into Tijuana, Mexico, and one trip to the Calgary Stampede in Canada, I've never been anywhere outside the forty-eight states before. I've heard that only about one-fourth of Americans even have a passport. How can we expect to understand other cultures if we never interact with them? Granted, one can see wide varieties of people, places, and cultures in different parts of our nation, but I've always known that traveling to another country would be different, special. Up until now, I've felt that international travel was a privilege I couldn't afford. I've daydreamed about flying to Hawaii, Europe, Australia, Mexico, or the Caribbean, but never Africa. I didn't think there were reasons to visit. I hadn't considered any historical places I wanted to see. No landmarks. No museums. No nothing. I stare out the window at the passing landscape, glad now that my first international destination is Ghana and that I'm not here on vacation.

Five hours later, and ninety miles farther down the main highway between Accra and Cape Coast, we arrive at our hotel. The narrow gravel entryway is partially blocked by half a rolling gate. Through the open side the drive opens into a courtyard. The white-and-gray hotel comprises two three-story buildings attached only on the ground floor. We pull through the roundabout and park. In the center of the large circular drive a garden grows. Varieties of tropical trees and trimmed bushes with well-manicured grassy areas grow throughout the front grounds.

Two guards stand at the top of the entry stairs in heavy black boots, dark-brown trousers, and gray short-sleeved shirts unbuttoned at the collar with white T-shirts underneath. Yellow cords drape over their left shoulders and attach to their left breast pockets. One has a club attached to his belt. I see no other weapons. They do not smile.

Inside the lobby, soft brown couches are arranged on either side of a large coffee table. The television plays in the background. Behind the counter, a young woman greets us with a smile. Above her head hangs a sign: "Cape Coast Hotel, Ltd. Where Success Begins."

Ledlie and I are assigned to Room 206. It's dark and the one low-wattage lightbulb doesn't help much. When we open the thick curtains to the glaring light outside, we expose bright red carpet and green spreads with flower-print sheets and pillowcases on the beds. The headboard is made of deep, rich wood. Twin beds fit together into one large bed frame. A desk sits below a mirror, between the door and a built-in armoire. Our room is equipped with air conditioning, a refrigerator, and television. We have a choice to make between the television and refrigerator, since there is only one electrical plug. We choose the refrigerator.

Down the hall a door leads to an outside balcony perhaps twenty feet square, with nothing but a small plant in one corner. The low walls are marble. I have my first real look at the whole of our hotel grounds. Two large gazebos rise from either side of the driveway with tables and chairs inside both.

A large, fat lizard with a black body and orange head stares up at me from the balcony railing. I can't see the ocean from here and I don't know how far away we are. I see palm and other varieties of trees. White houses stand across the road and apartment buildings cover a hill in the distance. The brilliant blue sky belies the fact that this is the rainy season.

Shortly after four-thirty we embark on the short drive to Elmina Castle, where we'll watch the Akwaaba Ceremony just outside the castle. Traditional leaders will conduct special rites.

Panafest—the Pan-African Historical Theatre Festival—began in 1992 and takes place every other year. People come from throughout West Africa, Europe, the Caribbean, the Americas, and elsewhere around the world to celebrate African history, art, and culture. This year, Panafest is combined with Emancipation Day, a celebration of the abolition of slavery in the British colonies in 1833 and in the United States in 1865. Also added this year is the first "Slave Route Pilgrimage," which traces the paths enslaved Africans took from northern Ghana to the waiting dungeons at Cape Coast.

The closer we get, the slower the bus moves, but this is nothing compared to the trip from Accra. I watch the ocean to our left as we make our way down the narrow road to the castle. People stare at us as we pass. I wonder what they think of this bus full of white people, something they probably don't see very often, since my understanding is that Ghana isn't a typical destination for many white people. The castle looms large as we approach. The red tile roof stands in contrast to the dingy white paint that peels from the exterior walls in some places and has worn off in others.

The moment we step off the bus, teenage boys swarm us. I'm separated from my companions and alone, surrounded on all sides by a group of boys at least a half-dozen deep. They compete for my attention by shouting that they want me to buy all sorts of things, from necklaces to wood carvings. Those without goods to sell simply join the crush and ask for money. They push each other around to gain advantage and grab my arms, trying to force pieces of paper into my hands. They want to give me their addresses and want me to sponsor them, whatever that means. With so many shouting simultaneously, I can't focus on any of them.

"Mister! Mister!"

"What is your name?"

"Are you from the U.S.?"

"Where are you from in the U.S.?"

"Please, Mr. Tom, I need you to sponsor me for school fees."

"Please, Mr. Tom, will you sponsor our soccer team?"

"Please, Mr. Tom, can I have your e-mail address?"

It is truly uncomfortable and I can't concentrate on anything except these boys. A policeman soon approaches and begins slapping them to chase them away. I'm startled and even more conflicted. I don't want him abusing these children on my behalf. It flies in the face of all the reasons we're here, yet it provides a few moments of respite and the brief opportunity to locate my cousins. Ledlie and I find each other and team up. It is, as he says when I finally manage to get close to him, "a battle of sorts."

Very mixed emotions well up inside me again. I'm torn between what I feel (I want out of here) and what I should feel—compassion. These are people with great need, and I have so much by comparison. I feel stifled and awkward. With the so-called assistance from local officials, and clasping hands to avoid being separated again, Ledlie and I finally make our way to where people have gathered for the opening ceremony. The young boys stay back.

Tarps are draped over poles so some can sit in the shade. The sun bears down on the rest of us. Speeches and drummers and dancers are followed by a parade of chieftains. A number of men walk by with long, ornate staffs. A group composed mostly of women and teenagers follows, carrying carved stools. Next a white cloth-draped palanquin—an enclosed litter—is borne on the shoulders of men below. Inside, an older man, presumably the chief, sits wearing a gold crown. In front of him sits a young girl, perhaps twelve years old, with closely cropped hair, earrings, and a necklace. She is as unobtrusive as he is boisterous in acknowledging the crowd as he passes by. Words on the side of the palanquin read "*Gye Nyame.*" Another man carries a gigantic white umbrella attached to the end of a long pole to shade the chief.

The enthusiasm of the dancers who perform next is contagious. I tap my toes in the dirt and sway to the beat. Kofi and Quaye were right, of course. There are other film crews here and no one pays any attention to Jeff, Liz, or the rest of our crew.

My attention is pulled in many directions. Speakers address the gathered crowd, but I can't focus. There must be close to one thousand people here. I feel exceedingly white. I can't blend in or disappear in the crowd. At first I think this is how it must feel for people of color back home when they're forced to work or live in all-white surroundings. But upon further reflection, I don't believe that's a very apt analogy. We may be in the minority here, but we're a very privileged minority; probably more similar to whites in South Africa than blacks in the United States. We try to be respectful and not push our way in to be able to see. At the same time, we gather in small groups so the film crew can tape us watching.

The ceremony ends, but apart from the dancing and watching the palanquins, much of it was lost on me. I walk away from the crowd toward the rocky beach. About a dozen abandoned, decaying cannon lie half buried in the ground with grass and weeds growing up and around them. A few palm trees reach high into the sky but otherwise there isn't much vegetation here.

I walk back toward our bus and boys begin to swarm around me again. One hands me a seashell, a small version of the kind you hold up to your ear to listen to the sound of the ocean. He has written on it, "To Mr. Tom from Eric."

"You didn't have to do that," I say.

"It is a gift for you," says Eric.

"Let me pay you for this."

"No. This is a gift so you will remember me and your time in Ghana."

I thank him and he smiles. As daylight begins to fade, most of the Family of Ten returns to the bus just to regain personal space. The kids continue tapping on the windows.

"Mister Tom! Mister Tom!"

"Please, Miss! Please, Miss!"

I feel invaded and I continue to feel conflicted by it.

After dark, most of the boys leave. While the film crew gathers night shots of the castle and ocean, I get off the bus and walk over to relax on a low wall outside the castle. I sit in the dark and watch the few people who remain. Elmina Castle is large and foreboding. The thick walls surrounding it must be twenty feet tall.

I listen to ocean waves crash onto the rocky shore and look up at the stars. I can't find the Big Dipper. I sit alone, taking it all in, until someone starts a car and the headlights shine on me. Eric and a few other boys see me and walk over. They are no longer so overpowering. The air has cooled and the pressure is gone. We talk until it's time for me to leave.

We drive back to the hotel and find our way to the restaurant inside. Ledlie and I order cocktails. We clink our glasses in a silent toast. We are a long way from the sea wall at the Lobster Pot.

Several of us decide to go to the Akwaaba Jam at the Cultural Center. Elly, Elizabeth, and I walk down the highway to the intersection to catch a taxi, but the only ones we see already have people inside. We end up hitchhiking, and are grateful to two Ghanaian men who kindly refuse payment. We learn that they went far out of their way to take us to the Cultural Center, a much appreciated gift at midnight.

Inside, it reminds me of a small county fairground. Several dozen booths offering carvings, jewelry, clothing, and food for sale line a wide, hard dirt path. People laugh, drink, eat, and socialize.

We pay ten thousand cedis—about a dollar and a half—to get into the concert arena and twenty thousand cedis for three beers and a coke. The music is high energy and comes in various forms: high-life, hip-hop, hiplife, reggae. My favorite musician is a popular local singer named Paapa Yankson. It is surprisingly uncrowded inside the concert area. Kofi eventually shows up and explains that the cover charge keeps people away. Tomorrow night is free and the concert will be packed. We dance until almost two in the morning before catching a taxi back to the hotel.

When we arrive, the hotel guards cradle rifles in their arms. I don't remember seeing rifles when we first encountered them earlier today. They're very casual and friendly now, much more than before. They flip their weapons around nonchalantly as they welcome us home for the night. I'm nervous watching guns periodically aimed in my direction as the guards swing them around. I make my way quickly to Room 206 and slip into bed without disturbing Ledlie.

CHAPTER 7

"UNDER A PATCHWORK OF SCARS"

Bought one man-boy slave. Gave for him one hogshead of rum...
six handkerchief for the women slaves. —*July 6, 1795*

It is a clear, hot Saturday morning, and the Grand Durbar of Chiefs, a parade of leaders, queen mothers, and elders from many tribes, will soon put on a display celebrating Ghana's rich culture. While waiting for the durbar to begin, I walk past Cape Coast Castle and down to the beach. Several dozen men work together in front of a group of huts nestled above the shore, enclosed by a tall picket fence. They strain to pull a giant net from the sea. Another dozen men standing in the water also pull toward shore. Eventually, the large blue net full of thousands of small fish lies at their feet.

Several dugout canoes rest nearby on the sand. Palm trees wave in the light breeze. It's another day in which the temperature and humidity will both reach the nineties. I look up the beach and stare at the immense walls of Cape Coast Castle. They loom, fearsome, towering above the rocky shoreline. Two dozen cannon aim toward the sea. I imagine things looked similar two hundred years ago.

A few more white people walk about today and we receive less smothering attention from boys. A man with a trained monkey tells his small pet to "shake hands with the white man." He then instructs me to give the monkey some money. His tiny soft hand snatches the coins I hold out. The monkey, who is dressed in blue jeans and a colorful shirt, is tethered to his owner by a thick chain. I watch them repeat their act for Ledlie, who laughs out loud at the monkey's skill in extracting coins from his hand.

We walk about a mile up the road leading away from the castle for the start of the Grand Durbar. Dozens of revered leaders in brilliant attire are carried by on palanquins, each litter uniquely decorated to show off its inhabitant. Most have colorful umbrellas or canopies for protection from the blazing sun. The men who carry them dance as they proceed, moving in circles, turning round and round at street corners, drawing attention to themselves and the venerated people they carry. Some chiefs and queens walk as subjects hold umbrellas above them. Drumming displays, horn blowing, dancing, singing, and laughter fill the street. For over two hours, the men carrying palanquins, the drummers, those marching on stilts, and those making music never stop, or even slow down.

I see Holly holding hands with a Ghanaian woman who carries a baby on her back. Holly says they've held hands most of the way as they walked together. She asks me, "Why didn't we do this on the Fourth of July?"

"This *is* the Fourth of July!" I exclaim.

People watch from doors, windows, balconies, ledges, and the roofs of cars. Some walk and others dance along with the slow-moving procession. A group of young girls adorned in resplendent full-length yellow, red, and blue dresses marches ahead of one palanquin. They clutch gold scepters. Amazingly, one man carries a throne on his head and shoulders with a man sitting on it. A group of men carries large drums with the skins directed behind them. The drums must be over four feet in length and over a foot in diameter.

I can't imagine bearing that load for the full length of the durbar. Drummers dressed in black and orange walk behind them, pounding out the rhythm. They never lose the beat as they walk. I'm certain the guys carrying the drums will be unable to hear by the end of the day. I spot the white *Gye Nyame* palanquin from yesterday.

A few cars try to snake their way through the parade route. People slide out of their way to let them pass. A young girl in a blue plaid dress glances at me as she walks by, carrying a basket on her head filled with small woven mats. A woman in a bright purple tie-dyed dress with a matching bandanna on her head dances with exuberance nearby.

I watch my step to avoid slipping into the three-foot-wide, four-foot-deep open sewer that flows alongside the street. Passing a demolished building, I watch a young boy enjoying the festivities from the rubble. A man on stilts rests on a roof above a sign reading "His Excellency Tailoring Shop." The long stilts make the roof an ideal perch.

"*Ye ye bako!*" the people shout. "Let's come together!"

Thousands and thousands of people line the street, hot, sweaty, alive, and proud. People of all ages fill every doorway and window, dancing, laughing, singing—honoring their culture, their ancestors, and themselves. At the same time, the durbar feels somber. The gravity of that which is being commemorated infuses the proceedings.

The durbar ends in a large field at Victoria Park, down the road from the castle. It fills with people as a man begins to address the crowd. I have no time to listen, since we will soon begin filming, so I make my way back up the street against the flow of people still walking to the park.

I purchase a bottle of water from a young girl just across from the entry to the castle. Her grandmother pulls me into her shop. Just like last night at the Cultural Center, merchants sell their wares at a variety of booths. One offers food and drink, the next displays clothing, and another sells souvenirs. The booths are colorful and the people friendly.

"I want you to buy something from me," Grandmother says. She puts a green shirt on me and buttons it up. "You look good," she smiles as we look at a mirror.

"How much?" I ask.

"Seventy thousand. No arguments."

"Will you take sixty-five thousand?" We were told that people expect us to bargain with them.

She frowns. Her smile does not return as we complete the transaction. I walk away and don't like the feeling. This is the last time I'll argue about a price. From now on, I'll either buy it for the stated price or walk away. No more negotiations.

At three o'clock in the afternoon we meet inside the thick white walls of Cape Coast Castle. With all the festivities outside, the castle sits quiet, mostly void of people. At the far end of the courtyard, past several graves embedded in concrete, past the cannon, I lean out and look down. Waves crash against the rocks far below that form the foundation of this fortress. In the distance, a small dog walks along the beach.

Around a corner to my left, narrow stairs lead up to a room where we meet Professor Kofi Anyidoho, distinguished poet and scholar from the African Humanities Institute at the University of Ghana, where he teaches literature. His chair, next to a large window, faces ours.

Professor Anyidoho didn't learn the complex and deeply rooted story of slavery and its impact on Africa from history books or in school—either in Ghana or elsewhere. He learned through poetry, drama, novels, and most significantly, through film. While researching Pan Africanism, a movement intended to unify African people globally and motivate them to understand who they are and where they should be going, he encountered a profound statement by an African American poet. "He said a people's view of themselves as well as the world has to be a long one if they are to be more than a footnote in history. Another African American scholar, Houston Baker, points out to us that to understand our origins we must journey through difficult straits even if in the end all we encounter is confusion."

He pauses to allow this to sink in. These first days have been filled with confusion. I've been taught to study for clarity, for understanding. I'm less and less sure that will happen for me in Ghana or anywhere else during this journey. Dr. Anyidoho adjusts his glasses. His graying goatee frames a friendly smile. His black, short-sleeved shirt hangs untucked over white pants. The calmness with which he speaks stands in stark contrast with the subject he begins to discuss.

"We sit here. The breeze is wonderful and I wish we could just relax and forget about what has brought us here. But this was the room in which the patrons did business, this room. This was where African people were sold into slavery."

I look around. Four walls, windows, a door, and chairs make up a simple room, nothing sinister at all.

"Just up to when Panafest started [in 1992], part of Cape Coast Castle was being used as a prison. Many forts in the country today are still used as prisons. Before the European presence we did not have prisons. The first prisons from the colonial period were located in the slave forts. Then we became independent and found it convenient to continue. In my own language, the word for prison is slave fort and the word for government is also slave fort. You can see how things come together."

He tells of a journey he and some colleagues took into Ghana's past to locate ancient fields of sorrow. They visited Gwollu in northeastern Ghana, where they saw walls erected around the entire town to minimize the danger of surprise raids by slave merchants. In another town, residents took refuge in a series of caves. Professor Anyidoho and his companions also traveled to Benin, which was once the Republic of Dahomey, to the town of Ganvie, built entirely on water.

"For every African, this was a state of war. When war comes, you quickly reorganize your life, suspend the things you have planned for yourself and reduce everything to the need to stay alive. The hope, of course, is that it will soon be over. In the history of Europe, the longest war was the so-called Hundred Years War. Fortunately that didn't mean people were fighting every day. But here you were under attack literally every day of your life. This went on for one thousand years. After two or three generations who would remember what normal life was like? Today, we find African people out of breath, trying to get a sense of where they are, where they were before the horror began."

Dr. Anyidoho stresses that the landscape wasn't like it is today. The rainforest was intact and there were no roads. If a person was captured in northern Ghana, he or she was four or five hundred miles away from the coast, and the journey was made on foot. Everyone's legs were chained and their necks chained to the necks of the people in front and behind. Sometimes people had to wait as long as twelve weeks for a boat to arrive. Given how people were packed into dungeons and the almost total lack of regular ventilation, and many other factors, there was a reasonable chance that many people would die before setting foot on a slave ship.

Professor Anyidoho looks around the room and out the window. "When we refer to this place as a castle, it was indeed a castle for some people. For the people who did business in this room, it was a castle. We will soon see the governor's rooms, rooms spacious enough for a tennis match," he laughs, "with wide windows and free ventilation."

W.E.B. Du Bois conducted one of the first major studies of the slave trade. He estimated that ten to fifteen million Africans landed alive in the New World. But Du Bois also concluded that every slave who arrived in the Americas represented others who died in Africa or during the Middle Passage.

"Between the point of capture, transportation to the slave forts, being held in the dungeons, and then, above all, the way they were transported across the Middle Passage, packed so tight it was practically impossible to walk through them, many people were lost."

Anyidoho points outside through the window behind us. Fort William, a small fortress, rises from the top of a nearby hill. It was built to provide protection for Cape Coast Castle from the Fante people, the Asante, and others. He tells us to look more closely as he points out several churches that dot the busy landscape.

In trading posts along the African coast that were controlled by the Portuguese and Spanish, it is reported that slaves were routinely baptized. Priests often baptized local African leaders, even while captive Africans moved into, and through, the forts on their way toward the Middle Passage. The professor gestures toward a window overlooking the courtyard below and says that when we begin our tour we'll see the church that was built directly above the dungeon. Referring to slaves who were baptized, he says, "You lose your name and take a Christian name. You become a slave in the name of God. Religion played a key role in all this. Africans have to live hopefully for the next world. We've already lost this one."

He explains that Christianity was the religion on the Atlantic side and Islam on the Saharan side of the slave trade. "There is nothing wrong with Christianity as a principle; there is nothing wrong with Islam as a religious faith. But there is something terribly wrong with each of these faiths being used to enslave other people."

"It's hard for me to understand why there are so many churches," I say, "as well as 'Jesus' and 'God' in the title of so many businesses around here. Is it that people don't remember, or don't know that these religions were partly responsible for this? Why is there such a strong religious belief here now?"

"It's very difficult for me to explain how this happened," Professor Anyidoho says. "This castle is actually sitting on the shrine of the most powerful of the local deities."

So not only did they force people into Christianity, they buried a shrine in the dungeon. They enslaved a local deity. The professor said earlier that slavery isn't discussed much in Ghana. Dain asks if the reason is because people want to forget, or because they want to move beyond it.

"Slavery on a certain level is a taboo subject. It's not a pleasant story. Each time we tell it, people weep. If you tell it truly, people have to cry. You don't want to spend all your time crying. It's only now that we are making a move towards giving proper prominence to this. It is the single most comprehensive experience that we have had as a people. So why do we reduce it to a paragraph, a small chapter in huge textbooks?"

"Our ancestors might have been in this room negotiating," says Jim.

"It's very possible that they did business here in this room. This one and Elmina Castle played very major roles."

Elly asks how the building is maintained. The environment near the sea, buffeted by winds, must cause rapid deterioration of the structure. The professor explains that those castles which have remained in use have been maintained. This one served as the headquarters of the British colonial administration. After independence in 1957, it was taken over by the Ghanaian government. The Cape Coast and Elmina castles have both been declared World Heritage Sites and thus receive some additional support for maintenance.

"The renovation has created a bit of a problem," he says. "Some of the more depressing evidence was found. In this one, the cell that was used for rebellious slaves [where they were left in a small unventilated room with no food until they died] was converted into a gift shop."

Speaking further with Professor Anyidoho regarding the number of African people who died during the centuries of the transatlantic slave trade, James explains that the slave trade database at Harvard University doesn't include some of the information Professor Anyidoho referred to. "You're talking about how many died in the villages on the way to the coast. We always talk about the Middle Passage as a horrific experience that killed so many. African American scholars usually don't talk about what happened in Africa before."

"We have not paid sufficient attention. This part of the story needs to be told." The professor pauses for a moment and then says, "Slavery is a tragic accident in which people today are still bleeding to death. Slavery is the living wound under a patchwork of scars. The only hope of healing is to be willing to break through the scars to finally clean the wound properly and begin the healing."

———•◦•———

Never before have I thought much about what took place in Africa. My knowledge is limited to southern plantation owners and their brutal mistreatment of their slaves. I read *Roots,* but the story of Kunta Kinte is about one boy living happily in his village with family and friends. I've never considered just how huge this whole enterprise was. In *Roots,* there were no slave forts. Kunta Kinte was kidnapped, tied up in a bamboo grove for several days, and loaded onto a ship. The professor now describes further agony, brutal and absolute, dirty and patched with scabs. How can I begin to understand the horror that African people have suffered? How do you clean a one-thousand-year-old wound?

During a short break I walk outside, back down the steps. Alone on the castle wall, my back resting against a cannon, I'm mesmerized by the waves breaking against the rocks below. Elizabeth sits a short distance away, also alone, staring at the ocean.

Winds blow and waves crash. So this is where the African diaspora began, the African Holocaust. Why have I heard so little about it before this journey? Of course I knew that Africans were brought to the New World under horrible conditions, but no teacher or textbook ever confronted me with the magnitude of this appalling enterprise. In one sense it reminds me of King Philip's War in that I don't believe it's highlighted in the curriculum because it flies in the face of the "land of the free and the home of the brave."

I imagine ships from Bristol arriving here: our ancestors rowed ashore in canoes like the one I now see a few hundred feet past the waves. They walked these steps, sat on these walls, negotiated in these rooms, and traded rum for African people.

They were here.

I feel them.

During my first trip to Washington, D.C., I imagined George Washington once walking where streets are now lined with the whitest marble and the reddest, whitest, and bluest flags I've ever seen. In Philadelphia, I've walked where Jefferson walked. I've bowed my head at Franklin's grave and touched the Liberty Bell. The tour guide said that in 1839 a group called the Friends of Freedom visited Independence Hall and read the inscription on the bell, from Leviticus 25:10. "Proclaim liberty throughout all the land unto all the inhabitants thereof." They knew that all the inhabitants of the land were not free. That's when the bell began to be called the Liberty Bell, inspired by the call for the liberty of enslaved African people.

Just one city block from where the Liberty Bell stands, I visited the reconstructed Graff House, where Thomas Jefferson wrote the Declaration of Independence with wording that implied that the enslaved deserve the sacred rights of life and liberty equally with all humanity. He later claimed this section was removed due to the objections of South Carolina and Georgia. Yet he owned many African people.[1] It is a paradox many have pondered and many more surely will.

Today I sit on a wall of Cape Coast Castle, thousands of miles from home, thinking of my family's ancestors. They built the

United States of America too, just as Washington, Jefferson, and Franklin did. But walking here, where our less famous forefathers walked two hundred years ago, does not inspire pride.

It inspires shame. It inspires guilt, embarrassment, and anger. What an utterly sad place to be.

The entire castle is white. The walls, inside and out, are painted to protect them from the elements, to keep them shining bright and looking clean. Cape Coast Castle is whitewashed, just like the history books from which I was taught in school.

As I walk away from the wall, I come upon Dain. He spoke with a Ghanaian woman who moved to the States and is here for Panafest. He overheard her talking passionately of her feelings about slavery. He attempted to invite her to talk with us, but when he tried to introduce himself, she said, "I hoped I wouldn't see any white people here. I would prefer not to talk with you." That was her opening and closing statement.

Centuries of scars cover unclean wounds.

———•+•———

James Amemasor recently graduated with a B.A. in history from the University of Cape Coast. He appears to be about the same age as Katrina. He and Professor Anyidoho lead us on a tour of the castle, one of the three largest of its kind—not only here in Ghana, but anywhere—with connections to the slave trade along West Africa's coast. The reason so many slave forts were built in Ghana is that so much of the coastline is solid rock. There aren't as many forts in Nigeria because most of its coastline is taken up by lagoons and marsh.

Every moment I am here makes me angrier. Context and rationalization are losing their influence. I think about the Jewish Holocaust. I've read books and articles. I've seen movies and television accounts about the shocking atrocities the Nazis inflicted upon the Jews. I've spent hours inside the Holocaust Museum in Washington. Six million Jews were slaughtered in less than a decade.

The Atlantic slave trade lasted approximately 425 years beginning in 1441.[2] During the first 75 years, Portugal transported Africans to the Old World—mainly Europe and offshore Atlantic islands. The succeeding 350 years involved numerous countries transporting a total of ten million or more Africans primarily to the Americas.[3] Through the traumatic uprooting of villages and families due to attacks on their homes, the loss of loved ones, and additional injuries and deaths, it impacted untold millions more. The trans-Saharan slave trade had been going on for more than five hundred years before that. Massive regions throughout much of Africa were pillaged for ten centuries, with families, communities, languages, religions, and hopes destroyed.

I know so much more about the Jewish Holocaust than the African one, though the number of people who were psychologically and physically battered or killed on this continent is staggering. I have a hard time paying attention during our tour and find myself stopping and staring out to sea.

Both to the east and west of the solid rock upon which this castle rests are sandy beaches. In addition to the many cannon, slots are cut in the tops of the highest walls. It is easy to imagine men with rifles firing from this protected spot. Just outside, in another courtyard below, stands a decaying building that once served as barracks for soldiers protecting the castle. Time and wind have worn away most of the shingles. Our guide explains that when Ghana achieved independence from British rule, there were understandably very negative feelings about the castles. Eventually, people realized that something positive could come from opening them to the public and telling the history of what happened here. In 1990, after renovation and cleanup, Cape Coast Castle was opened as a museum.

Down a long hallway in the living quarters, Professor Anyidoho says, "The governor's residence is located in such a way that it has a view over the courtyard. Every once in a while the female slaves would be paraded and the governor would look down and identify one particular woman to be brought to him. If you go to some of the other forts, you'll see a secret passage with a trap door that leads directly into the governor's rooms. Here the slave woman would come. That was part of the arrangement."

I stare out a window into the courtyard below. The area in which women were paraded lies directly in front of the entrance to the church.

We walk through the bedroom, dining room, and reception area, all quite airy and bright. It's easy to imagine a family living here, entertaining guests and conducting business.

Eventually, we descend through the courtyard toward the entrance to the dungeons. Professor Anyidoho tells us to notice the difference between where we've been and the place we're about to enter. "That will give us a sense of why this place was a castle for some people and a prison for others."

Dusk settles into night as we descend the concrete ramp. The low ceiling, winding passage, and lack of electricity make me feel like I'm entering a cave. Our flashlights show the way as we proceed. The passage leads to five large rooms that once held African men captive and two that held women. In total, these dungeons held as many as one thousand men and three hundred women at one time. We duck our heads to enter one of the cells in the men's dungeon. We wait as the film crew sets up their equipment. To pass time, I pace off the room from one end to the other, then side to side. Fifteen feet wide by thirty feet long.

The floor, walls, and ceiling are stone. Small carved trenches a few inches wide and a few inches deep once functioned as a toilet. They run around the outside as well as through the middle of the floor. They don't drain anywhere. The curved ceiling rises thirty feet over our heads. Three small openings, about eight inches wide and two feet tall, in the wall far above provide the only access to fresh air, but there is no way for it to circulate. At five degrees from the equator, the stagnant air is hot and miserably humid. I'm sweltering. My clothes are drenched. I'm disgusted by the images in my mind. I'm angry. I want out of here.

Suddenly we are plunged into pitch-black darkness. I literally cannot see anything. The battery pack for the camera lights just died. Jeff says it will take at least ten minutes to go to the van and replace it.

A male voice sighs. "Get out your flashlights."

A female voice replies, "Why don't we not? Why don't we just sit here quietly in the dark?"

Nothing more is said. It remains black.

I feel my way to the wall and sit on the rock floor. It doesn't matter if my eyes are open or not. The view remains the same. No one speaks. My thoughts drift in the silence. I breathe in deeply, exhale slowly, and calm my anger. I begin to put myself into another time, another body.

I imagine being here two hundred years ago with no lights, no comforts; only those three small holes far above connect me with the world outside this hard room and stifling heat. I can't focus in the blackness. I can only hear and feel and smell. What I hear and feel and smell are the worst things I've ever sensed in my life. My heart beats rapidly within my aching body.

Thoughts turn to those I love. Where is my wife? My last image is the utter panic on her face as I am beaten and torn away from her and our village. I tried to fight but they overwhelmed me; struck me; shackled me. Her screams still echo in my ears. I think in turn about my three daughters and my son and my inability to communicate with any of them. I want to hold them but I can't; to scream out, but I have no voice. They don't know what has happened, where I am—if I'm safe or in danger, alive or dead. I don't know if they are still alive.

Throughout my life, I have known my village and its surroundings. Never before have I traveled far from home. Now, forced to walk day after unending day to arrive at this dark stone dungeon, I wonder if I could ever find my way back home again, even if I were to escape. Many people died along the way. I see nothing, but hear groans all around. Some men weep. Others scream. I feel their anguish the same as my own. I can't move without bumping up against others. Our tears drop to the hard floor and mingle with urine and feces and blood from our wounds. I wrap my arms around myself and rock back and forth, back and forth.

A thunderous sound continues to roar through the openings above. The gigantic sound of the water fills the air. Over and over it crashes. Will it break these walls? Come through those holes and drown me? Breathing comes hard in the suffocatingly hot, unbearable air. Two hundred men lie crammed in this room. We sweat, breathe, cry, bleed, vomit, piss, and shit together. Yet I am alone.

My heart pounds.

I hear others weeping quietly.

For the first moment in my life I have an inkling of what total despair feels like. Unimaginable horror envelops me, pierces me. Tears stream down my cheeks.

I also know I am a white man in the year 2001. I will walk out of here soon. I will see my wife and children again. Someday, I'll walk hand in hand with my grandchildren on the beach back home. I'll barbecue salmon and sip wine with my friends. I can't know the real horror of this place, comprehend the totality of the loss, the despair. I feel worse, more alone than I have ever felt in my life. Yet I am only scratching the surface of the scar.

I take another deep breath. There is nothing else to do. I force my mind to go blank. I don't want to think about this anymore. Where's the damn battery for the light? I need this to be over. "Breathe," I tell myself. "Breathe."

I wasn't aware that my eyes were closed until I hear the professor's voice. The battery pack has been replaced. Lights are on. The crew films. I glance from face to face, at each of my cousins, and sense a new depth of knowledge that did not exist thirty minutes ago. I doubt that any of us was prepared to face the exhumed rotting corpse of a family secret buried in this place so long ago.

I sit on the original floor of the dungeon. Professor Anyidoho points to marks on the walls about eighteen inches from the floor. The coloration above differs from the shade of that below. When they were preparing to transform Cape Coast Castle into a museum, workers had to dig through a foot and a half of hardened human waste. The thought of six or seven hundred cubic feet of human excrement building up and drying over hundreds of years makes me nauseous. Momentary relief comes when the professor leads us out of this cell.

Down the hallway we walk, from one male dungeon to another, each roughly the same size. We pause at a series of rock shelves painted white, each smaller than the one below and built on a large base. I don't know if this is the original shrine Professor Anyidoho referred to or one that has been built here more recently to honor the original. An animal skin, many plants, beads, bowls, bottles, and flowers have been left by previous visitors. I shake my head in sadness.

The professor explains that the large hallway outside the five male cells, called the grand passage, is where slaves were conducted on their way to the canoes that would ferry them out to the ships. This long tunnel converges with a shorter one from the female dungeon.

I look around the cell and ask Professor Anyidoho, "This is the end of where they held the males—five rooms, each fifteen by thirty feet, holding a total of a thousand people?"

"Also at the time of course, because they're chained, people are mostly lying down," he says. "But there is usually not enough space to lie properly."

"You are talking about two hundred people in a room this size," I say. He nods, confirming my point. Unbelievable. Two hundred men crammed into 450 square feet without ventilation, lying in their own bodily waste. I realize that the number of people being held here would have fluctuated greatly, that perhaps it was even rare that there would have been two hundred people in this room at one time. But whether it was two hundred or fifty doesn't reduce the horror they experienced.

"What is also important is the psychology of being kept here in this darkness with the sea roaring in the background," he says. "You are dealing with people who have never had anything to do with the sea, sometimes from a thousand miles inland. Most of the arrivals would be timed to be in the night so that you get into this enclosed space in the darkness. Some people have said even to survive this you must have come with every possible strength of body and mind."

I am relieved to emerge from the hell below, back up the wide passageway through which we entered. I walk past the thick wooden doors at the threshold and fill my lungs with fresh air in the courtyard. Muggy air never tasted so sweet.

James Amemasor tells us about the people buried in the graves in the courtyard, including Phillip Kwaku, the first Ghanaian ordained as an Anglican priest, who served here. "He created a school to train mulattoes, the offspring of white fathers and African mothers. They worshipped up here." He points behind us. The church built in this castle above the dungeons was the first Anglican church in this country.

"Our ancestors were Episcopalians," says Katrina. "They are Anglicans, basically."

"And the same pattern in Elmina Castle, where it is a bigger church," says the professor, "but also stands right above the dungeon."

I am more and more amazed at the complicity of churches with the slave trade. I stare at the church door for a moment, and then turn away. We make our way toward the door of no return.

Katrina reminds us of the nephew of James DeWolf who committed suicide on the Slave Coast.

"The mortality rate of the Europeans was high," says Anyidoho. "Most of the officers did not come with their wives. Many of them didn't survive very long, partly at least because of malaria. The whole African coast was referred to as a white man's grave, especially if you ventured inland."

We continue to the door of no return, a giant passageway about twelve feet high and five feet wide. Hinged securely to either side of the thick block archway hang large wooden double doors. I ponder once again the uniqueness of the transatlantic slave trade, the only time in history when so many people were transported across an ocean and, at least in the United States, the attempt was made to entirely eradicate their culture. And for the first time in history, slavery became inextricably connected to one's race.

Professor Anyidoho addresses us for the last time today. He explains that this gate is not as dramatic or intimidating as the one at Elmina Castle. "That gate was so ingeniously designed that it narrows to where only one person can go through at a time. But history has its own way of nullifying some of our best plans. This Gate of No Return is also the gate through which many Africans of the diaspora are making their first contact with Africa."

Hundreds, or perhaps thousands, of descendants of Africans from the diaspora are here in Ghana today, in Cape Coast and Elmina, to participate in Panafest. Most people who walked through this door centuries ago never returned. But their descendants are able to return, if only to see where their ancestors came from.

"It is the history we have to wrestle," he says, "every one of us. There's no point running away from it. It happened. But different people played different roles. Whatever role your ancestors played is not something that you should run away from. The story is not a pleasant one. But we must begin to admit that it happened. No matter what role people played, this contact between Europe and the Americans on the one hand, and Africa on the other, left Africa much the poorer for it. The people of this continent are bleeding gradually. Slavery might not have killed us, but the consequences of slavery are threatening to wipe us out. All of us together can minimize the legacy of slavery.

"So at the Gate of No Return we welcome you back here in the footsteps of your ancestors, on the journey that you are taking to retrace their steps and see what you can do to minimize whatever damage we together may have caused."

I walk outside and stand with Dain, Jim, James, and Keila on the stone landing above the staircase that leads down to the sea. "We together" may have caused the damage, but it wasn't white Europeans or Americans who walked down these steps bound in chains to be rowed through the crashing waves out to a waiting ship. I sit on one of the steps and look down at a long canoe that rests on the beach. Dimly illuminated by the light from the camera just inside the door, I read the same words I remember from the palanquin: *Gye Nyame.*

The sound of the ocean washes over me.

CHAPTER 8

THE DOOR OF NO RETURN

Though people have lived along the West African coast for tens of thousands of years, European history there began when the Portuguese arrived in the late fifteenth century. They built forts—the first being Elmina in 1482—to stockpile the precious metal for which the Gold Coast was named before shipping it back to Europe.

The big fortunes turned out to be made in the slave trade. In the sixteenth century, Portuguese success in trading material goods for African people attracted the attention of other nations. Throughout the following three centuries, fierce competition raged as the Portuguese, Dutch, Danes, British, Swedes, Germans (the Duchy of Brandenburg), Spanish, and French built castles, forts, and temporary lodges along the West African coast to support their participation in the slave trade.[1] Out of approximately 110 fortifications, roughly 100 were built on the Gold Coast.[2]

During the eighteenth century, inland from the Gold Coast, the indigenous Asante kingdom acquired great power through their involvement in the slave trade by selling African people in exchange for weapons, rum, and other western commodities. They controlled the entire central region of what is now modern Ghana. Asante power eroded in the early nineteenth century when the Danes, British, Dutch, and United States each outlawed the slave trade. The Asante economy underwent a dramatic transformation.[3]

Over the course of the nineteenth century, as other nations abandoned the coast, Britain emerged as the main European power in the region. The British and Asante coexisted throughout the 1800s. Less powerful than they were during the slave trade, the Asante people still maintained enough control to make the British uneasy with their wealth and influence. After the Asante invaded the coast in 1873 the British attacked and burned the Asante capital of Kumasi in 1874 and declared the entire Gold Coast a colony of the crown. By 1902, Great Britain gained full control over the Asante kingdom and most of the area that is modern-day Ghana.[4]

Between 1876 and 1912, 110 million Africans, spread among thousands of chiefdoms throughout the continent, were arbitrarily divided into thirty regions with boundaries that separated many logically connected groups of people and forced others together who shared virtually nothing in common. The cultures, languages, and traditions of the indigenous peoples were ignored. Great Britain, France, Belgium, Portugal, Italy, Germany, and Spain would rule most of Africa for decades to come. Decolonization occurred primarily between 1957 and 1980, when most of Africa's current forty-seven independent nations were established.[5]

Ghana is merely one region in the vast continent of Africa that underwent dramatic transformation as a result of European imperialism. The violent conquest of the African continent was a naked competition among European nations for colonies and resources with almost total disregard for the needs and desires of the conquered Africans.

Historically, the many separate kingdoms throughout Africa had ruled themselves. Colonialism replaced local rule with European authority. Great Britain set up a system in the Gold Coast that allowed for a measure of continued local involvement. Local affairs were overseen, to a degree, by traditional rulers, subject to overall control by British colonial district commissioners. The rules changed regularly to preserve and increase British authority, and to spread English common law throughout the Gold Coast colony.[6]

Under British rule the Gold Coast thrived. Cocoa exports drove the economic engine, which also included timber, palm oil, rubber, and gold. African people benefited from good schools and civil services, but the greatest beneficiaries of the economic boom were exploitive European business interests.[7] And, as Kofi Peprah underscored to me, the schools were "colonial designed" and taught students the European worldview, not the African perspective. Imagine a Fante child writing an essay on "how we defeated the Spanish Armada in 1588."[8]

More than half a century passed before the Gold Coast became the first sub-Saharan African nation to win independence from its colonizers in 1957. The country's new name was derived from the medieval Empire of Ghana, which existed from the fifth to the thirteenth centuries far to the northwest of modern Ghana.[9] Breaking away from British rule after having been educated, supported, and dominated by it for half a century was traumatic for the new Ghanaian government. Cultural differences between traditional African governance and British governance were stark. The new government in 1957 reflected neither. Ghana experienced severe economic decline over the following twenty-five years. Rampant corruption led to military coups. Between 1966 and 1981, the Ghanaian people suffered through several corrupt, incompetent governments.

In 1979, Flight Lieutenant Jerry Rawlings staged a coup and dedicated himself to cleaning house. Rawlings turned management of the country over to a popularly elected civilian government, only to retake control by force two years later. Rawlings remained head of state for almost twenty years. Military rule ended when Rawlings was elected president in 1992. He was reelected in 1996 and was ineligible to run in 2000, when the reins of democratic government peacefully passed to the current president, John Agyekum Kufuor.[10] Posters of Kufuor are ubiquitous in Cape Coast. National pride must have soared when Ghanaian Kofi Annan became Secretary-General of the United Nations.

———•·•———

We're on our way to a restaurant Juanita has selected, where we will sample a genuine Ghanaian meal in place of the food our hotel prepares for our American palates. I look forward to branching out from eggs for breakfast and turkey sandwiches for lunch. Our bus turns off the main road onto a dirt street, past several homes and a small store, before turning again, and we park in a wide area between a group of reddish-brown and dark-yellow homes on one side and the Solace Spot, our destination, on the other.

Two young women walk by. Half a dozen goats and two dogs scurry out of their way. The Solace Spot is an open-air restaurant with umbrellas, some made from palm leaves and others like giant, upside-down woven baskets, offering shade to people gathered around the small tables underneath. A tattered green-and-white flag flutters in the breeze, advertising the restaurant's name.

A small white chicken passes, hops up the small step past the open metal gate under the arched entry, and walks in. We follow her until she gets nervous and flutters away. A young woman leads us to a small room with one large table and a few smaller tables that aren't visible from outside. Juanita explains our options and orders two different meals for the group. *Omo tuo* combines rice in palm nut soup with goat meat and beef hide. Her other selection consists of *kenke*, made from fermented corn, and *shitos*, a spicy black pepper sauce. Though these aren't delicacies I'll choose on a regular basis, I've never experienced flavors like this and appreciate trying them.

As we leave, a young man of about sixteen or seventeen stands just across the dirt space in front of the restaurant entry carving up two goats on a wooden table. I glance around again at all the un-tethered goats scampering about. For the rest of our time in Ghana, I will see not goats or chickens, but lunch and dinner.

A light rain begins to fall for the first time since our arrival in Ghana.

We return to the fort at Elmina late in the afternoon under far different circumstances than last time. There are no dancers, speakers, chiefs, or hordes of teenage boys. There are no tarps offering shade, no cameras other than ours. It feels far more isolated and desolate than two days ago.

In contrast to its counterpart at Cape Coast, which is located in the midst of the city with homes, shops, busy streets, and Victoria Park nearby, the Castle of St. George at Elmina stands separate from the nearby township, rising high above barren rocks and the crashing sea below. While both are battered by the elements, Cape Coast is bright white throughout. Elmina is darker, dingier. Its roof rises to the height of the palm trees growing inside the courtyard walls. Cape Coast boasts a museum and store. All Elmina has is a few curled postcards resting in a metal rack on the front counter.

Cape Coast is a focal point of Panafest. Elmina was merely the backdrop for the opening ceremony. Many more people visit Cape Coast regularly. Both forts are constant rock-solid reminders of centuries of European presence on these shores.

Construction of this castle began in 1481 by order of King John of Portugal. The oldest and largest castle in sub-Saharan Africa, and named St. George by its first governor, "El Mina" referred to all of the Gold Coast. The Portuguese assumed they would locate the mines from which all the gold came that they acquired in trade with the Africans. Though they never found any goldmines near the coast, the moniker Elmina remained.

The rain has stopped and brisk winds blow the leaves of the palm trees. There are no people on the rocky shore as far as I can see. A large canoe carrying about a dozen passengers floats offshore. A red flag flies from the front and one man steers from the rear.

The plank floor of the drawbridge entry is connected by heavy chains to a wooden frame above. We walk through two archways, one built of stone, the other lined in brick, to the main courtyard inside, where we face a two-story brick and white stone building with a sign above the door reading "Portuguese Church."

Ledlie reads aloud from a plaque on a nearby wall: "In everlasting memory of the anguish of our ancestors. May those who died rest in peace. May those who return find their roots. May humanity never again perpetuate such injustice against humanity. We the living vow to uphold this."

I listen to my roommate's voice, but it hurts to hear his words. The deeper I delve into all this, the more mystified I become at how people rationalized the cruelty perpetrated on others throughout history.

In the small entry room, Katrina brings out copies of documents she found at the Bristol and Rhode Island historical societies related to the DeWolfs and their activities in the slave trade. A letter to James DeWolf from Captain Ganver reads, "Arrived at Elmina Castle. I immediately went to shore and then made a barter for eight Benin slaves. I remain your dutiful junior captain. I hope that God spares my life."

There are more. "I will buy the woman; have inclination to sell her...I will buy also and use some prime men...Hundred and twenty dozen knives for one prime slave..."

A receipt from Cape Coast Castle is dated 1790.

Sitting inside these walls, listening to these words, and holding in my hands all this physical evidence that exists, I think about the hushed whispers of Keila's No Talk Rule and the shame-filled soil from which it grew. The letters, ship logs, receipts, and other records with the name "D'Wolf" on them, above all other evidence, reveal what this family did. Similar records with the names of so many other people, towns, colonies, and states reveal what New England and my entire nation did. I bow my head and rub my temples to ease the pounding within.

Against the wall, a black pedestal with an open book on top stands below a sign that reads, "Comments About Your Visit Are Welcome."

One page bears a long list of Americans with one note left on behalf of all. "Africa, please forgive us, and our ancestors."

I read on. "Excellent tour. Please put real shackles on the walls for more emotion."

A Ghanaian American wrote, "It's nice, but my only problem is, I'm finding it a little bit difficult to forgive the whites after going through this tour."

From a Dutch person, "Terrible thing my country did."

An American then wrote, "Glad I'm not Dutch." I wonder if this person has reflected on the role Americans played in the atrocities committed toward people of African descent.

Daylight begins to fade. We move outside into the courtyard and split up to wander around the castle. Alone, I ascend stairs behind the Portuguese church and amble along the wide walkway on top of the parapet looking out over the sea. Some of the openings in the wall still have cannon in place, others don't.

Descending, I pass the male slave dungeons and walk through several passageways, the door to each one shorter, narrower, than the one that preceded it. At each opening, I move more slowly as I experience how this design reduced the possibility of revolt. My flashlight provides the only illumination. I kneel low to pass through another archway, only four feet in height, and find myself in a small room with one final passageway, perhaps eighteen inches wide, with an iron gate that leads to the sea. Elizabeth sits alone in front of the gate, gazing through its bars into the darkness outside. A white sign, resting against the base of the gate, reads "Slave Exit to Waiting Boats." I turn off my flashlight. We sit in silence together for a few minutes looking out.

Listening.

Thinking.

While still staring through the iron bars, she says, "This is really incredible. It makes things a lot clearer."

I turn my gaze from the night sky to Elizabeth. "How do you talk to someone about this who has never been here?" I ask. "We've been immersed at a pretty deep level for months and it's been particularly intense in Bristol and here. And we're just scratching the surface of some of these issues. I couldn't understand—what little bit I think I've understood—without being here." I reach out and grasp one of the bars of the gate. "How could people design this door and the passageway and the cramped doorways leading to it? How could people design human ovens in Germany?"

"People are manufacturing weapons right now."

"But where does that mind come from? This represents the ultimate inhumanity."

I release my grip on the iron bar and fold my hands together in my lap. Elizabeth and I sit with our separate thoughts, the sound of crickets in the background; the darkness, the aloneness, that narrow, evil door through which we listen to the ocean.

———·•·———

Later, most of us gather outside under one of the large gazebos at the hotel. "The thing that I guess strikes me more than anything right now," I say, "is that we've talked, when we were in Bristol and Providence, listening to historians and scholars. We've heard people say, 'You've got to place it in the context of the times,' and 'this is the way things were done,' and 'this is how life was.' And I sit in that dungeon and I say bullshit. It was an evil thing and they knew it was an evil thing and they did it anyway. And I couldn't have said that before..." I pause a moment. "...before tonight."

I'm angry. I didn't expect such strong feelings tonight—certainly not as strong as last night. But another church above another dungeon and that damned door. I can't get these images out of my head. Then Ledlie says this is a natural place for prayer, that it's important that we pray.

"I have to be honest with you," I say to the entire group, not just Ledlie. "I'm really bothered by the role the church played in the institution of slavery—the role of people who claim to be Christians. It's like the role certain churches or church people played in collaboration with the Nazis and the Holocaust. I have a hard time reconciling it." I turn to Ledlie. "How does it feel to be a priest and to be in these castles knowing that above the dungeons, churches are built?"

He looks startled and hesitates before answering. He takes a deep breath and his eyes narrow. He says on the one hand he's outraged and trusts that he would never be involved in anything like that. On the other hand, he believes the priests at the Cape Coast and Elmina churches thought they were helping the governor and the soldiers. I'm incredulous, and what I want to do is scream, "Are you kidding me?" but I won't because Ledlie is a priest and my cousin and my friend. But he's basically saying he believes the church made an awful situation more bearable.

"We're all vulnerable," he says. "We all do hypocritical things." We stare at each other. Neither of us says another word.

The next morning, Ledlie and I discuss our mini-confrontation about the Church last night. He wasn't prepared for it and admits he probably came across as a bit defensive. He says, "But I need to come to terms with it. This is complicated, but I thank you."

I didn't mean to put him on the spot, but so much evil has been perpetrated in the name of God. Ledlie is a convenient target. Perhaps as I help him face the Church's complicity, he can soothe some of the fire burning in my soul. I've grown to appreciate Ledlie's acceptance of people. To watch him sit and talk with Elly, knowing they have diametrically opposite beliefs—Elly has told both of us she's an atheist—was a real revelation to me. In my experience, many people who are involved in organized churches are very judgmental, and Ledlie's lack of such judgment impresses me.

My thoughts turn to Ghana—so many people replete with religious faith. They appear to be at peace. We've heard about traditional healers and learned of ancient shrines like the one in the dungeon. But then, I don't know what to make of all the outward signs of Christianity. I'm baffled by signs with "Jesus" in them, like the Baby Jesus Hair Salon. But Ghanaians seem deeply spiritual, and in the midst of my uncertainty, it gives me pause.

In the 1960s Ledlie spent nine months in the Central College of the Anglican Communion in Canterbury, England, where St. Augustine's College once trained clergymen as missionaries to the colonies of the British Empire. Ledlie told me about a chapel there built from hundreds of memorial blocks, each engraved with the name of a person who had been connected with the church's mission on the west coast of Africa. Ledlie admits that after seeing the churches above the dungeons, he thought about those stones and —even though they commemorated missionaries who served after the slave trade was abolished—began wondering how many priests were complicit in the slave trade, and how many genuinely intended to bring understanding, light, education, and healing in the name of God.

"You believe that their intentions in many cases may have been honorable?" I ask.

"Yes."

Given my strong feelings about this, I find Ledlie's words difficult to hear. I can accept that most priests throughout history probably didn't think they were condoning slavery or the slave trade by accepting a position at a church located in a European trading post on the African coast. They may have thought they were doing what they could for the Europeans and perhaps even for the Africans. Ultimately, I have no idea what they thought, but looking into my cousin's eyes, I feel compelled to continue grappling with this issue together with him.

CHAPTER 9

"I HAVE TO DO IT EVERY DAY"

This afternoon we'll participate in what Katrina calls "a community dialogue." She informed us earlier this week that as we meet people, any people, we should invite them to join us today. There were no qualifications other than an interest in talking about the legacy of slavery. Several Ghanaians, as well as African Americans, have been invited. We are reminded to speak slowly. Here in Ghana, *we* have the accent.

During our drive from the hotel, Katrina and Juanita try to focus our expectations. We don't all agree. Some want to apologize for our ancestors' role in the slave trade. Dain thinks it would be inappropriate. He and Ledlie spoke with a Ghanaian priest yesterday who reminded them that Africans were full partners in the slave trade, so shouldn't they apologize as well? James agrees with Dain about the apology, but he does think it is important to say how terribly sad we feel.

Abiko Eghagha, a young woman of twenty-four and one of our production assistants, sits next to me on the bus. So far she's been mostly silent around me. Today she says, "Sometimes I think the African Americans who come here leave with hate. That is not helpful. It would be better if people would use their energy to make the world better."

Our bus driver, Sam, pulls through an open iron gate and parks on the hard dirt in front of a large building. The walls are dingy white like the walls at Elmina Castle. This appears to have once been a school, probably built during colonial times. A hand-painted sign reads, "Darosem Restaurant; Cape Coast Town Hall; Catering for Breakfast, Lunch, Dinner, Parties, Birthdays, Weddings, Etc." Wide steps, flanked by two twenty-foot-tall trees as high as the front of the building, lead to the front doors.

We enter a large auditorium with a stage at the far end. In places, its curtains have separated from the track above. Dozens of white plastic patio chairs are gathered in the middle of the open wooden floor. Far above, several ceiling tiles are missing. Others are cracked or discolored by leaking water.

Wide slatted doors to the outside are set into the sides of the auditorium. They remain open so air will circulate on this, another hot, humid African day. I walk outside and watch three small boys jostle and play together.

When I go back inside, Ledlie sits in the middle of a small circle of chairs that are filled with young girls in peach-and-brown uniforms from nearby St. Monica's School. They look to be twelve or thirteen years old. I stand a short distance away and listen as he speaks with them about slavery, rape, malnutrition, and the Middle Passage. One girl asks if Ledlie's ancestors bought her ancestors for a lot of money.

"No," he says.

"They lied to us," she says. "The white people said they are coming to make friends with us and trade with us. Instead they came and made us slaves."

"Are you not ashamed of coming here?" another girl asks. The other girls giggle. They look surprised by their classmate's boldness.

"Yeah, I am ashamed. It is a shaming thing."

As more of our guests arrive, Ledlie's intimate conversation breaks up. We soon sit among the students from St. Monica's and more than two dozen adults of various ages from Ghana and the United States. We begin by introducing ourselves to each other.

Then Kofi stands. "Good evening to you all. My name is Kofi Peprah and I'm the co-facilitator for this program. We are all gathered here this evening to create history. We have a family from the United States whose ancestors were directly involved in the slave trade and it has created a lot of tension in their heads."

Katrina explains the background of the project and Juanita then asks for a moment of silence to honor the ancestors who were taken from this continent, to honor the people who were taken on ships and did not survive the Middle Passage, to honor the people who made it alive to the New World. Their legacy is why we're here. "When we talk about slavery and spiritual decimation, we often talk about black folks. But something has happened to white folks in this whole process. This family is trying to figure out what that is and they want your help and your wisdom. You don't have to be nice. The last thing this family wants is for people to say things in a way that's overly polite and is not getting at the real stuff."

Abiko says, "If you are trying to ease racial tensions, why are you having this conversation in Ghana when the problem is really in America?"

An African American woman, Dr. Jessie Ruth Gaston, professor of African history at California State University, Sacramento, wears a bright fuchsia-colored wrap around her head and a light blue blouse. "Why Ghana? I say, why not Ghana? The participants in the slave trade are diverse. It's not just an issue with the U.S.; it's an African issue as well. Not all Africans participated. But some of the rulers did benefit from the trade. When I teach African history, it's a hard area to discuss. It's complex. Many times, when students learn Africa participated, they just throw the responsibility off."

She talks about the treatment African Americans continue to be subjected to: one group of people has been taught that they are "less than" while another has been taught they are "greater than." Everywhere in the world where there are black and white people, or lighter-skinned blacks and darker-skinned blacks, the images remain. The negative images connected to people of African descent impact them when they seek employment. The assumption is that they aren't qualified. People question whether she earned her job or if it was handed to her through affirmative action. People of color can have college degrees, she says, but "When people see me, they see black."

"That gets at the crux of the issue," says Juanita. "There are things that white folks don't understand that intensely affect present-day living for black people. How has this whole legacy impacted white people? What has it done to the ways in which they set up their families, their communities, the ways they move through the world, and the ways in which they deal with nonwhite people?"

We listen to example after example of incidents in which people of African descent are regularly suspected, followed, or looked down upon. We hear how young African American girls play with white dolls and how young black women want to straighten their hair to look whiter.

"When I was in college I read Toni Morrison's novel *The Bluest Eye*," says Katrina. "I had blonder hair than I do now and I cut my hair as short as I could because I was so upset that I had the kind of hair and blue eyes that were making young black girls aspire to look like me. It was such a quintessential white guilt thing. Until I started dealing directly with my family history, and working through my feelings, the guilt was all-consuming. When you hate yourself, you're not an effective ally in solving problems."

She says that one legacy of slavery for white people is that we don't notice racial inequality because it's too painful. "When you do notice, it's so upsetting that all you can do is hate yourself. A lot of people get stuck in one of those two places. What I'm trying to figure out is if there's some other place where I can absorb the horror, yet be in a better relationship with myself and others in solving the problems."

Kofi walks farther down this path. "Do you think the slave trade made the whites feel superior? Do you whites feel superior while you are sitting with us?"

"Whites of European descent have felt superior from the very beginning," says Dain, who sits next to Kofi. "In every new country we went to, people of a different color we considered barbarians and savages."

Kofi leans forward, looks directly at Dain, and digs in. "Do you still personally feel superior as a white person?"

"That's a wonderful question for me," says Dain as he taps his own chest and smiles. "I can say uncategorically no, I do not. I feel that everyone in this room is my peer at least, and some of you are probably my superior in many ways." He tells about growing up in Charleston, South Carolina, a terribly racist community, in the forties and fifties.

"I was terribly racist. I remember walking behind black people and yelling out the word 'chocolate.' I remember throwing pecans at the flower ladies across the street from us, all of whom were black, simply to harass them. That embarrasses me very, very deeply. Was it the environment that I was in? Absolutely. Was it more than that? I don't know, and that thought scares me. I may be afraid to dig for that answer.

"I feel very proud, frankly, that I have been able to overcome as much of that as I have. But it's taken a great deal of looking inside, and it's taken an enormous amount of risk to reach out and put my arms around those black people who I know. It has at times been very scary, because we've been taught to be scared of black people."

"So Dain," says Juanita, her head tilted slightly. "I'm curious. Do you really, really think that you've shed every single bit of the racial categorization and the racism? Do you really think it's possible that's where you are? Because I know a lot of black folks who would think that wasn't true." It's obvious that Juanita doesn't think it's true.

"And I would think that wasn't true also." He laughs. All of a sudden he's in the hot seat and his bald head turns red. "I'm not sure I said it was completely gone."

"You said overcome, and so to me..."

"Largely overcome," he interrupts. "Let me narrow that down." I feel a little sorry for Dain as he grapples for his next words. "My deep concern is that racism is a part of the human condition. People want to feel superior to other people. I don't think it can all ever be shed. What I can do is move how I interact with people beyond where I used to be, and embrace them. That is the best I can do."

Juanita calls on a Jamaican woman, Dr. Kaylene Richards-Ekeh, a professor of criminal justice who, like Jessie Gaston, teaches at California State University, Sacramento. She wants to address how the legacy of slavery impacts criminal law in the United States. She explains the disproportionate percentages of incarceration of people of color—that when black people violate the law, they're treated differently than Caucasians who commit the same crime. For the same offense, black people are more likely to be arrested, more likely to be prosecuted, more likely to be convicted and sentenced to longer terms in prison. "That is one of the legacies of slavery. When people violate the law I'm not saying they should not be prosecuted, but black people are less likely to be able to obtain a good lawyer, and justice in the United States depends on the lawyer you can afford."

She discusses images in our society that perpetuate certain myths, such as that black people are criminals and drug addicts. And even though most people on welfare in the United States are white women and their children, the prevalent notion is that it is black people on welfare.

Eli Jacobs-Fantauzzi teaches video production at Berkeley High School. He came to Ghana for the first time to study and to trace his roots. Eli tells about his Puerto Rican and Jewish heritage. He's traveled to Israel, Puerto Rico—where his African ancestors are from—and elsewhere in the Caribbean. He says, "If you look at the whole world today, you have to ask yourself why blacks and Africans are at the bottom everywhere. In Africa, in the Caribbean, in South America and North America, the darker skin you have, the lower you are in society. That's the effect of slavery.

"For the family that came here today, and for we of privilege in the United States, whether white folks or folks of color, do you really want equality and justice? We're here today on top. If we weren't on top, we wouldn't be able to be in Ghana. Are you really willing to give up what you have to be equal? I figure the answer is no." His voice becomes more animated. "You can talk about Nelson Mandela, and what he did was great. But the situation in South Africa is the same. The same people have the money. It's easy to play around with, but when we're talking about action and being real with ourselves, where are we willing to go with this?"

Ledlie sits across the room from Eli. "I'm a retired priest of the Episcopal church. My brother here asks the right question, and it's very disturbing. I think of the parable of the young wealthy man who went to Jesus and asked what he could do and Jesus said, 'You can give up your wealth.' And he turned away sorrowful." Ledlie says he's scared of that image; that he would be that man.

"When I began this journey," says Elly," I thought I needed to return transformed into a disciple of a new vision or that I would need to be done. And I'm not going to be done. This conversation has to happen every day, every hour, with whites among whites, with blacks among blacks, between blacks and whites—every combination. We need to keep talking."

"I've been a primary teacher for thirty years." I turn my attention to an African American woman with a powerful voice and presence. Josephine Watts sits next to Jessie Gaston and sounds like someone who could keep the attention of a primary school classroom. She works with teachers who teach English as a second language. She says, "You asked what you can do. Take a closer look and try not to deny that racism exists, that injustice exists. You can do something about it. Minorities cry about it, and nothing is done. But if the dominant culture accepts it, then something can be done."

Josephine says that at schools we need to ask the educators to accept blacks and whites on an equal level. Many black children have felt the stigma of a white teacher believing they cannot learn, that they have nothing to offer. "I sat in a class observing a white teacher. She only had two black kids in her class, and she was asking questions. A little black boy had his hands all up." She waves her arm like a young child. "She kept telling him to sit down. This is in Sacramento. These things are happening to our black children. They grow up to be adults and here we are."

"Can you help me?" I ask Josephine. She nods and smiles. "If I as a white person stand up and talk, whether I talk about Dr. Martin Luther King or about Nelson Mandela, I have the impression that people think I'm just trying to be politically correct. I don't know how not to sound that way. Are there words or images that I could bring to this dialogue so black people don't think I'm full of crap; so that black people can see that I'm trying to be a sincere person who wants to do better?"

Josephine's eyes bore into mine from fifteen feet away. She says February is the only time we talk about black people. Throughout school curriculums the focus is on European culture, and subjects like Shakespeare, with which black students have little or no connection. When teaching math, why not include the contributions the Egyptians made? When education is broadened to include contributions by Africans and African Americans, blacks can start feeling good about themselves and then they'll know we're sincere.

"But if you just dwell on one thing, well, everybody knows about Martin Luther King."

I respond that I don't work in a school, and ask how to apply it in daily life.

"Daily life, okay. I was a teacher; only black teacher in my school. It took years for the white teachers to even invite me to any functions they had. Then, if we were going to a movie, they didn't ask me if I was interested in the movie we were attending, and it was the most boring movie I ever went to." Her comment elicits laughter. "Reach out to any minority person you're working with and invite them into your home, into your circle. That's a step. And once you invite them, don't think it's a token. Ask what they want to do this weekend. Just sit in our shoes. Make it a point to go to a black play or a black concert, so you can see how it feels. That's a step."

"See, that's hard." I'm not sure why I said these words. They just came out. I look at Josephine and shake my head.

"That *is* hard." Josephine leans forward as she slings her words at me. Most of the group laughs and claps, but I don't look at them. I focus on Josephine, who also doesn't laugh. "Hey, I have to do it every day. I'm almost the only black teacher in my district. When I go to a conference, I'm the only black person sitting in that conference. Is it easy? No. But I have to do it. You have to do it. You have to do it in order to feel what I'm feeling."

"Thank you," I say. I continue to stare at her for several moments.

Dr. Gaston says, "What the family has hooked onto is the truth. Once a group of people get hold of the truth, they don't just sit still on it. In African history or black studies, everybody used to say, 'What is there to teach anyway?' I have one African history class, to cover from ancient times to present. Now, what can you do with that? How can you teach the history of a continent four times the size of the United States all in one term?

"Once the truth starts coming out it will cause this kind of confusion amongst members of the dominant society, which sets off a chain. So I think it's a good beginning. And what Eli was saying too, 'But what now?' " She asks if we're willing to talk about reparations and other types of programs. Becoming conscious of racial injustice and the legacy of slavery is only the beginning. "What then?" she asks.

That is the key question, I think to myself. What next? The truth is confusing. Actually, that's not accurate—it isn't the truth that's confusing. It's what to do with the truth that upsets the ordered world I've been raised in and taught to believe in. That's confusing, and very challenging.

"I want to comment on walking in people's shoes," says Eli. "I never believed that would work. You'll never get the experience the other person has." He looks toward Josephine, "You said, 'I have to do it every day.' They don't have to do it every day. So they'll never understand what you're talking about—ever. So don't even think that you can. It's not comparable. The direction you're going is great, but if you're not going to devote your life to it, they'll never take you seriously. You can talk about Martin Luther King, or whatever, but they'll know after you leave the podium you're not real because you haven't devoted your life to it. It's not something you can turn on and off. It has to be a path, a walk of life."

Eli's comments ring true. It is my privilege that allows me to be here. Before this journey I never considered my own privilege. Of course I've known I'm better off than many people, but it has always been generic. It was "we Americans" or we "middle class" who had it better than "those poor people" over there. It was never me.

Listening today, I realize even more that I've been trained, invisibly and unconsciously, not to see my own privilege as a man or as a white person. I look down at the little notebook in which I write. Even this twenty-five-cent pad of paper is evidence of my privilege.

I have every confidence that all these notes I'm taking, and cassette tapes I'm recording, will one day become a published book.

I look around the auditorium and marvel at this moment here in Cape Coast, Ghana. I'm part of an amazing conversation with several Ghanaian people, but mostly with African Americans. Why don't we talk together like this at home? Why did it take all of us coming to Africa? How can we whites understand what African American people experience, and how can they understand us, if we don't talk with each other?

CHAPTER 10

GYE NYAME

The next morning we drive to a wildlife preserve featuring a tree canopy walk. Ninety minutes after leaving our hotel, we park at Kakum Rainforest Park. The peaceful, lush jungle offers a stark contrast to the harsh and cluttered city, and is a refreshing change of pace.

Led by a guide, we begin our hike. The lizards are larger and more numerous than at our hotel. We walk along a path of flat rocks and steps embedded in the hard dirt; the foliage is rich and thick. The smell of the forest, the soil, is so alive compared to everywhere else we've been in Ghana. We slowly ascend a steep incline.

We stop by a gigantic tree where our guide, Roxan, introduces himself. He tells us that he's also called by the common name of Yaw, because he's Thursday-born, and explains that Ghanaians, specifically the Akan people, name according to the day of one's birth. "When born on Monday if you are male, they call you Kwadwo; if female they call you Adjua. Tuesday males are Kwabena..."

After he tells us all the names, Katrina asks him to repeat Monday's names.

"When born on Monday, male they call you Kwadwo, female Adjua."

Katrina explains that we're here because our ancestors were involved in the triangle slave trade, and that one of the slaves brought to Rhode Island was named Adjua.

"That means she was born on Monday," confirms Roxan.

I stare at Roxan, taken aback by his words. I've read Adjua's name in *Mount Hope*, the book about Bristol and the DeWolfs written by Elly's grandfather, listened to the nursery rhyme about her and Pauledore, and stood before her grave, a few steps from that of the man who presented her as a Christmas gift to his wife. Roxan's words remind me of Adjua's humanity and her circumstances. She was a young girl who lived here with her family and was raised in the culture of her community before being kidnapped. Roxan's matter-of-fact response also drives home the fact that Adjua was just one of millions stolen from this continent. The ache I feel from this evil commerce in human flesh continues to grow deeper and more personal.

Roxan smiles, turns, and leads us further up the trail.

He describes the different animals that live in the preserve, including elephants and bongos—the largest species of antelope. There are duikers, leopards, and monkeys. He makes no promises that we'll see them because they are most active at night. He explains the wide varieties of tree and plant species.

We soon arrive at the first platform at the beginning of the canopy walk, which juts out over a steep drop in the terrain below our feet. From here, we'll cross a series of seven rope bridges—metal ladders tied together, with two-by-twelves laid between the rails, secured inside nets held up by thick horizontal ropes that serve as handholds to protect us from falling. The ropes are tied off to platforms, like tree houses, in several giant trees. The distance from the walkway to the ground increases the further out we walk. The highest point is almost 100 meters from the jungle floor—over 300 feet.

I soon stand approximately 165 feet above the ground listening to birds. The variety of sounds is rich beyond description. Butterflies are everywhere. Thick vines extend from the fauna far above us all the way to the ground.

Our peaceful morning eventually ends. Though we saw no elephants or monkeys, the smells of the jungle, the expansive view of miles and miles of Ghana from its treetops, and the songs of the birds result in a morning I'll not soon forget. I stare out the window and think about Adjua on our drive back.

———•———

Since our journey began, we've spent several days learning from historians and touring sites, and two days interacting with groups of people of African descent, both in Rhode Island and here in Ghana. We've talked in small groups over meals, but today for the first time we gather alone to confront the issues that are foremost in our minds as a result of all we've absorbed.

How can the damage caused by slavery be repaired? How do we all heal? What are we, as white people, willing to give up? Can giving up something like money make a difference in the world? Are we responsible for everything our ancestors did and everything that will happen in the future? Who are we in respect to all this? Why would anyone care? Elly wants to know what Juanita thinks. How can she not be angry?

Juanita sits between Ledlie and Keila on the floor, their backs resting against the wall. Katrina and Juanita designed this journey to have a strong focus on white people talking with white people and coming to terms with our past—with racism, privilege, and power. Juanita helps lead the interracial dialogues, is Katrina's trusted advisor, and is an integral partner in this project, but they didn't intend to include her on camera beyond her facilitation. But no matter how things were designed, many of us have grown close to Juanita, spent time with her, and relied on her for advice about Ghana. She has become a sounding board for our questions regarding racism.

So she joined us today, though it was just going to be behind the scenes.

So much for plans. We turn our focus toward Juanita as Elly speaks of her own uncertainty. "We talk about white family issues. We don't always have another perspective to reassure us that it's okay. It doesn't feel okay. It feels grotesque."

Juanita agrees to share her feelings. She and Elly sit on the floor and face each other, holding hands. Tears flow from Elly's eyes. Juanita says, "Given all that's happened, am I not angry? The entire truth is that in this moment, you're just a good person to me. It is very easy to see your goodness. And also the truth is, of course I'm angry at white people. I think white people have been cowards. They have chosen to give up their integrity and their humanity for so long. It's ridiculous. If you grew up where I grew up, you'd be pissed off. Anybody who's alive or who's paying attention should be pissed off. The fact that white people are *not* pissed off means that they are *not* paying attention."

Since childhood, I've read about and watched images on television of black people denied access to schools and the right to vote, beaten, sprayed with fire hoses, imprisoned in disproportionate numbers, and lying dead from lynching or an assassin's bullet. What have I done to combat blatant injustice? Precious little. In my silence, in living my normal day-to-day life, I haven't been pissed off. I haven't been paying attention. Have I collaborated with injustice?

Juanita continues. "The reason I'm doing this project is because it's important for me that white people take responsibility. Ultimately, it's about human liberation. It's also about liberation of my people. It's about liberation of you guys. And that's the truth."

Elly continues to cry and asks Juanita how she manages to stay dry.

"I cry a lot about this stuff," she says.

"And you don't need to." Ledlie's voice is quiet.

Juanita's voice remains calm. "We've been taking care of you for centuries and we're sick and tired of taking care of you. We're sick and tired of taking care of you for survival. We've had to study you and learn what it is that makes you upset and learn what makes you comfortable. We've had to do that in order to save our lives."

Responding to Ledlie's comment, Dain says, "We need to be able to cry together." He looks at Juanita. "I don't mean you, right now, but the two races must be able to cry together. Otherwise it doesn't happen. If the abused is unable to forgive the perpetrator, there will never be the kind of peace or redemption we need to have in the world."

Elizabeth sits on the floor against the couch between Dain and Katrina. As he speaks, I watch her face harden as she slowly, and almost imperceptibly, shakes her head in disagreement.

"To me, it's an order and a sequence thing," says Katrina. "From a human, theological, emotional level I agree with you. But it's not for us to say that before we've done everything in our power, in word and deed, to apologize. Then step two is for black Americans to decide what they want to do with that."

"Blacks have to come to the table too," Dain argues. "We have to go through the traveling together." Dain clearly disagrees with Katrina about who should be talking with whom.

"But Dain," says Ledlie, "haven't you heard that they've been at the table all this time?"

"Yes, in a lot of ways."

"And we haven't," says Jim. "Whites don't even talk about race. How can we ask for forgiveness from black people?"

"I am not asking for forgiveness today," says Dain. He explains that in order to achieve reconciliation, there must ultimately be forgiveness.

Holly sits on the floor opposite Dain, near me, and tells him we can't have any expectations.

James jumps in to defend his uncle. "I do not hear anybody saying they *expect* forgiveness."

"But we do have somebody saying that if we don't get it it's not going to work," I snap and point at Dain, "which is pretty much the same damn thing."

"That is not what Dain is saying," says James. "Dain is saying eventually, eventually, there must be forgiveness. But that could be a long way off. What I hear him saying, and certainly what I'm trying to say, is we must come to the table. Katrina's right. It's not fair to expect black Americans to come to the table. With the legacy that black Americans have had to endure, it's not fair. But the reality is it's necessary if there's to be progress, for black Americans to come to the table at least with those white Americans who are trying to talk."

Every black person I've encountered on this journey has said that white people need to talk with white people, so I tend to agree with Katrina. But I continue to look to Juanita for understanding, friendship, and justification. When Juanita told Elly that she's angry at white people, I was surprised. She's spent most of the past month with us and I believe she feels comfortable with us. Yet there's a wall between us, and I believe we're separated by gender as well as race. Once again I'm reminded that we lack a common language for this incendiary conversation.

Elizabeth picks up on the gender issue as well. She points out how messy this is. Just as white people can't look to people of color to make ourselves feel better about our own racism, men can't look to women to feel better about our own isolation and sexism. She says that racism and sexism are very much connected. She believes white men, and "WASPs"—white Anglo-Saxon Protestants—in particular, are incredibly isolated, and just as white people need to talk to each other about racism, men need to talk with each other about overcoming their sexism.

James disagrees with the concept of whites talking only among themselves. He thinks there's a danger of becoming self-indulgent.

"I want to know what you meant by self-indulgent," Holly says, "because to me this barely scratches the surface of self-indulgence." She narrows her eyes and clenches her teeth. This feels more like a battle than a conversation.

"I think there's a danger in isolation that we end up giving ourselves forgiveness. We give ourselves permission to move on because we've decided we've dealt with it and we feel better, rather than dealing with the living consequences today." When James stood in the dungeon, it was clear to him that he could do nothing for the people who suffered there hundreds of years ago. There are people we can do something for today who still suffer the consequences of slavery.

"James, this is all analysis," says Keila.

Keila, Holly, and Elizabeth consistently question James's comments, accusing him of being too analytical and not emotional enough.

Eventually Ledlie comes to the rescue when he asks, "Is this need for women to reform the men a critical element in dealing with racism?" When Dain and Jim stop laughing, Ledlie reminds everyone what his personal agenda is. "I want to know more how I am a white racist. Then I want the help to change. That's all I want." He pauses, and then adds, "Boy, that's a hell of a lot."

Ledlie says it's as though if we don't solve the "emotional female" versus the "intellectual male" conundrum we won't be able to solve racism either. Holly accuses some of the men of patriarchal behavior and lack of emotion. This is becoming a common theme.

Dain claims that he *has* exposed his own raw emotions, like yesterday when he revealed the racist attitudes of his youth in Charleston and received no support from anyone in our family. That explains why, other than during this conversation, I've noticed that he's become quieter around our Family of Ten since yesterday. Now that I think about it, I don't recall him joining the rest of us for breakfast this morning.

Holly becomes defensive. I feel immersed in a maelstrom. Everyone's talking, no one's listening. We aren't getting anywhere other than in each others' faces, which pushes us further apart.

"Juanita said this is a project about liberation," says Elizabeth. "We're talking about liberation not just from racism. You can't talk about one type of oppression in isolation. The stuff that's caused white people to oppress black people as long as they have is the same stuff that has caused men to oppress women; that causes straight people to oppress gay people; that causes adults to think of children as less than fully intelligent human beings."

"And when she said 'liberation,'" adds Katrina, "she also meant for everyone. Patriarchy oppresses men and racism oppresses white people."

Elizabeth says that the way Dain and James speak reminds her of her father—that men commonly speak as if their feelings and thoughts are absolute truths. The message she has received throughout her life is that she is there to be taught. This is the definition of patriarchy. She believes this is what needs to be undone in order to achieve liberation.

Dain again stresses that he feels like he's being vulnerable emotionally and not being respected. I try to connect with him because I empathize. I explain that I was raised to assume I'm right all the time. My dad told me from birth that I could be anything I wanted to be. That is my training and Dain's as well. We feel like we make ourselves vulnerable, and if we don't get the reaction we expect, we hide behind our often sarcastic humor. Though I've only known him for one month, I'm amazed at how similar Dain and I are. Yet I disagree with most everything he said today.

I'm relieved when dinner arrives.

———•———

Prior to the Emancipation Day vigil at Cape Coast Castle tonight, there will be a candlelight procession along the same route as the

Grand Durbar from the other day. We continue riding our emotional roller coaster from this afternoon on our bus ride from the hotel. Some aren't sure whether we should participate. If we do, should we walk in the front, middle, or back? Should we walk as a group or separately?

I'm grateful when we arrive because I feel impatient and need distance from some of my cousins. When I climb off the bus, a Ghanaian woman walks up and offers me a torch, simple as that. I smile and thank her. It feels as if so many roadblocks to reaching out to people from different races and cultures have been constructed by white people ourselves. We think. We worry. And then we think and worry some more. For the most part, I've felt warmly and enthusiastically welcomed.

When the long line begins to move, I walk alone, lost in thought in the dark stillness of night. The only light comes from the hundreds of candles we hold.

A young black woman walks up beside me. "Hello."

From her voice, I know she's from the States. She wears a white, long-sleeved blouse and her hair is tied back with a white band, exposing large hoop earrings. A video camera hangs by a strap around her neck. Our torches light our faces and the road ahead.

"What is your group doing here?" She's seen a few of my cousins and correctly assumed the white people are together. I tell her about our project.

"What about you?" I ask.

"I'm Latisha. I'm from Chicago. I teach art to sophomores in high school."

I mention that one of the women in our group teaches art in New York, and ask Latisha if she enjoys her work.

"It can be challenging. Last year, my white students petitioned the school, claiming I'm racist for forcing black art on them. The school administrators told me to give my students options. I dropped it altogether because they never give blacks options. History books don't reflect the contributions of blacks so black kids don't care about school."

Latisha and I walk together the rest of the way, wish each other well, and then part. Inside the castle courtyard, I look around at all the chairs filling up. I haven't seen any of my cousins since the beginning of the walk. A banner hangs from above the performance stage. It reads "Akwaaba!! Panafest Foundation Welcomes You." People look down from the upper level of the castle, leaning over the wall directly behind the stage, and crowd the stairways on either side that lead down to the courtyard level, where hundreds of chairs are soon filled.

The ceremony begins when a man walks to the middle of the stage and welcomes the crowd. Musical and dramatic performances are interspersed with speeches, mostly by African Americans. I keep expecting to see the high school students from the Du Bois Center, but I don't. Perhaps they performed elsewhere. There are choirs from Jamaica, dancers from different African countries, speakers from the United States.

I'm struck by the irony of the joy I witness onstage, knowing they are dancing and singing directly above the dungeons. After the last of the performances, a man invites everyone to enter the dungeons for a concluding ceremony. A choir begins to sing as the crowd makes its way to the door leading down the ramp into the darkness.

I look around and see Elizabeth waving to me from a short distance away. We make our way to each other through the crowd. Elizabeth doesn't think it's right to enter the dungeons tonight. It would be disrespectful to the African and African American people here. I agree. It feels like we'd be invading a sacred place. We hail a taxi and return in silence to our hotel.

When I wake up the following morning, one thought permeates my thinking. I'm not ready to leave. Our week here has passed by so quickly. But Ledlie and I take one last glance around our hotel room, and then carry our bags down the stairs and into the lobby, where Elizabeth sits on the couch next to Kofi, who rests his bare feet on the coffee table.

We load ourselves back into our two buses and drive to the Donkor Nsuo River, known as the Slave River, which is about forty kilometers off the road leading to Accra, near a town called Assin Manso. We join a throng of people making their way through a gateway into a walled-off area. We stand near the back of the crowd that surrounds two graves. Many people are dressed in traditional, multihued garments made from kente, the boldly designed cloth of the Asante people, worn on important occasions. Some wear dresses and others sport jeans and T-shirts.

The graves hold two formerly enslaved people who were brought back to Ghana, one from Jamaica and one from the States. I remember Professor Anyidoho telling us how they were brought back through the door of no return, symbolically coming home. Everyone who visits the Slave River must pass the two huge marble crypts, about twelve feet long and six feet wide. They rise like hospital beds from about eighteen inches at the foot to four feet at the head with a large brass plaque on top of each one explaining the significance of the reburial here. A wreath rests atop each of them. They are surrounded by a four-foot green, red, and yellow fence.

We stand in silence while two women pray over them and invite us to remember all the other African people who were sold into slavery. After hundreds of years, these two people finally made it back home.

After the brief ceremony at the graves, we walk down a long pathway and through a large, arched gate with a sign that reads, "Akwaaba to the Ancestral River Park." The two large painted gate panels bear striking life-size images of a man and a woman in shackles, each against a bright-blue background. We pass a brown stone building with a thatched roof where a woman sits breast-feeding a baby outside. After a quarter mile, we pass through another, smaller archway that reads, "Welcome to the Slave River" with two more gate panels with chained African people painted on them.

We arrive at the place in the river where, we are told, captured African women, children, and men were given their final bath before being taken to the dungeons. Young Ghanaian men play drums while other young men and women perform traditional dances. They are dressed in red and black with yellow ties around their waists, and their energy is high.

As I watch the festivities, I remind myself that the bathing here was part of the whole marketing process by which people were sold like any other trade goods. Deals were made. People's names were taken away. They were shaved and their skin was oiled here. I walk through one last archway, which says "Last Bath," and head down a set of steps to the river.

What an enchanting and peaceful setting, with foliage so thick it almost blocks the sky above and the jungle beyond. It smells rich and alive, like the Kakum Rainforest. The flat, wide bank allows many people to gather together on the shore. The shallow river flows gently by.

A man performs what appears to be some kind of cleansing ritual for people just upstream from us. He holds large leaves in his hand and dips them in the water. He then brushes them down each person's body from head to foot. It reminds me of baptism.

Nearby, Dain also watches the ritual as person after person is brushed with the leaves until there is no one left. I watch him approach the man at the edge of the river and speak with him for a few moments. Dain soon turns and walks away. He joins Elly and me on the steps and says he asked the man to perform the ritual on us. He declined. He said we needed to deal with our own issues and then have our own white elders perform a cleansing ceremony for us.

I jump from the shore to a large rock that extends into the middle of the river; a good vantage point. I don't feel nearly as overwhelmed and emotionally drained here as I have elsewhere. I'm pleased we're concluding our time in Ghana here near the water in a tranquil setting.

I'm one of the last of our group to walk back to our buses, along with Juanita and Kofi. The hundreds of people who were here a few hours ago are now reduced to a couple dozen. By a quarter past four we are on our way to Accra. We exchange gifts with our Ghanaian crew members. Abiko and Joyce, another production assistant, hand each of us a carved, rounded, wooden case, approximately sixteen inches long and two and a half inches wide, which opens up on hinges to become the game board.

"This is called Oware," says Joyce. "It is the oldest board game still being played in the world. It began in Africa and has spread around the world. It is the game of the Asante kings."

They do their best to teach us to play. Seeds, six on each side, are moved around a series of twelve hollowed-out pits according to the rules they explain, and a few of us begin to understand the fundamentals. Each case is carved with a different symbol on the outside. Mine looks familiar.

"What does this mean, Abiko?" I ask.

"It stands for *Gye Nyame* in my language, which means 'except God' in English."

I remember the words *Gye Nyame* as well as this symbol, from one of the litters carrying a king in the Grand Durbar, and on the canoe at the bottom of the steps outside the door of no return. "Accept God?" I ask. With so much overt Christianity everywhere, it doesn't come as a surprise. "It encourages people to accept God in their lives?"

"No, 'except.' Nothing can stop me except God. *Gye Nyame* creates much power and responsibility. It offers freedom to those who will work for an end to oppression."

I thank her for the perfect gift. Having spent so much time with them this week sharing meals, bus rides, and waiting around for filming to begin, I will miss Abiko, Joyce, Africanus, Kofi, Quaye, and our other new friends. We arrive at the airport to begin the long wait for our flight.

Several hours later, I sit next to Elizabeth as the jet begins to taxi. There is no cheering like there was when we arrived.

CHAPTER 11

THE MIDDLE PASSAGE

In the plane, my mind begins to wander. We will fly across the Middle Passage over the next several hours. Two hundred years ago, this same journey took up to three months.

A few nights ago, while sitting in the darkness on the hard rock floor in a dungeon in the belly of Cape Coast Castle, I was overcome by emotion, by the weight of a sordid history in which our ancestors played an integral part. Now I fly over the Atlantic Ocean aboard a modern airliner headed home.

My mind turns to the experience we've just had. I think of millions of African people being kidnapped from their homes and taken across the sea under incredibly inhumane conditions in wooden boats. What images of home, family, and friends jarred their minds? What did their despair sound like? What pain did they endure as they struggled against the fetters that bound them? Which emotion was more powerful, hatred or fear? How many simply did as they were told under the threat of a vicious beating, quietly surrendering, as hope fell away like so many drops of sweat?

Recent studies of captains' logs, seamen's diaries, owners' records, and other archival materials reveal the magnitude of the Middle Passage with more clarity than ever before. Records identify more than seventeen thousand slaving voyages from the eighteenth century, for instance, but only a few brief accounts describe daily life aboard slaving vessels. Very few people, black or white, recorded details about life aboard these ships.[1] Combining available historical facts with hints and pieces of stories from a variety of sources offers a sense of what it must have been like.

A ship leaving Rhode Island was outfitted to carry a full cargo of rum, along with a variety of other goods and provisions for the crew and ship on the long voyage to the coast of West Africa. Once it was anchored near the castles of Cape Coast, rum, tobacco, and other goods were traded for African people. The crew then refitted the ship to haul a cargo of humans instead of barrels, building platforms below deck into which they would cram people for the next long voyage. They also built partitions on deck to keep the men and women separated and to protect themselves in the event of a revolt.

Rhode Island ships were significantly smaller than their European counterparts. A British slaver may have held upwards of five hundred captives, but the average number of Africans on a Rhode Island ship was just over 113.[2] Consequently, the crew could unload their cargo at the Gold Coast, purchase their payload of African people, and depart more quickly than their larger competitors. Less time in Africa meant less exposure to disease for the captain and crew. It meant less time for enslaved Africans to be held in dungeons. It meant a higher chance of survival for all, which I find an ironic benefit. It meant more Africans survived to be enslaved for the rest of their lives.

Trying to comprehend the Middle Passage is to imagine the unimaginable. I have no concept with which to compare it. Based on what we've learned so far on our journey, and upon evidence that has been analyzed by scholars, I know that colonial America, later the United States, was a tiny player in the worldwide transatlantic slave trade. Recent estimates place the total number of Africans who, over three and a half centuries, survived capture, the dungeons, and the Middle Passage, and arrived in the Americas (including the Caribbean islands and North and South America) at roughly ten million. In the eighteenth century alone, the British shipped two and a half million. Of these ten million people, estimates are that 400,000 Africans arrived in the colonies prior to independence and in the United States after independence. Rhode Island was responsible for transporting over 100,000 enslaved Africans into the Americas.[3] Of approximately two thousand total slaving voyages originating from North American ports, half departed from this smallest of states.[4]

Over the roughly seventy-five years that Rhode Islanders participated in the slave trade, the mortality rate of captive Africans traversing the Middle Passage averaged 12 percent. Disease killed traders and crew as indiscriminately as those sold into slavery. Just as indigenous Americans succumbed in huge numbers to new diseases brought to the North American continent by Europeans, so did Europeans succumb to afflictions in Africa they had never been exposed to before. Though data for Rhode Island crews is sketchy, mortality rates for British, Dutch, and French seamen were higher than those of the Africans they carried.[5]

Prior to departure for the West Indies, it was common to brand captives by country of origin or destination, or by individual proprietor, to ensure ownership. Some slavers branded their captives with heated pieces of silver wire fashioned into the merchant's initials. The wire was hot enough to blister, but not to burn the skin severely.[6] Other slavers used red-hot irons. The spot on the body to be branded depended on which nation owned the ship.[7]

Olaudah Equiano published a written narrative in 1789. He wrote of being taken captive as an eleven-year-old boy from his home in the kingdom of Benin around 1756. He describes his childhood in the province of Eboe in idyllic terms: it was a nation of dancers, musicians, and poets. He said their manners were simple, their luxuries few. Cattle, poultry, and goats supplied the greatest part of their meat. The soil was rich and produced plentiful vegetables including plantains, yams, beans, and corn. Tobacco, cotton, and pineapples were also abundant. The wants of the people were modest and easily supplied. Equiano's father, the head of a large family, owned several slaves. He also sold others into slavery—prisoners of war or those who had been convicted of a crime.[8]

Equiano's happy childhood ended abruptly when he and his sister were kidnapped and sold.

The first object which saluted my eyes when I arrived on the coast was the sea, and a slave ship, which was then riding at anchor, and waiting for its cargo. These filled me with astonishment, which was soon converted into terror when I was carried on board. I was immediately handled and tossed up to see if I were sound by some of the crew; and I was now persuaded that I had gotten into a world of bad spirits, and that they were going to kill me. Their complexions too differing so much from ours, their long hair, and the language they spoke (which was very different from any I had ever heard), united to confirm me in this belief. Indeed such were the horrors of my views and fears at the moment, that, if ten thousand worlds had been my own, I would have freely parted with them all to have exchanged my condition with that of the meanest slave in my own country. When I looked around the ship too and saw a large furnace or copper boiling, and a multitude of black people of every description chained together, every one of their countenances expressing dejection and sorrow, I no longer doubted my fate; and, quite overpowered with horror and anguish, I fell motionless on the deck and fainted.

Soon afterward,

the blacks who brought me on board went off, and left me aban-
doned to despair. I now saw myself deprived of all chance of re-
turning to my native country, or even the least glimpse of hope
of gaining the shore ... my present situation ... was filled with
horrors of every kind, still heightened by my ignorance of what
I was to undergo. I was not long suffered to indulge my grief; I
was soon put down under the decks, and there I received such a
salutation in my nostrils as I had never experienced in my life:
so that, with the loathsomeness of the stench, and crying to-
gether, I became so sick and low that I was not able to eat, nor
had I the least desire to taste any thing. I now wished for the last
friend, death, to relieve me; but soon, to my grief, two of the
white men offered me eatables; and, on my refusing to eat, one
of them held me fast by the hands, and laid me across I think the
windlass, and tied my feet, while the other flogged me severely.

Typically, the captors shackled the right arm and ankle of one
man to the left arm and ankle of another to restrict their movement
and prevent rebellion. The crew packed the Africans tightly together in the hold of the ship. As in the dungeons at Elmina and
Cape Coast, there was little room to stand, sit, or lie down. Each captive's space in the hold was smaller than a coffin. Sleep must have
been fitful at best, and never restful.[9]

As described by Equiano, the typical hold below deck was dark,
hot, and humid. I try to imagine the reek of human misery, sweat,
urine, excrement, and death. Men and women were separated. They
all laid or sat on hard, rough-hewn wooden slabs, wedged together
like so many spoons in a drawer. Their bare skin must have been
scraped and cut as the ship rocked back and forth. With so many having never experienced sailing before, nausea must have been ram-

pant. The stink of vomit would have mingled with the rest of the disgusting odors.

Keep in mind, this is a description of conditions before a ship even left the coast of Africa. While still in view of the shore of his homeland, Equiano wrote,

The stench of the hold while we were on the coast was so intol-erably loathsome, that it was dangerous to remain there for any time, and some of us had been permitted to stay on the deck for the fresh air; but now that the whole ship's cargo were confined together, it became absolutely pestilential. The closeness of the place, and the heat of the climate, added to the number in the ship, which was so crowded that each had scarcely room to turn himself, almost suffocated us. This produced copious perspira-tions, so that the air soon became unfit for respiration, from a variety of loathsome smells, and brought on a sickness among the slaves, of which many died, thus falling victims to the im-provident avarice, as I may call it, of their purchasers.

This wretched situation was again aggravated by the gall-ing of the chains, now become insupportable; and the filth of the necessary tubs, into which the children often fell, and were almost suffocated. The shrieks of the women, and the groans of the dying, rendered the whole a scene of horror almost incon-ceivable.

Happily perhaps for myself I was soon reduced so low here that it was thought necessary to keep me almost always on deck; and from my extreme youth I was not put in fetters. In this sit-uation I expected every hour to share the fate of my compan-ions, some of whom were almost daily brought upon deck at the point of death, which I began to hope would soon put an end to my miseries. Often did I think many of the inhabitants of the deep much more happy than myself. I envied them the freedom they enjoyed, and as often wished I could change my condition for theirs. Every circumstance I met with served only to render my state more painful, and heighten my apprehensions, and my opinion of the cruelty of the whites.

Once the ship was on its way, the sound of the sea and of the creaking wooden ship must have been drowned by the moans and cries of those nearby. Rats, lice, maggots, and other vermin were the only living creatures free to roam about the hold. Captives couldn't scratch themselves or swat an insect without tugging at the person they were shackled to. Chains rattled. Wood groaned.

The journey from Africa to the Americas lasted anywhere from five weeks to several months. Day after day, week upon week added up to months of staggering misery.

Against all this adversity, people survived. If it is true that 12 percent of Africans who left the Gold Coast of Africa did not survive the Middle Passage, then 88 percent of them did. Most of the African men, women, and children who came to the New World overcame the most inhumane and cruel of conditions.

Ironically, the slave ship captains and owners needed to ensure the safe delivery of their human cargo to market in order to achieve high profits. Consequently, some restraint and care were practiced on most voyages. Most owners cautioned their captains against overcrowding the ships so their "cargo" would not die. There were brief daily opportunities for the captives to exercise by jumping around or dancing on deck. A large number of manifests listed vinegar, indicating that the hold was cleaned and disinfected occasionally with the common cleaning solution of vinegar and water.[10]

Food mostly consisted of rice, beans, and corn. Equiano described a "large furnace or copper boiling." He feared being thrown into it by his captors. What he most likely observed was the crew preparing food. As he soon discovered, those unwilling to eat, or attempting to starve themselves and end their own misery, were force-fed. Fresh food and water were obviously unavailable.

Some captives died of the "bloody flux," or dysentery. Some succeeded in committing suicide by jumping overboard. The dead and the sick that the captain believed would infect other captives and crew members were thrown overboard, as in the case of the woman who, after apparently contracting smallpox, was tied to a chair and thrown overboard in 1791 by Captain James DeWolf.[11]

Stories of revolts aboard slave ships were not unheard of. Most did not succeed. The *Amistad* mutiny made famous by Steven Spielberg in the film of the same name was an exception. Seventeen revolts were recorded on Rhode Island–owned ships between 1730 and 1807, about one for every fifty-five voyages.[12] This was due, no doubt, to the fact that men, much more than women and children, were kept shackled as a general rule in order to prevent uprisings. Far more Africans and crew members died of disease than from combat aboard the slaving ships.

As days on the ship became weeks, the African people must have anguished over their homes and loved ones left behind. Lying in the stinking hold of a ship surely stripped away all optimism. Hope for any decent future vanished. After weeks and months of horrid conditions, millions of Africans survived. And for what future? Equiano described it thus:

> *At last we came in sight of the island of Barbadoes, at which the whites on board gave a great shout, and made many signs of joy to us. We did not know what to think of this; but as the vessel drew nearer we plainly saw the harbor, and other ships of different kinds and sizes; and we soon anchored amongst them off Bridge Town. Many merchants and planters now came on board, though it was in the evening. They put us in separate parcels, and examined us attentively. They also made us jump, and pointed to the land, signifying we were to go there. We thought by this*

*we should be eaten by these ugly men, as they appeared to us;
and, when soon after we were all put down under the deck again,
there was much dread and trembling among us, and nothing but
bitter cries to be heard all the night from these apprehensions.*

I'm aware of no diary from any African survivors of the Middle
Passage aboard a ship owned by the DeWolf family or any other
Rhode Island–owned ship. Is Equiano's account typical of so many
others who survived the journey? I believe that white and black
people alike heard the cries of children, the screams of women, and
the swish of the lash as it tore into the flesh of those who challenged
the white men's authority. Captive men surely agonized as they saw
black women used for the sexual pleasure of their white captors.
The putrid odor in the hold must have been a universal experience.
Rotting food and stagnant water were not atypical, even for crew
members.

And yet, most captives who entered the ships off the coast of
Africa survived to stand on auction blocks in the Americas. Like
Equiano, they found strength, a will to live that overcame the desperate situation they found themselves in. Too soon they would be
bought by white men and become their property for the rest of their
lives. The same fate awaited their children, their grandchildren, and
future generations.

CHAPTER 12

LA HABANA

After spending the night in New York City, I ride the subway back to the airport. With the U.S. embargo against Cuba, arrangements are complicated. Our cultural exchange visas were acquired through the Massachusetts Foundation for the Humanities. A company called E-Trav arranged our flight, accommodations, tour bus, guide, and many of our meals. The woman from E-Trav is a godsend at JFK, walking us through all the procedures and checkpoints.

Our plane touches down in Havana at 1:11 a.m. The applause from the passengers, most of whom appear to be Cubans returning home or visiting family, mirrors that in Accra. Warmth and humidity greet us at José Martí International Airport. The ground crew rolls steps to the exit door of the plane for us to disembark. As I look down from the top of the stairs, my first preconception is blown immediately. I expected to be greeted by uniformed guards with Russian-made Kalashnikov rifles lined up watching us, taking pictures, and pulling people out of line for questioning. But not a single person waits on the tarmac. We simply walk to the terminal. If it weren't for the language being spoken, this could be Redmond, Oregon.

Customs, again, is a breeze. Our bags and equipment have yet to be inspected by anyone in the world. We climb onto the bus we'll use all week. It's the size of a school bus, but with large cushy seats. A Cuban man speaks into the microphone at the front as we pull out of the airport. "Welcome to La Habana. My name is Raúl. I will be your tour guide all week. Feel free to ask me anything about religion or policy or anything else about Cuba and I will be completely honest with you. If national policy is different from my own views, I will tell you both."

Raúl Izquierdo is a small man with short hair, a mustache, and a tiny goatee. He seems open and friendly and speaks fluent English. I've been listening to my Spanish CDs for months so I can find my way to the bathroom, the hotel, or a restaurant. I can order a beer and offer a genial greeting, but I harbor no illusions. My Spanish remains quite limited. Having an English-speaking tour guide is most welcome. Raúl advises us not to carry our passports, visas, or airline tickets. The hotel will issue us a guest pass, which is all we'll need to carry with us. Ledlie and I finally get to sleep around four-thirty in the morning.

I awake less than three hours later and tiptoe out to avoid waking my roommate. Breakfast, which comes with our tour package, is served at the restaurant on the top floor of the five-story Plaza Hotel. I'm the first of our group to arrive. The feast spread before me includes omelets, fresh fruit, fresh-squeezed guava, papaya, and orange juices, pancakes, and wide varieties of breads, salads, and meats. I carry my full plate outside to eat on the expansive balcony. Long white walls trimmed in peach are set off by white window shutters. Plants grow in all the window sills. I sit alone looking out over the city.

There will be no filming today, so after breakfast Elly, Elizabeth, and I decide to do a little exploring. We walk along one of the many roads leading through downtown La Habana. I find it jarring how quickly we enter a completely different world. We move from the opulence of the Plaza Hotel to abject poverty in just two blocks. One building stands solid and well kept; the next is in decay; another is uninhabitable. Clothing hangs to dry from balconies above. Cars from the 1950s are parked on the street. An old woman ambles by, pulling a cart. There are bicycles and a variety of taxis. Small dogs run free everywhere.

Shortly after noon we arrive at the Malecón, a wide street that runs parallel with the coastline, and rest on the seawall, which stands about three feet tall and three feet thick. I kick off my sandals and look out across the water, knowing I'm only ninety miles from Florida. In certain ways I feel farther from my country than when I was in Cape Coast. I'm American. I'm not supposed to be here. I feel like Adam taking a huge bite out of the forbidden apple.

As we stroll down the Malecón, men check out Elly and Elizabeth with obvious prurient interest, which I never saw happen in Ghana. Kids of all ages sit on the wall. Many jump or dive into the ocean twelve feet below. At the end of the Malecón, I gaze across the bay at what looks like a fort. It reminds me of Cape Coast Castle. We spend the next two hours in the Museo de Música, viewing Cuban musical instruments dating from the sixteenth century to the present.

We meet the others back at the hotel and soon depart for dinner. Inside a nearby well-appointed restaurant, a seven-piece band plays. After being seated at our long table, I tap my toes in time with the music and watch two dancers, a man and a woman, move perfectly in sync with each other. He sports a thick gray mustache with huge muttonchop sideburns. She wears a bright red and blue wrap on her head, and jewelry dangles and jangles from her ears, neck, and wrists.

Ledlie and I discover El Mojito, Cuban rum mixed with sugar, lime juice, crushed mint, seltzer water, bitters, and ice: the perfect drink for the hot weather. As we finish eating, the woman dancer approaches. I agree to join her and we make our way through the tables and dance in front of the band. With every step, we shout, "Bah!"

"Bah, bah, bah!" Juanita now dances next to me with the woman's partner. What a way to end our first day in Cuba. My thoughts focus on music, food, drink, and dancing, and not on slavery at all.

The following morning we ride our bus through the tunnel under the entry to the harbor. The port at La Habana was once one of the largest slave markets in the world. The fortress I saw yesterday from the end of the Malecón is larger than either the Elmina or Cape Coast castles. It was built over four hundred years ago to protect La Habana from invasion. A prominent lighthouse, added by the Spanish colonial government in 1845, guides ships into harbor. Although it is popularly called "El Morro," the castle's proper name is El Castillo de los Tres Reyes del Morro or the Castle of the Three Kings of the Nose, which refers to the three kings of Bethlehem, the patrons of its chapel, and to the way the land juts out at the point, similar to a very large nose.

When our bus emerges from the tunnel and pulls to a stop in the parking lot, we are left on our own to explore the fortress, now a popular tourist attraction. I leave the others to wander alone and enter a nondescript yellow building with a tiled roof. No sign indicates what's ahead. I step into a long, narrow room and find myself in what was once Che Guevara's office. His gun, backpack, and desk are on display. The walls are covered with pictures of Che, the Cuban national icon. In my short time here, I've seen fifty images of Che for every one of Fidel Castro.

Back outside, I cross a courtyard and climb a long set of stairs. I emerge onto the high roof of another building, several hundred feet long, and walk to the far end. Going back down the stairs at this end, I open the door at the bottom to find myself face to face with a man in uniform holding a rifle. He's young, in his twenties. He tries to talk with me but knows virtually no English. I try, but cannot communicate with him at all. I smile and say, "*No entiendo.*" I can't tell if I am in a place I'm not allowed. He smiles, so I feel no threat, and after several minutes of struggling to communicate, we give up. We shake hands and I walk away unhindered.

I rejoin my cousins near the castle's outer wall. Elizabeth sits, sketching by the cannon, and I sit nearby to watch. A man far below fishes from the end of a pier. A warm breeze blows. What an idyllic setting, and what a contrast to the heaviness that permeated Cape Coast.

Back on the bus, we're driven to the home of Maria del Carmen Barcia, professor of history at Universidad de la Habana. Thick bushes and a green cyclone fence surround her small white house. A young child, perhaps five years old, stands outside awkwardly holding a dachshund in her arms. As I enter the well-kept home, with its comfortable furnishings and an eclectic collection of art, I'm certain that Carmen is better off than many people we've encountered here. Carmen is a woman with skin as light as mine and a confident smile. She wears a multicolored dress of green, black, blue, red, and yellow squares and sits in a tall-backed wicker chair. Large plants are plentiful. Carmen speaks to us in Spanish as María Teresa Ortega, or Tete, our main translator, interprets.

Carmen has studied slavery for many years and has written articles and books on the subject. Tete points out that there were no Cuban natives available to provide a labor force for the Spanish conquerors. "We were more thorough than you were in the U.S. We killed them all." Most of the indigenous Cubans died within a few decades of Columbus's arrival in 1492. The Spaniards needed laborers, so African slavery in Cuba began in the sixteenth century.

Carmen explains that early on, many of the enslaved were able to purchase property, as well as their freedom. Some even owned other enslaved people, reproducing aspects of domestic slavery as it once existed in Africa. The United States outlawed the slave trade in 1808, and Spain followed suit in Cuba in 1820. Both Americans and Cubans ignored the laws to continue in the trade. The sugar industry was booming and the cost of purchasing Africans was high. Not only did the slave trade not end in Cuba, it increased. From 1815 to 1816 the number of enslaved African people entering Cuba doubled. From 1816 to 1817 the figures quadrupled. Enslaved Africans continued to enter Cuba until 1873.

———·•·———

I suspect that most people like me, with a standard public school education in the United States and a typical interest in the news, lack even a rudimentary understanding of the not-so-little island barely ninety miles off the coast of Florida.

Cuba, with a land mass of 42,800 square miles, comprises more than half the total land mass of the Caribbean and is larger than seventeen of the United States, including Tennessee, Ohio, and Virginia, as well as Austria, Portugal, and Costa Rica. Its population of over eleven million outnumbers that of all but seven of the United States, as well as Greece, Bolivia, and New Zealand.

Cuban history encompasses far more than a half century of Fidel Castro, but Cuba's longtime authoritarian leader continues to capture the major focus of the media and of U.S. high school history texts. Americans tend to view Castro as a caricature, when the reality is far more complicated, and European and American involvement in the history of Cuba is largely ignored.

As Tete pointed out, the indigenous population of Cuba was almost completely wiped out soon after Columbus's arrival. The story of Hatuey was recorded by Bartolomé de Las Casas, a Dominican friar who became known as the protector of the Indians and an outspoken critic of the cruelty of the Spanish toward native peoples.[1] Hatuey fled Hispaniola (the island on which modern-day Haiti and the Dominican Republic are located) for Cuba to escape the inhumane acts of the Christians and was eventually captured and tied to a stake to be burned. A friar told him what he could do before he perished in order to be saved and go to heaven. Hatuey inquired if all Christians went to heaven. When told that they do, he stated that he preferred hell.[2]

The Spanish mistakenly thought Cuba was bursting with gold to be mined. When that proved false, Cuba's importance to Spain remained largely strategic. Its location allowed Spain to control the Caribbean seaways, and thus the flow of silver in other parts of the New World. The island's inhabitants maintained a meager existence until the rise of the tobacco and sugar industries in the eighteenth century. In 1700, the population of Cuba was approximately 50,000. Then, over the next hundred years, sugar production in the West Indies attained an importance in the world economy equal to that of steel in the nineteenth century and oil in the twentieth.[3] Sugar production required a massive labor force, which was provided by the import of Africans. By 1791, Cuba's population had grown to over 270,000, including almost 65,000 slaves, and this occurred even before Cuba's sugar industry became consequential.[4]

Several incidents toward the end of the eighteenth century contributed to Cuba's transformation from a small force in the world economy into a significant one. Spain relaxed its laws limiting Cuba's ability to trade with other nations. The creation of the United States resulted in a conveniently close trading partner. The most significant turn of events, however, was the slave revolt that erupted in the French colony Saint-Domingue (which occupied the western third of Hispaniola) in 1791, led by Toussaint L'Ouverture, which culminated in independence thirteen years later and a new name: Haiti. The former colony had been the Caribbean's premier sugar producer and financial power, but the Haitian revolution resulted in the establishment of the first free black republic in the New World—and the demise of its sugar industry. This provided

Cuba an immediate and dramatic opportunity for increased sugar production.

Between 1790 and 1820, the year trading in slaves became punishable by death in the United States and the slave trade to Cuba was legally abolished by Spain, more than 230,000 slaves arrived in Cuba. Between 1821 and 1865, more than 200,000 additional Africans were illegally imported,[5] and by 1869, Cuba's population ballooned to 1.4 million, including over 360,000 enslaved Africans.[6] Slavery itself wasn't outlawed until 1886.[7]

Cuba became the dominant island in the West Indies in the nineteenth century, which benefited the DeWolfs and other American investors greatly. Economic success depended upon the free labor provided by enslaved Africans and the business acumen provided by slave traders and plantation owners. Most, like the DeWolfs, were absentee owners (though a few DeWolfs would later reside in Cuba). The introduction of the latest machinery, along with the railroad for transporting crops, resulted in Cuba's rapid and dramatic economic development.[8]

The complicated relationship between the United States and Cuba goes back to shortly after the American Revolution. Thomas Jefferson hoped Cuba would become part of the Union.[9] In the mid-nineteenth century, Presidents Polk, Pierce, and Buchanan all attempted unsuccessfully to purchase Cuba from Spain.[10]

Fearing a slave revolt similar to the one in Haiti, some major Cuban land and slave owners supported annexation by the United States, a strong and sympathetic partner employing the same slave-based economy, as a way to ensure continuation of the slave system. The end of the Civil War and the abolition of slavery in this country ended such efforts for a time.

The first Cuban war for independence, the Ten Years' War (1868–78), was launched to achieve independence from Spain, universal suffrage, and the end of slavery. Revolutionary forces were led by General Antonio Maceo. Neither the Spanish nor the Cubans prevailed, and the signing of a peace agreement ended the fighting.[11]

The war resulted in such widespread destruction that many Cuban and Spanish elites lost their fortunes. Taking advantage of a rash of bankruptcies, U.S. business interests made significant new investments in Cuban plantations and mines. Spain still controlled Cuba, but American influence quickly grew.

José Martí led the second Cuban war for independence (1895–98). Martí is considered the father of the Cuban nation. "In exile in the United States, he successfully forged alliances and developed the ideologies of a popular, antiracist, and anti-imperialist nationalism that still has enormous resonance for Cubans today."[12] Martí was killed in 1895. The war lasted three additional years and ended after war broke out between the United States and Spain in 1898.

Stateside business interests were threatened by the revolution. National interests were at stake—in particular, security for the future Panama Canal. Expansionists in this country set their sights on Cuba. Spain could not quell the revolt. The U.S. government sent the battleship *Maine* to Cuba in January 1898. When it exploded in the harbor of La Habana in February, the United States blamed Spain, declared war, and destroyed a Spanish fleet near Santiago, Cuba. The Spanish-American War lasted less than four months, was fought in both the Pacific and Atlantic, and resulted in the United States's emergence as a power on the world stage for the first time. Peace was declared with the signing of the Treaty of Paris in December 1898. Spain was expelled from the New World and the United States became the dominant power in the Caribbean, gaining control of Puerto Rico, as well as Guam and the Philippines on the other side of the world. Though the treaty granted Cuba its independence from Spain, the reality was that we also gained control of Cuba.[13] When the Spanish flag was lowered it wasn't replaced by the Cuban flag. The stars and stripes flew over La Habana.

By late 1899, an economic invasion of Cuba began as U.S. commercial interests moved in as never before. With their control over Cuban money, the U.S. government invested in Cuban infrastructure such as schools, mining, transportation, health care, sanitation, customs, and postal services. An American military government was installed with the goals of feeding the starving population, controlling the spread of yellow fever, disarming the revolutionaries, and drawing up a constitution for Cuba's self-governance.

The United States agreed to turn the government over to the Cubans provided that certain features beneficial to this country were adopted as part of the new Cuban constitution. The Platt Amendment imposed a number of conditions. Cuba could make no treaty that would impair its independence. It allowed no foreign debt whose interest could not be paid through ordinary revenues after defraying the current expenses of government. It allowed for U.S. military intervention to preserve Cuban independence or to maintain a government adequate for the protection of life, liberty, and property. It declared all acts taken by our nation in Cuba during military occupation to be valid.

Cuban leaders were outraged, believing the amendment essentially made a colony out of Cuba, but our government would not budge. The terms of the Platt Amendment were incorporated into Cuba's constitution and the United States was given legal supervision over governance in Cuba. A permanent treaty was signed in 1903 in which the United States also received the permanent right to maintain a military base at Guantanamo Bay.[14]

Over the next three decades a series of U.S. military interventions and political manipulations were constant reminders of who managed Cuba. A succession of corrupt and incompetent governments faced challenges by students, communists, business interests, army veterans, labor unions, and Cuban nationalists, whose goal was true self-governance. Cuba was economically dependent almost solely on the United States.[15]

In 1934, army chief Fulgencio Batista forced Cuba's then president to resign. He appointed a provisional president and the United States soon officially recognized the new government. They saw Batista as the one leader in Cuba capable of maintaining order. Batista retained control by ruling through a series of handpicked "puppet" presidents.[16] In 1952 Batista took direct command in a coup d'état and canceled all elections. His military dictatorship would last seven years.

Perhaps the future of Cuba would have been different had the United States made an effort to help local citizens during the first half of the twentieth century, but farmers who needed financial assistance cultivating their land in order to grow crops were refused U.S. government support. Consequently, corporations like United Fruit and a few sugar and railroad barons were able to purchase vast tracts of property from desperate Cubans very cheaply. Many formerly independent Cuban farmers thus became wage earners for large land-owning corporations. Tobacco and sugar industries, once controlled by Spain, came under the control of the United States.

By the late 1950s, American sugar companies controlled three quarters of Cuba's farmland. American financial interests controlled 90 percent of Cuba's telephone and electric utilities, half of its railways, and 40 percent of its sugar production. Cuban unemployment reached 25 percent.[17] All of Batista's arms, planes, tanks, ships, and other military supplies came from the United States, and his army was trained by U.S. armed forces. Cuba was, for all intents and purposes, controlled by this country for the principal benefit of its businesses. Cuba became one of the more highly developed countries in Latin America, but its well-being and destiny were at the mercy of outsiders.

The Cuban revolution began when Fidel Castro led an attack on the Moncada barracks in 1953 that ended in disaster. Over the next few years, the legend of Fidel grew to mythic proportions.

On January 1, 1959, after several years of unsuccessful guerrilla attacks against Batista's army, revolutionary forces, led by Fidel Castro and Che Guevara, took control of Cuba's capital. They established a nominally socialist state, and Castro has ruled ever since over a largely poor and isolated egalitarian country. Castro has committed human rights violations, but he also overthrew a repressive regime, and for the first time since Columbus landed on this island and claimed it for Spain in 1492, Cubans governed Cuba.

———·•·———

"I'd appreciate hearing why you have been studying slavery," Ledlie says to Carmen. "Why you are concerned about it?"

Carmen explains that she studies slavery as well as the various classes in Cuba. The upper and lower classes originated from different types of immigration—primarily Spanish immigration and the African slave trade. "Our culture comes from these two roots," says Carmen. "If you don't understand these roots, you cannot understand Cuba."

She explains that her students did not understand that the root of slavery is in capitalism. Slavery disappeared when slaves were no longer necessary to the financial success of the plantations.

I ask her about slavery's legacy in Cuba—whether people are still treated differently based on their race or the pigment of their skin.

"Slavery leaves very large marks on a society and still today you can find reminiscences of things. In the fifties there were still separate black clubs, mulatto clubs, and white clubs. Blacks walked one way and whites walked another way in the same park. Today this is not the case, mostly with young people, who have grown up in another type of society."

Holly asks for Carmen's reaction to our making this film.

"You are looking for your family roots, to know what was good and what was bad. It is very natural that people want to know where they come from, where they are going or perhaps what they're doing to be better."

I don't think this is the answer Holly was looking for.

———◦•◦———

Later that evening, several of us walk to a restaurant called Floridita for dinner. Their menu claims it was Ernest Hemingway's favorite restaurant. A chain hangs between the end of the bar and the wall, blocking one bar stool, Hemingway's favorite, to prevent people from sitting on it. There are pictures of Hemingway with Fidel, a picture of Mariel Hemingway sitting on the stool, and a bust of Hemingway on a small shelf. This corner of the bar narrows so that from the stool, you can lean forward on the bar, lean back against the wall, or lean to your left against the adjacent wall. They say Hemingway preferred it so he would not have to talk with more than one person at a time. The other stools are bright white. Hemingway's has yellowed with age. Floridita also claims that the daiquiri was invented here in this restaurant and was "Papa's" favorite drink.

After dinner, we head back to the Malecón to enjoy the excitement and spectacle of Carnival. We find a section with enough room for our group in one of the many bleachers set up along the road. We buy brightly painted handmade masks, maracas, and posters from people walking by and settle in for the festivities.

One of the most highly anticipated celebrations of the year, Carnival is one gigantic street party. The vivid colors and rhythms remind me of the Grand Durbar in Cape Coast. Though the origins of Carnival are uncertain, it is the final festivity before Lent that Italian Catholics began celebrating long ago. Because one of the Lenten practices included abstaining from eating meat, the term "Carnival" may derive from one of two early Latin terms, *carnem levare* or *carnelevarium*, which, roughly translated, mean "to take away, or remove, meat."[18] The celebration spread throughout Europe. As the French, Spanish, and Portuguese took control of certain parts of the Americas, they brought Carnival with them. Over hundreds of years, the European celebration of Carnival in Latin America absorbed influences from Caribbean arts and ancient African traditions of marching and drumming through villages in costumes and masks. The resulting combination of the three cultures evolved into the modern celebrations of Carnival we witness in Cuba.

The distinction between observer and participant blurs. Group after energetic group of festively costumed people dances past our bleachers. Spectators from the sidelines join in. All vehicles are completely enveloped in colorful decoration. Multileveled platforms protrude out and above whatever truck is hidden within. A particularly large float pauses in front of us, with dancers high above as well as below on the street. Women wear bright yellow dresses and gigantic ribbons atop their heads. Men walk on stilts. Huge, lighted flowers cast a warm glow. Next come dancers in tiny bikinis and then others in full skirts. Men play drums for women dancing in metallic silver blouses with short orange skirts. Some walk with enormous masks on their heads. One man in a white-polka-dotted red shirt dons an oversized blackface caricature mask with a huge cigar poking out of its mouth. Ribbons flow wildly from people's wrists. Dancers laugh as more people jump out from the stands to join them. I dance for a few moments with a woman in a bright-green dress with large feathered plumes radiating from her head in all directions. She smiles and then quickly moves along.

In the Grand Durbar the colors were equally brilliant, but other than the dancers and drummers, the rest of the participants seemed more subdued. The focus in Cape Coast was solemn by comparison as people made their way toward the castles that once held so many in bondage. Tonight, though I'm with total strangers, I laugh, eat, drink, and dance, swept away in celebration.

CHAPTER 13

"OUR NICE PROTESTANT SELVES"

Due to the lateness of our return from Carnival last night, our morning is our own. I spend a few peaceful hours eating breakfast, writing postcards, staring at the ocean, filling my lungs with warm Caribbean air, and window shopping down narrow Obispo Street around the corner from our hotel. My feeling of relaxation is absolute.

When the late morning "camera call" comes, we drive to the home of Natalia Bolivar—a scholar in Afro-Cuban studies and one of Cuba's foremost experts in, as well as a practitioner of, the Santeria religion—where we meet with her and Zoila Lapique, a professor, historian, and research librarian with expertise in nineteenth-century Cuban cultural and social life. Both are experts on slavery and the slave trade in Cuba. Natalia appears to be in her early or mid-sixties. She has light skin, short gray hair, and glasses. She wears many different types and colors of necklaces and rings on five fingers. A nearly spent cigarette rests between two of them. Zoila, about the same age as Natalia, also has light skin and short gray hair. Unlike Natalia, Zoila speaks no English. We sit informally around Natalia's living room. There aren't enough chairs, so a few of us stand or sit on the floor.

Natalia discusses spirituality in the lives of the enslaved. Santeria, the syncretistic Afro-Cuban religion, means "the way of the saints." Traditional African sacred beliefs, primarily from the Yoruba people of West Africa, were combined with elements of Roman Catholicism. When the Africans first arrived in the Americas, having been baptized, their native religions were suppressed. To preserve their traditional beliefs, the slaves equated each of their ancestral gods with a corresponding Christian saint. Slave owners in Cuba were satisfied that the Africans were worshipping like good Catholics, and the Africans simply used the new names to refer to their traditional gods.

"From your knowledge of Santeria and the different African religious practices here, what would those traditions say we need spiritually, given who our ancestors are?" Katrina asks.

"Remember that you are living in the twenty-first century," says Natalia. "Do not judge them as you would judge them in our time. Most of the black people whose ancestors came as slaves know they suffered very much on the plantations, but they won't like to go back to Africa. They wouldn't judge it so seriously. What is terrible is the racial injustice with black people in the States."

"I am curious what your reactions are to why we are here," Holly says to Natalia. I suspect she's hoping for a different answer than the one she received yesterday from Carmen. Holly seems frustrated by the conversations we've participated in yesterday and today, and I think she feels like the seriousness of slavery and its impact on people today has been somehow minimized in Cuba.

"You are the first ones I have seen who are interested in your ancestors as slave traders," says Natalia. "Everyone should know from where they come and about their families, but it's not for judging. You are interested to perhaps influence others in their attitude against the racism. That's very nice. You have to wait another one or two hundred years for racism to be eliminated. You didn't create the problem. It's a problem of the system and it has to pass many, many years so that things can be eliminated."

Zoila pulls out a photocopy of a map from the late 1800s with a few places circled in green. Tete translates as Zoila explains. She found the name "Wolf," but not DeWolf, marking three sites that were coffee plantations. Each is referenced not with the name of the coffee plantation but with the family name. One can also see the geographic coordinates.

"They say Wolf?" asks Katrina.

"Wolf," says Zoila. "In those days, since lots of names were similar, they referred to the plantations using the family names. The name 'Wolf' was not common in this area. It was very outstanding, specific. This map was made in 1875."

This gets Katrina's attention. "What?"

"It covers the time from 1860 to 1872."

Upon closer inspection, one of the "Wolf" sites is labeled "Mariana," the name of one of James DeWolf's plantations. Katrina looks surprised. We know James DeWolf left Cuban plantations to family members in his will in 1837, and we're pretty sure that at least one stayed in family ownership until the 1850s. We also know from a Rhode Island Supreme Court case regarding the estate of one of James DeWolf's descendants that there were a number of them—at least a dozen—still living in Cuba in 1893, though we have no evidence that they still owned plantations at that time. The result of the case was that a Bristol estate went to Cuban descendants of James DeWolf.

But if they owned, or even oversaw, one or more plantations in 1872, that's post–Civil War, post–Emancipation Proclamation, and well after every northern state—including Rhode Island in 1843—had officially outlawed slavery. However, slavery wasn't banned in Cuba until 1886. Now we learn that DeWolfs may have still owned plantations in the 1870s. A name written on an old map doesn't prove they were still in family ownership, but that doesn't prevent many of us from speaking at once, asking questions, and speculating about the family's potential continued involvement with slavery in Cuba in the late nineteenth century. Boris Iván Crespo, our line producer in Cuba, has located the Mariana, as well as Arca de Noé (Noah's Ark), which was owned by George.

As we prepare to depart, Natalia makes a recommendation. "Take a little of the earth and keep it. When you have a bad conscience over what they did two hundred years ago, you have your little bag and you say, 'This is dead.' It's like taking out all the bad influence."

"Maybe our destiny is to feel a lot of pain and confusion," says Elizabeth.

"You are a woman and you are living in another century," says Natalia. "You should not feel the weight of the history. You're not living in the Inquisition."

Late in the afternoon, our bus pulls off the side of the road. We park near a series of old, abandoned single-story buildings. Many miles have passed since we've seen people or towns. This is a former sugar plantation, but not connected to our family.

A dark, skinny man, shirtless and wrinkled with age, emerges from one of the buildings. I'm not sure if he's the caretaker here, a historian, or a government representative, but he's clearly expecting us. Martinas introduces himself with a big smile, gesturing broadly with a half-full, two-liter bottle of Cuba Libre (rum and cola) in one of his hands, from which he periodically drinks. Lisa Maria, our production assistant in Cuba—and interpreter when Tete is unavailable—translates his rapid Spanish.

"In spite of all the pressures, the slavery and the revolution, today we are free. You come out to this country and you are brothers. You are family and I welcome you. The victory of Fidel's revolution is that all people are treated the same. We are all one family in Cuba."

He explains how the buildings, now in ruins, were first constructed in 1796 as part of a coffee plantation. "When the coffee trade failed, the sugar trade came. The result was a surge in the slave trade. They disembarked at the bay, at Baja Santana, and then relocated here in these houses." He continues talking, then pauses and smiles.

Lisa Maria stutters and gulps. "He says...he says...um, I'm sorry I'm a little disturbed about his comment, perhaps we should talk about it."

Something just happened, but I don't know what.

Lisa Maria says, "He looked over towards Juanita and I didn't realize what he was looking at, and he said, 'I think I see a slave coming. I see a little slave over there in a straw hat.'" She says that it was obviously meant as a joke, and that such jokes are part of Cuban culture, but still, she looks upset, probably concerned at how Juanita, and the rest of us, may react. She says she feels her own heart pounding.

Martinas blows a kiss toward Juanita and speaks to Lisa Maria. She turns to Juanita. "He says he threw you a kiss to let you know that there is no racism and no hard feeling. He says you're very beautiful."

Several people begin speaking at once until Lisa Maria intervenes. She explains that she and Boris were talking earlier about how in Cuban culture many jokes focus on race. It usually doesn't translate very well to Americans because of the difference in race relations there. In Cuba it is very normal to refer to somebody, or to call them over, by their skin color. "So, somebody would say, 'Oye, negra, ven acá,' or 'Mira ese blanco sucio.' And this is very normal."

The look on Lisa Maria's face expresses her concern about whether Juanita, or any of us, understands without getting offended. She says, "In my family, growing up, because I am darker in my family, I'm called, '*Mi prieta, mi negrita, mi mulatica.*' These are still used as terms of endearment."

Dain asks if it's fair to conclude that Cubans have moved beyond the confusion and sensitivity that perhaps we're still stuck in.

Lisa Maria thinks so. She says Cubans by nature are very open and they joke a lot. "That's how we deal with life. People say the Cuban worker is not very efficient because he'll be out in the sugar cane and someone will come by with music. People will drop their machetes and talk and dance. It's about living life and having fun."

A few of us nod and the tension eases a little. Juanita doesn't appear offended. Maybe Dain's right, but I don't know.

"All right," says Elly, "so where were we?"

Martinas looks across the open courtyard, with its grass and trees, toward some abandoned stone buildings with tile roofs. Weeds grow from the tiles. The large *barracón*—barracks—were in use as slave quarters from 1796 to 1875. He points across the yard toward a bell tower above the roof of one of the buildings. "In the mornings, the bell rang. The slaves came together and went out this entrance to work the fields. The one thing they had against them was their skin color. That was their disgrace. In being black, they were slaves and, in being slaves, they were dogs. Before the revolution people were separated and had their own social groups by race. There was no mixing. Once the revolution triumphed, the social class by color was eliminated. That is the triumph of the revolution. Your family arrived and you are my family. If others arrive they are my family."

Elizabeth says to Lisa Maria, "I want to ask the gentleman how he knows all this. Was it handed down from his family? He seems like an expert."

"I learned from reading books and studying. I don't invent anything. I don't lie. Historians are the great liars."

Katrina wraps up our conversation and thanks him. Martinas

smiles, waves farewell, and saunters back toward the building from which he first emerged.

Boris performs the same functions here that Africanus Aveh did in Ghana—coordinating people and locations, and taking care of other production tasks. I'm not sure how Boris found Martinas, but this has certainly been our most interesting encounter so far. With each of the people we've met in Cuba, we feel a disconnect between what we're searching for and what they have offered us. Katrina and Boris attempted to arrange meetings with relevant black schol- ars in Cuba, but these scholars were unavailable during our time here. Would their views have been different? Maria, Natalia, Zoila, and now Martinas have all attempted to paint a picture that doesn't quite fill the canvas of our expectations, which is a reflection on us, not them. I'm not sure what we're looking for, but we haven't found it yet. Cuba since the revolution is a very different place from the Cuba that existed before Castro. We've learned certain facts about the past, but they seem to float in a fog that is largely disconnected from the present.

We enter the roofless shell of a building that was once part of the slave quarters during the Spanish colonial era. The door is long gone. Crumbling walls appear to be held together by vines and lichen. A large open window looks out on the road. We hear birds singing and the occasional sounds of horse-drawn wagons that seem to be going from nowhere to nowhere. The wind blows through the trees but doesn't make things any cooler. My sweat-soaked shirt clings to my skin.

Katrina has set aside this time for us to debrief on what we've experienced in Cuba so far. She tries to kick-start a conversation. "So what did you think about Natalia saying we shouldn't beat our- selves up so much?"

Elizabeth believes Natalia's background is similar to ours—

privileged—and she's chosen to deal with it differently than Elizabeth chooses to. Holly expresses frustration with the responses both Natalia and Carmen gave to the question of why we're on this journey. She says we may be researching our ancestors, but the scholars we've encountered don't appreciate our attempt to understand the legacy of slavery. They don't understand racism in the United States.

Elly agrees, but says we don't need endorsements from Cuban people. Racism back home isn't their problem, and racism is different here. Though slavery in Cuba led to racial stratification, she's come to the conclusion that slavery here under the Spanish was kinder and gentler than its exceptionally vicious and hateful counterpart in the States. "We hated the people. We didn't allow drumming. We separated people from their tribal origins. We didn't allow people to use their languages. We wanted to eradicate who they were, as opposed to utilizing their bodies while allowing them to be who they were. "

As is often the case, Dain's take is different. Seated on the ledge of the large open window, away from the rest of us—which has become typical for Dain since our last few days in Ghana—he says he has a more hopeful view of what can happen in our country because Cuba appears to have minimized racism. "They've shown it can be done."

I'm not sure I agree. In spite of what Martinas said, we've heard from two people who claim there is no racism in Cuba. Yet I've read that darker-skinned people wouldn't be allowed to work in the nicer hotels. A definite class system exists here that we haven't been exposed to because we've only been here a couple days. "I don't know if we can conclude that they have a sweeter racism here in Cuba than we do at home," I say.

Katrina believes the people we've met are being protective of us. No one wants us to feel bad. Perhaps many light-skinned Cubans, those with more privilege than others, have a vested interest in our not taking racism too seriously because it would have implications for them.

Cuba feels like a small-scale illustration of the challenge people face back home trying to overcome racism. Ignoring racism, arguing that it doesn't exist, or blaming others for it has allowed fearful white people to insulate themselves from it for many generations. No one can study history's hidden and ugly chapters without being changed by the results. I haven't been told the truth about slavery in the North. The real history of U.S. involvement in the Caribbean remains largely hidden. What else don't I know?

Keila stands next to me. She appears upset as she fidgets and looks down and then up at the rest of us. "I feel a lot of confusion, a lot of emotion. I'm having a real problem with, I don't know what to call it, the itinerary. It just feels way out of balance to me. I'm history-ed out. What we did in Ghana, when we started doing processing with each other as a family and we started doing our own personal communication work—I think that is really important for this project and we haven't really done it again since then. I'm trying to be a good girl because I don't want to make too much trouble, but *damn!*"

This last word explodes from her mouth and Keila bends over at the waist. I watch her, but I don't move a muscle. She rises again and says, "I need to have us connect more with each other on a feeling level. A lot is going on between us and we're just being our nice, Protestant selves and I'm *sick of it!*"

Holly rocks back and forth on the other side of me, smiling as her sister continues to release her pent-up frustration. I don't like standing between the two of them right now. I watch Elly pull on a vine dangling from above her. She smiles. I wonder what she's thinking. I'll do just about anything to avoid connecting with this anger.

Jim says he has the same feelings as Keila. "I'm real interested in Ghana and Cuba, but here's a group of ten people who seem to be together, ready to talk about race in the United States, and we're not talking about it."

I don't get it. It feels like race is *all* we've talked about.

"And how it's feeling right now," says Keila about the film, "is that it's gonna show up as a really neat travelogue about slavery."

"It won't be," says Elizabeth. "It won't be." She waves her hand from where she now sits, next to Dain, in that opening in the wall away from the rest of us, who stand in a circle in the middle of the crumbling ruins. "When I've been in Bristol and stood in front of Linden Place, I've thought, 'This is a beautiful piece of architecture and a beautiful setting. This whole street is beautiful and it came from slave money. It came from stuff that was not beautiful.'"

She explains how that feeling was so different from when we were in the dungeons in Elmina and Cape Coast. *Traces of the Trade* is about how history gets buried and glossed over and prettified. She says that now we're in Cuba with all these distractions. We sleep in a lovely hotel with amazing food. We're surrounded by beautiful architecture, upbeat music, and museums. Carnival adds to the festive air. The atmosphere is sensuous and seductive. We aren't focused. We're becoming fractured.

"Suddenly we're not feeling this heart-wrenching, blood-and-guts rage and torture like we were in Ghana," she says, "because it's not so hard core. Everything's a little bit softer and nicer."

All these nice and pleasant things are set up for people like us. It's quite tempting to be distracted and easily lured back into amnesia. "This disconnection is the very thing we're here for," she concludes.

She's right. This feels more like a vacation than what I felt in Ghana. It's easy to get distracted with a Mojito in my hand and a band playing nearby. I'm receiving a great lesson on how easily the disconnection transpires.

I move away from Keila and Holly. It's itchy, hot, and muggy. I swat at a bug buzzing in front of my face. Keila still looks like she's ready to burst. When Jude, our codirector, asks her what's on her mind, Keila says there's a "program" that keeps happening. There are certain things Dain has said that feel very patriarchal to her. She doesn't feel safe in bringing them up because she doesn't want to begin such an important conversation and have it end prematurely. Working on important issues in relationship with others takes time, and our schedule never allows enough time. I stand to the side silently wondering what this has to do with issues of race.

Elizabeth, now standing, says she wants to hold the men in the group accountable for the underlying "silent stuff" that is so strong in WASP culture. Juanita asks her to explain.

"It's the 'Daddy Knows Best' bullshit, like 'we know what's best for you.' I feel that with you, Dain." She looks at him but gets no reaction from Dain.

She also feels like she's supposed to protect him. As a woman, she's not supposed to tell him these things because it's going to be too hard for him. Consequently, it won't be safe for her. It sounds very similar to the way Juanita described the feelings of black people in relation to whites in Jim's room in Ghana.

Elizabeth says she's never been allowed to say she's angry. Growing up, she was ridiculed for being angry. She describes a systematic mode of operation in which men make many choices that women are supposed to go along with, and which, she says, also extends to race and class relationships. Juanita asks her how she has experienced white men who come from a background similar to hers.

Elizabeth pauses. Tears well up in her eyes. She says the best thing to do is just keep her mouth shut. If she doesn't, she'll be labeled as overly emotional, overly sensitive, told that she thinks too much, or that she's a bitch. "I'll get called a dyke, or get my space violated, my body violated, you know?"

Birds chirp wildly in a tree nearby as Elizabeth continues. "I go into situations trying to be open with men and that's what happens.

It's very confusing, and it's very painful, and I don't know how much men are aware of that." She shuffles from side to side and explains how it happens in both large and small ways. "It happens with people slapping your ass when you're walking down the street and it happens in polite cocktail conversation. It happens a million ways."

Katrina says she sees the parallels to what black people must go through trying to explain what they experience, and how hard it is for anyone to talk with people who have more power than they do. Powerful people have been given a certain entitlement and they've internalized it. "It's important to name it," she says. "That's how men get taught, and it's how women get taught."

"As a white woman in this WASP culture, I've been handed this plate of being the keeper of all that stuff," says Elizabeth. "I know exactly what to do, and how to read every little nuance, so that men don't feel uncomfortable."

James accuses the women of having a double standard. They accuse Dain of knowing what's best for them, yet they are doing the same thing to him. Though challenged by Jude to respond, Dain refuses. In this emotion-filled atmosphere, he says he knows what the result will be. She tries several times to get Dain to open up. He repeatedly answers, "I'm not going there."

I'm surprised by Dain's reaction, since he's the main target here and he's rarely at a loss for words. But then I'm not sure how he could respond. From where I stand, off to the side, trying not to be noticed, it feels like the protective walls that separate us are much stronger than those of the *barracón*. They feel like the impenetrable walls of the Tower of Babel.

Ledlie speaks for the first time in a long while. "I startled myself in our session last week in Ghana when I said, 'What are you trying to do, reform us men?' I realize that's a step on the way. I can see how women more readily understand the relationship between racism and sexism. If I would do with Roxana [his wife] what I know

I ought to do, and give up some of my male privilege, it would prepare me for the racism question."

We stand in silence for a moment as Ledlie's words sink in. Then
Holly says she's beginning to realize that what men don't understand about women is similar to what *she* doesn't understand about
white privilege. She says there are things she isn't aware of about
being white. Now she hears men speaking in the same way of things
they're unaware of regarding women. Many times in such situations with men, she's silently rolled her eyes and thought, "Oh,
brother," but now she sees the parallel.

Juanita says, "What's being discovered here is there's no group
of people that should be made out to be the villain any more than
anybody else. We live in a society where a certain group of people
holds most of the power. They happen to be white, Anglo-Saxon,
Protestant, wealthy men."

She points out the connection between the ways men are conditioned and how society looks. It's not about attacking men. But in
order to create a more just society, we need to blow the whistle on
harmful patterns, behaviors, and ways of thinking.

The fading daylight signals that it's time to leave. We climb
slowly back into our bus for the ride back to La Habana. I stare out
the window. Initially, I thought Keila and Elizabeth may have been
leading us far from the main subject of our journey. Veering off into
sexism felt a bit like a red herring, as if perhaps racism and privilege are just too difficult for us white folks to handle. Then Ledlie's,
Holly's, and Juanita's words reminded me that by digging just a
little deeper, I can see how inextricably racism, sexism, and other
"isms" are tied together. They grow together in the same fertile soil
of fear.

CHAPTER 14

ARCA DE NOÉ

Dain's occasional absences, which began toward the end of our time in Ghana, continue. After what happened yesterday, I can't help but notice.

After driving thirty-some miles southwest from La Habana along a road with few other travelers, past fields and telephone poles, our bus pulls to a stop in the middle of Artemisa, an aging sugar plantation town in the La Habana Province. We're told this is an urban center with a population of more than forty thousand, but you wouldn't know it from where we've pulled up. Artemisa prides itself on the fact that two dozen of Fidel's original 150 freedom fighters came from here. A sign reads, *Hay sangre de Artemisa brillando en la bandera* ("There is blood of Artemisa shining in the flag"). Somewhere near Artemisa, James DeWolf's plantation, Mariana, once produced crops for my distant cousin's financial benefit.

Climbing down the steps of the bus onto the street, I watch people stare at us. Two children play nearby and periodically glance in our direction. An older man sits on a chair just outside a business of some sort, looking warily. Others stand in doorways or against the wall along a covered walkway. Across the street, a tall cyclone fence surrounds the town's sugar mill. Nearest the fence stands a low, bright-pink building with larger buildings behind it, and two gigantic concrete smokestacks reach skyward.

Standing just inside the door of a small market, a woman with dark-blond hair offers the first welcoming smile I've seen in Artemisa. She spins fresh cotton candy and pauses to offer us a sample. This is definitely not that pink or blue stuff we get at county fairs back home. I never knew sugar could taste so good.

We are soon joined by three people: the historian of Artemisa, the executive director of the Center of Sugar, and the director of a local museum. As it turns out, there isn't much to see. No buildings remain from James DeWolf's time, just fields of sugar cane. James initially grew coffee here. Sugar came later. All five DeWolf plantations in Cuba produced one or the other.

A small black man in a dark-blue shirt approaches. It appears he's learned why we're here and agrees to talk with us. Lisa Maria translates as Mario Chappotin introduces himself and tells us his grandparents were slaves on a nearby plantation. His grandfather died before he was born, but he grew up with his grandmother. "Obviously, as you can see with me having the name Chappotin, and being black, I am a descendant of the slaves of the Chappotin plantation."

Katrina asks him if his grandmother told him any stories from being enslaved, but he says it was too long ago. He's almost sixty years old. He lives in what was once the slave quarters where his grandfather was housed.

Elly asks if he considers himself Cuban or Afro-Cuban. He answers with a firm nod of his head, "Cuban."

Orlando Garcia Blanco, the historian, and Alberto Beltran Moraro, the director of the Center of Sugar, say that everyone here is Cuban first. They explain that all Cubans are part black, regardless of how they look. Alberto has very light skin. His wife is black. They carry no resentment, Alberto says, because none of our family alive today is responsible for what happened in the past.

Though our conversation with Mr. Chappotin is brief, two interesting pieces of information emerge. First, the Chappotin plantation was located next to the Mariana. Second, James DeWolf's son, Mark Antony DeWolf (grandson of the first DeWolf slave trader), married Sophie Chappotin in 1821. The Chappotins, owners of that neighboring plantation, were French refugees from Martinique, another Caribbean island long involved in the slave trade.[1]

After Mr. Chappotin says good-bye, we walk toward a few long, decaying, abandoned buildings. They were once the slave quarters for all the plantations in the region, one of the first areas where plantations were established in Cuba. We walk along a dirt road for half an hour, stopping when Orlando points across a field toward a line of trees that is the approximate location of the edge of the DeWolf plantation.

We can't get close to it and it doesn't really matter. A line of trees marks what used to be the edge of the property several hundred yards away. Much has changed, and very little history from that time seems to have been preserved. Everything fits with our map.

Katrina brought a copy of an inventory that was written by the manager of Mariana in 1818. Jim reads it. "One hundred and three negroes of both sexes, ninety-six from Africa, seven born on the estate, eight oxen, one bull, six cows, seven calves, two American horses, two colts, four mules, and eighteen sheep."

I stare at the line of trees and try to conjure up in my mind a working plantation. I wonder how often James DeWolf visited here. I wonder if he stood where we now stand. I don't feel him the way I did in Ghana. I don't feel much of anything. We soon turn and walk back into town.

Standing once again in front of the store where the woman makes cotton candy, we are surrounded by curious people. I don't understand it. They wouldn't come anywhere near us a couple hours ago. One man explains. "A bus like yours never comes here. Everyone thought you were the authorities. This is only the second time in anyone's memory that a group of people have come to our town like this."

Several miles away lies our next destination. Arca de Noé, Noah's Ark, is the plantation owned by George DeWolf, James's nephew. He was an absentee owner, like his Uncle James, until he fled Bristol in disgrace in 1825 and moved here. Our driver, Guillermo, stops and says this is as close as we can take the bus. The road from here is more of a wide path, so we begin to walk, past houses made entirely from palm trees. Raúl explains that these are typical cabin houses for Cuban farmers. The houses are not very strong, but they can be easily rebuilt after a hurricane—just walk into the nearby forest and gather the materials. The walls are constructed from the wood of the royal palm tree, and the roof is made with the leaves.

We pass an eclectic mix of trees, bushes, cacti, and flowers large and small in many shades of yellow, red, and orange. A large bunch of bright-green banana-like fruit hangs over our path.

After walking about a mile, we turn right onto a smaller dirt path that continues for a few hundred yards and ends at a small farm. Pigs squeal and chickens squawk, intruding on the quiet of the past half hour's peaceful walk. Even the cows join the cacophony of screeching from within a series of enclosed pens and stalls. I think they're nervous about the thunder roaring in the distance.

We stop under the canopy of a gigantic ceiba tree near the edge of a thicket. Revered by practitioners of Santeria, its massive roots, sometimes a foot or more thick, snake above the ground away from the trunk. Arca de Noé lies somewhere within a massive thicket another quarter mile or so beyond this majestic tree. We wait in the shade for everyone to arrive. The animals eventually settle down and Katrina asks for some stillness. She suggests that we let go of all the logistics and the noise. She stands for a long moment with her eyes closed, breathing deeply, then looks slowly around at each of us.

"We are close to the land that was owned by George DeWolf," she says. "There were probably two plantations bordering each other in this vicinity: Noah's Ark and Good Hope. Three of the De-Wolf plantations had the word 'hope' in them [just like the Rhode Island state flag, I think to myself]: Good Hope, New Hope, and Mount Hope. Hope for some, hopelessness for others. Before we go in, we'll listen to some readings from the diary of a man who worked on DeWolf plantations here in Cuba."

Katrina has brought diary excerpts by Joseph Goodwin, who was hired by George DeWolf in Connecticut to work on the plantations in Cuba, including Noah's Ark. [2]

> *February 13, 1821: [Goodwin describes La Habana as] a strong, filthy place, but the business that is done here is immense and shipping very numerous.*
>
> *April 9, 1821: Negroes look wild.*
>
> *April 14, 1821: The first Negro I struck was this evening for laughing at prayers.*
>
> *May 20, 1821: Two Negroes deserted.*
>
> *September 28, 1821: Found two bosals [a term for slaves from Africa as opposed to those born in Cuba] this morning suspended by a rope in the woods not too far distant from the house. They were the two best bosals on the plantation. I have not yet learned the cause of the unfortunate circumstance for the present. Suffice it to say they are no more. They had been hanging undoubtedly three days previous to the discovery.*
>
> *January 20, 1823: The two that deserted yesterday came back this day. They are the two largest, stoutest, fastest Negroes on the estate. Their punishment will be as follows: four days in the Sapo [stockade] heavy ironed. Four days in succession after Prayers. Twenty-four lashes on the naked bottom each, after which lanced and well rubbed down with rum and salt. Weather warm, wind strong at South East.*

April 24, 1825: For the last ten days I have not been pleased with my situation. George deWolfe, [Captain] Bradford and Muckler have very plainly shown a disposition to make trouble and difficulty on the estates with the Negroes. Notwithstanding, I have cautioned them repeatedly. I have given Mr. DeWolfe one Negro to do with him as he pleases, thinking it would be better to spoil one than more, with express orders not to say any thing to any other Negro on the estate; but to no effect. I shall go on patiently a few days longer.

As we finish reading, thunder begins to roll. Lightning flashes. We all look up at the sky, which has become darker in the past hour. Jude questions whether we should proceed. "Let's go in," I say. We've come this far and I don't intend to miss seeing this place up close. Boris leads the way. After crossing an open field, we walk along the outskirts not of a thicket, but of a dense forest. Then at some access point only Boris seems aware of, we follow him into a jungle so thick in places that he swings a machete to cut branches and widen the path so we can make our way, camera gear and all, to where he says he found the ruins of a building from the plantation. This reminds me of Kakum Rainforest Park in Ghana, only seen from ground level instead of from above. Hacking our way through to God knows where, I don't know how on earth Boris found the ruins of anything in here.

Forward progress is slow. Though it's hot and extremely humid, the foliage is now so thick that if it does rain, I'm certain we won't get wet. We continue farther and farther in. Just as I'm beginning to doubt Boris, we climb a final small mound, emerge into a clearing, and stand before what remains of George DeWolf's plantation.

I've come to the conclusion that George was the ultimate S.O.B. in the family, the epitome of the evil slave owner. We heard earlier how Goodwin described the trouble George caused with the slaves. It may be conjecture to conclude he raped enslaved females, but we've heard that story, and such was the widespread practice of the day. Katrina has one letter that appears to complain about a man taking such liberties here, but the name is scratched out.

There's no question he continued trading rum for African people after it became a federal offense. He's the only one in the family who we know for certain did. His own uncles, James and John, didn't trust him, didn't invest in his ventures, and considered him "slippery."[3] His portrait in *Mount Hope* looks like one that would hang on the wall in an old horror movie with the eyes cut out so the bad guy could spy on the room's inhabitants.

We now stand in his ruins. There's no knowing whether this was George's home or slave quarters, or what. Thick walls of rock have crumbled. Trees and bushes grow over and through the walls, adding to the sense of evil. Liz and Jeff begin to film, but no one wants to stay. Dain stands near the trunk of a tree whose branches have grown into and broken down the walls. What strikes me is how similar, in an eerie way, this is to James DeWolf's grave site: a mound, creepy roots that look like tentacles strangling what lies below, and a tree growing from within.

Mount Hope describes a landing dock thirty minutes' walk from here, on the Gulf of Batabanó. On a clear day, George could see the Isle of Pines in the distance from his dock.[4] Katrina says, "Obviously we can't imagine that right now because of how overgrown it has become, but the proximity to the gulf allowed George DeWolf to see the ships come in. This was during the illegal period, so having his own little inlet and cove where his ships could come in, rather than going into Havana, was part of what enabled him to carry on his business. Linden Place was built from his fortune made during one year of the illegal trade after 1808."

"Actually," Elly says, "George DeWolf sounds like a bastard. I'm glad he's dead."

"What made you say that?" Jude asks.

"Oh, I guess I didn't have as much information this morning

as I do this afternoon, but if he's messing around with his slave girls and he's doing illegal stuff when everybody else has decided to move on ..." Crashing thunder punctuates Elly's comment.

Dry branches, twigs, and stones crack and rattle under our feet as we walk about. "Let's have some time where people can just be here, and do whatever you need or want to do," says Katrina.

"Let's piss on the building," says Ledlie. "It can be a ritual."

"Spoken like a true Episcopal priest," says Jim.

"With these bugs and this heat, all I'm aware of wanting to do is get out of here. I'm sure the people who worked here felt the same way but they couldn't," says Holly.

"I'm ready anytime too," says Jim. He and Holly start out. I stand next to Elizabeth, not quite ready to leave.

Jude asks me how I'm feeling. I share with her my desire to be proud of my family, but with the slave traders, it's hard to view them as products of their time. They knew what they were doing. "Maybe that's obvious to some people, but we don't spend a lot of time talking about these sorts of things in history class. It's kind of glossed over; ignored. Slavery is brought up as a principal reason the Civil War was fought and the mighty North took care of that problem. On we go to the industrial revolution and flying at Kitty Hawk and then men on the moon. But being in these places ..."

I look around at the disintegrating walls in the darkness. Though hours of daylight remain, the foliage overhead blocks out much of the light. Elizabeth, who was listening, points out that Natalia said yesterday that it was part of the times. It's what people did.

"How do you react to that?" asks Jude.

"It's hard to say, because I didn't live then," she says. "But there's stuff going on today that we all accept as normal. In a hundred years people might look at us in the same exact way. Virtual slavery happens all over the place because of American corporations. I buy stuff made by people who aren't getting paid what they're worth. I've heard people who don't want to deal with this whole subject using 'context' as a way to not deal with it. I agree with Ron Bailey, the historian we met at the Old State House in Providence. He said it's always been a moral issue. You can't enslave another person without making a huge decision."

We've attracted a larger group. James asks, "What does that say about people, then, if so many societies had slavery?"

"People get greedy," says Elizabeth, "but not everybody."

"No," James says, "but many people in every society seem to be willing. It's not a few evil people. It's a lot of very ordinary people."

"They say the same thing about German soldiers in World War II," I say. "They annihilated people and then said they were just following orders. There are also many times when good people stand up and say no. We're dealing with the people who did not stand up and say no."

"I don't feel like there are good people and evil people," says Ledlie. "Everybody is capable of good and evil. To characterize a person as one or the other is to get into simplification. That doesn't work."

"What makes it hard for me to imagine," says Katrina, "is what they risked in order to do what they did. Sailing across the ocean, given the dangers involved, means the greed had to be so strong. To hear the moaning of people below deck, for as much as Africans were supposedly viewed as animals or subhuman, the sounds of their voices were human sounds. If your own wife or child were sick she would groan in the same way. So to hear those sounds and . . ."

Ledlie finishes her thought. "And submit them all to your desire for quick money and comfort. What a son of a bitch."

"And his grandson, Samuel Pomeroy Colt, was a son of a bitch," she adds.

"It's harder for a rich man to go through the eye of a needle than enter into the kingdom of heaven," I say. "Am I close on that one?" I look to Ledlie, who nods. "You get used to a certain level of comfort. We're here because we have the luxury of being able to be here.

It's hard to keep clear thoughts when you have certain luxuries and privileges in your life."

"When you have a lot, it's hard not to value it," says Ledlie, "and if you value it, then you become subordinate to it."

I remember what Natalia said, and I pick small pieces of decaying rock from the wall and place them in an empty film canister. Once I get home, I'll cook the stones in a microwave to relieve myself of any worries about parasites. This place makes my skin crawl. I swat mosquitoes and other bugs, even when they aren't there. This place makes me itch.

On the long walk out, we move more slowly than on the way in. Once we're out of the jungle, Elizabeth sits down in the grass and opens her book to sketch another ceiba tree that grows nearby. We talk in small groups as we walk.

"I feel better, getting out of that rat hole," Elly says.

"It is a rat hole," I say. "I don't know how much of it is because it's George, and how much is just because it's a rat hole."

"It's a rat hole and a mosquito den, a den of bloodsuckers."

Once we pass the giant ceiba and the farm, Ledlie, Elly, and I walk together on the road back to the bus. An elderly woman, about eighty years old, stands in front of one of the palm houses we passed hours ago on our way in. We strike up a conversation and Elly, who speaks passable Spanish, translates. The woman says she was born in the house we just left. She calls it La Luz, which means "the light."

The house fell to ruin twenty years ago, more or less. She knows it was once called Arca de Noé, but is not familiar with the name De-Wolf. I'm glad they changed the name of the place. It gives me some comfort to believe that not only evil things happened in that house, that someone besides slave traders owned it. I can see in the eyes of the woman before me that loving people lived there. Children were born there.

A boy riding a bicycle stops to offer us a pile of fresh fruit that I don't recognize. He shows us how to eat it, skin and all. It's delicious. Eventually, the others make their way back to the bus and we drive to our hotel.

———•———

It takes most of the following day to drive from La Habana to the Cuban city of Trinidad. I notice that Dain engages in long conversations with several of our female cousins. Today must be his day to "go there" with them about their issues.

There are fourteen provinces in Cuba. The city, and province, of La Habana is located in the west. Trinidad is in Sancti Spiritus province in the central region. We arrive at our hotel, Playa Ancon de Trinidad, late in the afternoon. Ledlie and I check into our room on the sixth floor. After dinner, I stand at my window staring at the Caribbean Sea as the daylight fades. It's taken well over a century for the DeWolf family to return to this beach in Cuba to consider the harm our ancestors inflicted on the world.

After breakfast the following morning, we board our bus and drive the eight miles to the town of Trinidad and "Valle de los Ingenios" (Valley of the Sugar Mills). Named a World Heritage Site by UNESCO in 1988 due to its exemplary architecture and historical importance in the sugar trade, Trinidad was once the third-largest city in Cuba. It no longer registers in the top twenty-five.

Tobacco long ago replaced sugar as the main crop. We're given time to explore this well-preserved colonial city. No modern architecture mars the sixteenth-century atmosphere. The cobblestone streets are narrow, the buildings colorful. Purple smacks up against green and peach blends into red. A patch of brick shows through where plaster has fallen off. I walk around a small dog sitting on the sidewalk near a horse tied to a post. A man in a blue shirt and white hat rides by on one horse and leads another by a rope. Another man smoking a cigar sits on a step holding a rope tied to a small burro.

Several of the cobblestone streets converge at an open square in the center of town, surrounded by a white metal fence. Within, stone pathways encircle and partition four small grassy areas. Several benches and large palm trees line the square.

Vendors fill a side street with tables covered by jewelry, blankets, clothing, hats, and all sorts of other handmade items. A woman in a white wedding dress with a wide hoop skirt and daisies in her hair stands on the sidewalk talking with three younger girls. Another woman holds out a sample of her crocheted shawls to me and smiles. I walk into shop after shop. In one, I watch a woman roll cigars.

Next we drive a short distance outside the city and up a hill to an overlook where we can view the expanse of Valle de los Ingenios. Here we meet Martha Castellanoz, a local expert who will spend the rest of the day with us. Standing at the overlook, we gaze out over miles and miles of lush, green valley below. Martha explains that seventy-three mills once dotted this valley. I try to imagine all the people it would take to work all these acres and acres of land to support so many mills. The fields are lined with trees and dirt roads; the entire valley lies encircled by distant mountains. Once again, the beauty is marred in my thoughts by what was done to people forced to work here against their will. Trinidad's wealth during the nineteenth century came from widespread sugar production that owed its success to the labor of black people.

We drive to a former sugar mill that is now home to a museum, open-air market, and restaurant. Outside behind the main building, we rest on benches surrounding a metal contraption about four feet square that is mounted on concrete blocks three feet tall. Martha explains how this manual sugar press squeezes liquid out of cane, which can then be made into molasses. A ten-foot-long pole sticks out of the center horizontally about five feet above the ground. Katrina and James begin to push it around, turning the large drums in the center while Ledlie feeds a stalk of cane between the drums. Sweet liquid sugar soon runs out a spout into a pitcher at the base.

Inscribed in metal letters is one more piece of innocent-looking evidence of the connection between the North and slavery. This machine was built in Buffalo, New York.

Martha points out the tall bell tower in front of the museum, which stands forty-three meters high. Many of us climb the 134 rickety steps to get to the top. I soon stand where mill and slave owners once stood to oversee their kingdom and servants.

Returning to our bus, we stop along the road at a sugar cane field. Keila tries to cut the cane with a machete, followed by Dain and Jim. From their less than successful efforts, it becomes clear this is not a simple task for the inexperienced. Jim finally shears one cane off and I chew a piece of the sweet plant.

As I step into one of the rows between the tall sugar stalks, the air is instantly sticky and stiflingly hot. It must be twenty degrees hotter than it is ten feet away on the road, and twice as humid. The leaves cut my skin. I'm not usually bothered by enclosed places, but this is seriously claustrophobic. It is impossible for me to imagine anyone working in these conditions. And to envision them slaving away from dawn to dusk, day in and day out, boggles my mind. This is the most unpleasant feeling I've had since being in the slave dungeons in Cape Coast.

We drive back into Trinidad for a "slave meal" that is being specially prepared for us. We're told it is representative of the food that slaves were fed to keep them strong for work. We sit down to a table filled with fruit, bowls of corn soup, and a variety of breads. The chef describes our upcoming five-course meal. Martha translates. Our late-afternoon supper won't be exactly what slaves ate because they don't have all the ingredients, but we're assured it will be similar.

First, drinks are served. Martha says, "This is called 'canchanchara.' It is made of spirits taken from the sugar cane, plus honey and lemon. They didn't use ice with it and they had it mainly in the mornings. They called it fire water."

Obviously, the ingredient from sugar cane is rum. The canchanchara is refreshing on another hot day. Next come malanga fritters, made from a starchy tuber, similar to a potato or yam, ground up with garlic, onion, and salt and fried by the spoonful. The fritters come with okra salad. Our chef explains that okra salad has been part of the Afro-Cuban diet since very early times. It remains a staple in the diet of peasants. The main course of fish, chicken, and rice is served next. This is a typical slave meal? It seems more like an extravagant tourist feast at a nice restaurant.

Juanita tells us she was brought to tears when the food was served. Regardless of whether this meal is representative of what enslaved Africans were served, they were fed in order to work. They cut sugar cane for the benefit of the DeWolfs and thousands of other white plantation owners. Part of the sugar was made into molasses and later distilled into rum. Part was refined and spooned into cups of tea by people who gave no thought to what brought that sugar to their dining table in Philadelphia or Baltimore. We sit in this pleasant space, enjoying light conversation, rum, and an abundant banquet, one of the best we've had on our entire journey. Juanita's presence reminds me to take each bite mindfully.

———••———

The next morning, after breakfast at the hotel, we load the bus and begin our long drive back to La Habana. Thunder cracks, lightning flashes, and rain pours from the sky. I sit next to Elly. She says, "Being here now makes this so real, but we won't be able to stop it from becoming the past and fading into a dot on our road map."

My fear is that Elly is right. Throughout my life, whenever I've had an experience that I thought would change me forever, it rarely has. The emotional charge of the moment eventually fades and I slip back into the habits of my everyday life.

We've been so well taken care of in Cuba that it has occasionally been difficult to focus on anything but the delicious food and drinks and the music. But when I do think about it, all the disparate pieces begin to fit together into a larger picture. American descendants of European immigrants wanted the best life for themselves and their families. They expected free labor from people they considered separate and worthless except for the work they produced. Plantations were far enough away to be out of sight, but still accessible. A manual sugar press from Buffalo, sugar in my coffee, cotton for my clothes. A nation of ordinary people giving no thought to where the sugar and cotton came from or how they were produced. "Complicity" and "amnesia" are the two words that come to my mind.

Our plane lifts off around four in the morning. As I watch the lights of José Martí airport fade, I have conflicting thoughts about Cuba. Most people here cannot legally leave the country or even own a car. My sense is that the only way to make socialism and its philosophy of relative equality survive is through dictatorship. It takes away any incentive for hard work because advancement isn't likely. Yet the peaceful joy we found in the Cuban people we met is something I don't often see back home. I've witnessed a sense of community, a national identity, and a happiness I didn't expect. It does appear that Cubans are ahead of us in the effort to overcome racism, and in spite of the obvious restrictions, there remains something I can't adequately explain: an odd sense of freedom that we lack in the United States.

CHAPTER 15

IN THE FISHBOWL

The weeks since we first gathered together feel like a lifetime. We began our journey in Bristol, just as our ancestors did two centuries ago, to retrace the route of the Triangle Trade. We have now completed that triangle by returning to Bristol. After driving from New York to Rhode Island, Ledlie and I slept comfortably last night once again in Nancy's home.

I walk to the Burnside building across the street from St. Michael's on Hope Street, where we'll participate in another interracial dialogue. This conversation is described as a "fishbowl," where people sitting in a center circle of chairs do all the talking while those in the outer ring listen. We then reverse roles, and then finally we all participate in one large conversation together. As we settle in, we are encouraged to be open and honest and to listen *actively*. In other words, don't just listen in order to prepare a response. The Family of Ten begins in the outside "listening" circle.

Kimberly James looks to be in her early thirties. She lives in Boston and was invited by a crew member. She participated in the Interfaith Pilgrimage of the Middle Passage, in which a group of people from different faiths and races spent a year, beginning in

May 1998, retracing the history of slavery in the United States, the Caribbean, South America, and West Africa. From Kim's description, *Traces* and the Interfaith Pilgrimage were similar projects. Filmmakers traveled with them as well, but, to her disappointment, have so far been unable to raise the funds to complete production.

Myrna Cook, who was with us for the first dialogue six weeks ago, says it doesn't make any difference which group finishes its film first. She's just glad it's being done. Myrna worked in the music, television, and film industries in Hollywood for twenty-five years. She says there are black people who could finance the Interfaith Pilgrimage film if they chose to.

Kim doesn't dismiss the value of *Traces;* she just finds it odd that this family could find funding when black filmmakers could not. "Again here in America we have whites outdoing us and it's being applauded and funded."

I want to interrupt. I want to say, "Wait a second. This project isn't completely funded; far from it. There have been some grants for filming, but debt is financing a lot of the effort this summer." But the fishbowl rules of "active listening" require me to remain silent at this point. And besides, even if *Traces* is struggling to find funds, it may not be struggling as much, and there is access to loans. The playing field still isn't level.

So I say nothing. I listen. The United States has such a long history of keeping black and white people apart that I know I still have much to learn. I suspect most white people believe that with the passage of civil rights laws, everyone is on equal footing now.

Harold Fields is a friend of Holly's and Keila's from Denver, where he works to combat racism. Harold succinctly expresses how unequal our footing remains. He likens the impact of America's ignorance of history with trying to cure skin cancer with Clearasil. "It will take a force equal to the four hundred years that got us into this situation to get out of it. You can't turn the spigot off and see the effects of this just evaporate. This country was founded on stolen labor and the stolen land of a lot of people."

"From a historical perspective, what land hasn't been stolen?" questions Keith Stokes, who was also with us six weeks ago. Keith says one of the facts of history is that we're all equally responsible for the slave trade. Africans actively participated with white traders. The solution is not to evoke guilt, but to understand historical facts and try to move forward despite these atrocities. I find Keith's words somewhat comforting in that he doesn't lay the entire blame at the feet of white people. But Keith's opinion doesn't appear to be shared by other black folks in the room.

After we switch circles, Elizabeth says one of the issues at the crux of racism is whites not having relationships with people of color. Katrina has been questioned about our group being made up strictly of white family members. She believes that racism is a "white problem," so the focus of our energy should be with ourselves, untangling our issues. I wonder. I've tended to agree with Katrina, but now I wonder if it isn't equally important to work with blacks. Is the real problem that we don't have many relationships with black people, so working with whites is easier?

"What prevents you from forming friendships with people of color?" asks Wayne Winborne, who joined us six weeks ago and today serves as one of our facilitators.

"I live in a county of 115,000 people," I say. "In the 2000 census there are 222 who identify themselves as black." And though I don't say it, I was surprised that there could be over two hundred black people in my county. I would have guessed a couple dozen. I don't have much opportunity to establish relationships because there are so few black people in Central Oregon. I don't want to do some token act just so I can say I have a black friend. I'm trying to be conscious about this.

Holly also struggles with the issue of establishing relationships with people of color. She wants to have black friends but doesn't want people to think she's being nice just because they're black.

Ledlie was able to get past his own reticence about approaching black people while we were in Ghana. We took on the responsibility of approaching people on the street, telling them what we were doing, and inviting them to take part in a dialogue with us. He approached three young men in Cape Coast. One of them closed his eyes and pulled back. When Ledlie explained that we're concerned with what has been inherited by both blacks and whites, this fellow's response was "I know what your inheritance is. You're masters."

Ledlie asked him to join our discussion, but he said, "When I see white men, I see wickedness." He said he was filled with bitterness and wouldn't join us. Ledlie says he was thankful for the exchange. The vast majority of encounters we had with Ghanaian people were pleasant. Ledlie believes most Ghanaians expressed themselves to us in sort of a postcolonial reflex kindness. This man didn't. He spoke honestly about how he felt.

We move our chairs into one large circle and Wayne zeroes in on the issue of anger. With our increased focus on race throughout this journey, what do we fear more, the potential angry reactions of white people or black people? Elizabeth says white anger is much scarier. Holly agrees. Harold points out that black people live with white anger all the time. It has been expressed violently. It has been expressed through congressional legislation. "White people control the police and the armies. You might be afraid if we controlled them and sometimes we fantasize about that." He smiles.

Harold says that as we develop relationships, it is important to be aware that in this country, to be accepted, black people are expected to act "more white." They are expected to give up their blackness, their culture, and who they are. He hopes our experiences in Cuba and in Ghana help us understand what it's like to not be in control, what it's like to be a minority. Most white Americans don't have any clue what that feels like and how it takes its toll over time.

He then suggests that white people need to be careful about having black friends if they're only willing to do things or go places where the white person is comfortable. "Are you real? Well, come on over and let's hang out in the hood sometime." His words remind me of my exchange with Josephine Watts in Ghana.

Kimberly's parents tried to instill pride in her about being African American, but when she walks down the aisles of any store, she still sees most products using white people as models in their advertising. It's difficult when everything you see, almost every image, is not you, and what is perceived as beautiful is not you. She encourages us to try having a simple conversation. She's had people begin conversations wanting to know how she got her hair done in her small, tight braids. People have actually asked if she washes it. "You wouldn't go up to any other person and say that to them."

She acknowledges that a white person might ask about her hair just to start up a conversation, but she doesn't want to have to explain her hair. Maybe she wouldn't mind it after a relationship has been established, but questions about her hair are questions about her blackness. "I can't speak for all black people. But people ask if I only listen to hip-hop music. Just try to know me as a person. I am a black person, but try to see me as a person first."

I say to Kimberly, "The most common phrase I can remember, in talking with white people about this project, is 'Why can't they just get over it?' It was two hundred years ago. The Civil War's been over for a hundred and thirty-five years. Why can't everybody just get over it? It's only through this process that I'm beginning to get the inkling that my definition of what 'it' is, is different than your definition of what 'it' is."

"It's not over for me," she says. Our eyes are locked on each other. "I wasn't a slave, but new things are happening in the present day—what I have to live with every day—so it's not over for me."

I've never experienced life from Kimberly's side of the racial divide, but as I learn more about the disparity between blacks and whites I continue to be amazed at all that I and, I believe, most other white people haven't seen.

Holly is frustrated with herself over all the times she's remained quiet instead of speaking up about injustice. In a diversity training video she watched, a black woman said we'll get somewhere when white people get as animated, outraged, and angry as black people. I'm sensitive to what Holly is expressing. I've listened to racist jokes without saying anything. I don't tell them myself anymore —not about any race. I don't laugh at them. But I don't always say anything either. When I have told people I'm offended by their humor, they've been surprised and apologetic. Maybe it had an impact. Mostly I felt the impact on me. Each time I've said something, I've felt a little bit more prepared for the next time.

I lean forward and rest my head in my hands, elbows on my knees. Wayne says, "Remember, the choice to do nothing is an expression of power. People of color, for the most part, don't have the choice to not think about race. You don't know what to do yet, right?" He looks at me. "But understand that if you take two years off from this and do nothing, you have perpetuated."

Harold is struck by how difficult change is. The privilege that whites have inherited is frightening to explore because if what we take for granted in one part of our life isn't right, what else about our lives isn't right? What about our religious, political, or other beliefs? Harold doesn't even believe the core problem is racism. Racism is a symptom of a much deeper infrastructure. Harold's father was a plumber. He buried pipes under houses. They were the unseen, but critical infrastructure for the distribution of water and waste. In society, we have infrastructure in place to distribute wealth, influence, education, and other resources. The patterns of distribution define, support, and perpetuate our system. "The old pipes are rusty and they are corroding," he says. "It is hard to repair or replace them, but this is our work. Past the illusion of race, we are part of the same human family that must eventually be reconciled."

We're asking white people to explore our very foundation, to question aspects of our birthright that have been rendered invisible to us. Though I realize we'll never be completely aligned, I wonder how we can ever hope to confront something as gargantuan as racism when ten white people can't even get on the same page about how to move forward.

———•••———

Later, the Family of Ten meets alone with Tammy Bormann, a white woman who, along with Wayne, helps facilitate our conversation. She asks us to try a process called "dialogic learning," in which intellectual knowledge does not trump instinct or gut level response. The power dynamic that exists in traditional learning is set aside. In order for dialogic learning to take place, equality is the key. Participants must respect the value of everyone's input.

"We're used to debate and argument in this culture," says Wayne. "The goal is to win, to get my point of view over on yours. We embrace many skills and techniques to do that. I trot out my credentials to you when I introduce myself. I couch what I say in facts. Dialogic learning asks us to hear things in a mode we are not used to hearing."

Dialogic learning respects the wisdom a child offers. Learning can occur across age groups, cultures, races, and genders. Wayne says men often don't listen to women. We don't listen to young women a lot. Dialogic learning provides a way to get somewhere we're not used to being: on equal footing. It doesn't mean that Ledlie and I will ultimately agree about religion, but it means we'll listen to, and respect, each other. With Ledlie, at least, I'm pretty far down this road already. But then, we're two old white guys and on equal footing in terms of race and gender to begin with.

The focus of our journey was intended to be about black and white issues, and yet a lot has come up between men and women, between feelings and intellect. Perhaps the question that matters is whether I can accept other people who are quite different from me, believe differently than I do, and who I've been raised without understanding or even interacting with. What's challenging is that I've always assumed my way is the right way. Dialogic learning asks me to relinquish my pride and certainty so that I can have the opportunity to grow.

I explain to Tammy that, for example, I don't understand women. We're raised differently. I look at Dain and Jim and pretend to plead with them, saying "We've got to stick together"—a lighthearted attempt to make the point that in the midst of conflict between the sexes, men should understand and support one another. The group laughs. "And even *we* can't. I mean, these guys like the Boston Red Sox. I can't go there."

I glance around the room, enjoying the payoff of another small laugh for my joke, when Tammy—who isn't laughing—stresses that dialogic learning is about trying to "go there." Not making an effort is a way of removing yourself from any possibility of growth or challenge or movement.

"But sometimes you don't want to trust somebody who might be destructive," notes Elly.

Tammy agrees that there are times when one's instinct is not to trust but insists that when there's an opportunity for learning, one must try and embrace it.

"I've had a hard time that some people in this group have not wanted to go where I'm willing to go," says Holly. "It's pissed me off."

"That's about expectations," says Elly. "You're coming at this at different points. Your destinations are going to be different. So we can't force other people to go to the same place we do."

Wayne adds two more insights. First, shunning such interactions is an expression of power; men can decide that they don't want to deal with gender issues, but women don't have that luxury. Second, to "not go there" is an active decision.

Elizabeth says there may be things that white people, or men in particular, don't notice because they've been in positions of power. She thinks perhaps Dain has felt attacked by her over this very issue and wants to know when he stopped trusting.

"After some of the discussion groups we had," he responds. "I felt like there was no effort to hear what I was saying and I was getting an automatic backlash coming at me. I've felt betrayed."

"I see you as a very dear and thoughtful person," Elizabeth says, "but I think there are ways where you might think you're being thoughtful and considerate but you're still missing a lot."

"And maybe I'm right," Dain says. "I think that's fine for us to disagree as long as we can be loving and respectful of each other."

There remain a million unanswered questions and unresolved issues. Where I've ended up is someplace I had no idea I was going. I never expected to get into gender issues. Perhaps because we ended up being a group of five men and five women, that became one of the predominant issues in many ways. They're all interrelated: race, class, and gender issues. I'm old, I'm white, and I'm male. I carry all the baggage we're talking about. Yet I look at what I've learned about women in this group and I want to scream, "You think I'm powerful? You have the power to shut me down, the power to force lessons upon me that I'd rather not learn, the power that, with the turn of a phrase, I will shut off for fear of rejection."

It may be a different kind of power, but it's power nonetheless. It controls me in ways that I don't like to admit. Everything is about acceptance versus rejection, about believing I'm right all the time. It defines how I deal with women. How do we accept people who are different from us, who walk a different path than we do, and accept them as equals, their beliefs as valid?

I'm frustrated. It appears others are as well. Elly thinks we've healed some of our rifts. I don't. Dain thinks we missed the opportunity to deal with the real issues we intended to deal with. Elizabeth doesn't think we missed a thing. It feels like "dialogic learning" and "active listening" pretty much went one way. We all liked the idea of others listening to us as equals. I'm not sure how much effort any of us spent really listening to each other.

When we conclude, Dain approaches. He says, "We haven't talked in a long time."

"You sort of checked out."

"I had to. It was the only way."

I don't know all of what happened between Dain and some of the others, and I don't ask. Their experience symbolizes one of the challenges we all face in nurturing and enhancing relationships in the face of difficult issues. How do we "go there" with each other in ways that honor and respect our differences?

Dain and I agree to catch up soon. Then we embrace.

When the Family of Ten gathers for a final meal together a heated discussion begins, but it isn't about racism. It's about flowers. A member of our crew has created a centerpiece of fruit and flowers. Dain says the table setting looks very upper class and doesn't represent a meal that we would ever have together. The dishes and wine glasses are also too fancy. James and Jim agree. They don't believe the formal-looking table represents us.

Jim is concerned that Katrina won't present us as we really are, that she may caricature us as something we're not. "I think back to when you were interviewing me. I've forgotten why the conversation went that way, but I said, 'After college, I . . . ,' and you stopped me and asked me specifically to say Harvard. My going to Harvard wasn't about privilege. I earned my way to Harvard."

"You don't think going to Harvard is a privilege?" I ask.

"I think going to Harvard is a privilege," he says, "but I'd have gone to Harvard if I had grown up in a very different family."

"I never could have imagined going to Harvard," I say.

"You would have or you wouldn't have?" Katrina asks Jim. I'm not sure if she didn't hear his last statement over the sounds of dinner being consumed, or if she's seeking clarification.

"I would have, because I taught myself to read before I was four years old. I worked my butt off at every level at school."

"But you can't assume if you were in a different family, that you would have been in an environment that would have nurtured that," says Katrina.

"I would have. I had plenty of classmates at Harvard who were from different families. It was schools where it was nurtured," he says. I can't believe what I'm hearing. If Jim had been born in my family, Harvard never would have been on his radar screen.

"Like my father, I went to Harvard," says James. He points out the advantage of being raised in a family that understands that an Ivy League education is at least a possibility. "I want to say this very clearly, because it seems to me that's all about white privilege and the privilege of being in a particular white background and not another white background."

"Your dad also went to Harvard?" I ask Jim.

He and James both nod and say, "Yes."

"Okay," I say, "my dad worked for the phone company and he went to night school to get his college degree. For me it was the University of Oregon, um, go Ducks." With all the Harvard talk, my humble alumni plug just slips out. Dain laughs and quacks.

I face Jim and raise both hands in a gesture of sincerity. I pause to think of the right words. "When I sit back, I don't think you're lying. I don't. But when I think, okay, your dad went to Harvard, that's an up."

"Didn't most of our parents go to Ivy League schools?" Holly asks. She points across the table to Katrina. "Where did your dad go?"

"I'm either third or fourth generation Princeton."

Holly then points to each person, in order, around the table to identify the alma mater of each of our fathers. Starting with Katrina, I hear "Princeton, Princeton, Brown, Harvard, Harvard, Harvard, Brown ..."

"Yeah, we're representative of white America," I say sarcastically.

"Wait," says Holly, pointing to me, "night school." Then she points to Elly.

Elly says, "Harvard."

Holly reaches over and pats my back. "Everybody but you, honey."

"I'm going to go eat in the kitchen," I say, still joking.

I think more seriously about this later. When you are born into a family of privilege you inherit that privilege. A family with an Ivy League background typically passes on to their children Ivy League expectations and advantages. With reasonable effort, your parents and teachers will encourage and help you. Opportunities present themselves more readily. Sitting with my cousins, I feel miles distant from their Ivy League world of privilege. And if I focus on our differences, it's easy to convince myself how removed I am from them. But when I'm honest with myself I see more of what we enjoy in common. It becomes difficult to deny the many privileges that all white people share.

CHAPTER 16

MY HARVARD EDUCATION

Several years passed and *Traces of the Trade* remained unfinished. Katrina continued to struggle to raise completion funds. I continued to work on my book about our journey when I could fit it in, but life got busy. As Elly predicted, the summer of 2001 faded into a dot on my life's road map.

Then events in the summer and fall of 2005 brought the issues of power and privilege roaring back into my life in ways I never could have imagined. I found myself embroiled in a scandal that ultimately led me to resign from my elected position.

Working as a commissioner in Deschutes County at that time required my full-time attention. Three elected commissioners served as the administrative and policy-making board responsible for overseeing the operation of county government. In addition to serving as the public's elected advocates, the commissioners watched over an organization with 850 employees and a $200 million budget. We created and enforced county ordinances, hired and supervised department directors, and tried to resolve conflicts that arose between citizens and county departments, of which there were more than twenty.

My position afforded me the opportunity to make a difference in my community and in the lives of my constituents. For the most part, I found my work satisfying and rewarding. But long hours, meeting after meeting after meeting, too-frequent frustration with some of my colleagues, and an acute lack of privacy and time for other interests took its toll. I began to question my commitment to, and interest in, my job.

Then an amazing opportunity presented itself. After all the conversation—and joking—around the dinner table with the Family of Ten about Ivy League schools and privilege, in the spring of 2005 I was accepted into the Senior Executives in State and Local Government program at the John F. Kennedy School of Government at Harvard. I spent three weeks in Cambridge, Massachusetts, that June, focusing on results-driven government and the ethical and professional responsibilities of leadership. I interacted with a diverse and energetic group of classmates and faculty. We studied choices made by government officials in response to everything from weather emergencies and infectious disease outbreaks to corruption and interaction with religious organizations. We studied the media, history, finance, ethics, and how to achieve better results through our professional activities.

On Wednesday of our second week, Dr. Ron David stood before us, a pediatrician as passionate about health and healing in communities as in individuals. Dr. David pointed to words he'd written on the chalkboard. *Relationships are primary. All else is derivative.*

This statement is the common thread in all the subjects he teaches, and the philosophy by which he lives his life. He says that nothing matters more to us as humans than to be in relationship for the sake of being in relationship. "We tell each other our stories and disclose our innermost selves in order to fall in love with one another. The burden of disease, despair, and early death is not the lack of access to health care. It's the breakdown of relationships. If we examine the underlying damage to relationships and repair them, we will become healthier people and communities."

I felt like I won the lottery. Ron David's words captured the essence of what every great teacher throughout history has tried to tell us about right living. He explained that the challenge for him is that being African American so overwhelms everything else that he doesn't explore his own areas of privilege, such as being male and heterosexual. He can use his presumed victim status to hold me responsible for his pain. By blaming me, he participates in, and perpetuates, the system of privilege.

"As long as I keep you locked into a conversation about racism," he said, "I can avoid dealing with my own stuff like sexism and homophobia."

I raised my hand to tell him this was the first time I'd ever heard a black man state so clearly that he shares responsibility with me in the whole racism and privilege discussion.

"When I see what you and I have in common instead of what keeps us apart, then we can move forward in a new way," he said. "Think of hydrogen and oxygen. There is nothing about either of them separately that would lead you to believe they belong together. But when they are united they become something that neither can experience alone: water. We don't have to have privilege forever. We can transcend it through integration. Together we create something that doesn't exist. When I'd rather protect my miserable 'known' than risk joining you in the possibility of an unknown that will really be better, that is fear."

He said that if he focuses on him being black and me being white, he focuses on that which separates us. "When I use the fact that we are both men and use our commonality to help us understand each other better, things will improve. We must get beyond 'my experience defines all experience.' I am not the norm. Black folks need to take ownership of their part in this. We all have our parts to play."

I have the greatest difficulty when dealing with dogmatic people, especially those who claim they've received spiritual guidance for their political beliefs. Dr. David encouraged us to stay in the conversation with such people. Be committed to repairing broken relationships. People hunger for that conversation. We're all struggling to figure it out. He said, "It's worth the risk of being told you're going to burn in hell."

He agreed to meet with me after class one day to discuss *Traces of the Trade*. After I explained our project, he observed that *Traces* is similar to what we'd been discussing in class. We're creating an invitation to a deeper conversation. This is not a spectator sport. It involves mutual participation, which is the key to deeper relationships.

I came back from Harvard reinvigorated. The entire experience, particularly the relationships with faculty and classmates, sent me back across the country excited about my future as a county commissioner.

After a week at home, I flew to Honolulu for the annual conference of the National Association of Counties. While there, my climb up the leadership ladder reached its pinnacle when the new president of NACo appointed me chair of the Justice and Public Safety Steering Committee.

———

Soon after returning from Hawaii, I was asked to meet with two men who were checking into allegations of gender discrimination in the county juvenile department. During my absence at Harvard, my two fellow commissioners agreed to look into complaints that had been filed by a few employees. On Monday night, July 25, 2005, I met with the two investigators.

While they were examining the complaints, someone informed them about an incident that had occurred almost two years earlier involving me and a female employee of the juvenile department, a friend of mine whom I'll call "Heather" (not her real name; for reasons of discretion, and to respect the privacy of others, these events are described in general terms only).

Heather and I were friends. We socialized, and our families socialized, outside work. At a restaurant with a large group of colleagues one evening, at a statewide counties conference in 2003, what began as socializing and joking over drinks crossed the line to inappropriate sexual contact on my part.

We spoke by telephone the following day. She told me how upset she was with me over my behavior. I apologized. She accepted and we remained friends. I figured everything was resolved. But the investigators told me that my actions caused more harm to Heather than I knew. The county placed the director of the juvenile department, another close friend of ours, on administrative leave for not reporting the incident almost two years earlier. Both the director and Heather were instructed not to discuss anything about this with anyone, including me.

The problem with secrets is that even when you think you're in control, you're not. I was an elected official. I knew confidentiality would crumble and this would become big news in our community. The first difficult conversation I had after I left the investigators was with Lindi. I felt terrible. I apologized for the disrespect I'd shown her by my actions. I knew I'd hurt her. She told me she wasn't surprised by this; I'd always been outgoing and flirtatious, and sometimes completely inappropriate, especially after a few too many cocktails.

But Lindi stuck firmly by me. I thanked her so often over the next few weeks that she got sick of hearing it. "That's what marriage is," she said. "Being here for each other in tough times is the payback for all the years we've spent together."

I began seeing a psychologist. Talking with a professional with whom I had no previous relationship helped. I called each of our children and spoke to them of things I never imagined we would discuss. Once they got over the shock, each of them expressed their love, concern, and support. Admitting my own failings to my children brought us closer in ways I hadn't anticipated. It's as though I fell off the almighty "Daddy" perch and became a fallible human in a way they'd never experienced before. I dreaded calling my parents. They have always been so proud of me, so supportive, even when they've disagreed with choices I've made. My mom had expected to be a minister's mother. Now she would become a disgraced politician's mother. They didn't judge me, they simply loved me. I couldn't ask for anything more.

In consultation with my attorney, Lindi, and a few trusted friends, I broke the news publicly. I released a statement two weeks after meeting with the investigators in which I acknowledged my inappropriate behavior, promised not to allow it to happen again, and apologized to my constituents. I chose my words carefully in order to be as discreet as possible and to protect Heather's anonymity and privacy.

The resulting public spotlight embarrassed and shamed me like nothing I've ever experienced. The image I'd worked so hard to build could not protect me from the grenades I felt exploding around and inside me. I asked myself, "When life is already so hard, why do I make it harder?" Why had I pushed the self-destruct button? Imagining the pain that Heather and the director of the juvenile department must have been going through with their husbands and families created far more guilt than I'd ever felt before.

Naively, I hoped the storm would pass. But it only got worse. The district attorney in Lane County, where the incident occurred, launched an investigation into my actions for potential prosecution. Prosecution? I had been stupid, insensitive, and several other inexcusable things that night, but a criminal? I went from standing on top of the world to having my life spin hopelessly out of control.

Between bouts of feeling sorry for myself, I unloaded my frustration on my psychologist. It all felt so unfair. It was resolved two years ago. It felt like everything I read or heard seemed nuanced to make me look as horrible as possible. Whatever harm I'd caused two years earlier, the county investigation, coupled with the legal one, felt far more damaging. More people were dragged in and hurt by it.

I received additional counseling from Eileen Lock, a dear friend and counselor to our family for many years. She listened patiently for a while to my explanations and justifications. Then she began shaking her head. "You need to take one hundred percent responsibility for your actions, Tom. Nothing else matters. I understand that you don't want to face yourself and your stuff, but you need to get clear about you."

"I just want it all to stop. I want to have that stupid night back."

But I couldn't make it stop. I controlled nothing. The following weeks became a confused blur of media pressure and lawyers, as I waited to learn if I would be prosecuted. Friends and strangers offered commiseration and encouragement. Some confided how they had caused harm to others. I lost count of how many people said, "I'm glad I'm not in politics," or "If people only knew what went on at my office parties," and "I'm glad no one knows about the skeletons in my closet."

In mid-October, my attorney called to let me know the district attorney would not prosecute. My relief lasted all of two seconds as he then told me someone from the DA's office had held a press conference to announce his decision, describing how I had touched Heather without her consent and revealing that a similar incident had occurred with a different woman twelve years earlier.

The front-page headline read, "DA says DeWolf groped two women; no charges."[1] The article laid out several explicit details about what the investigators concluded. In a second front-page article, a representative from the DA's office said the statute of limitations ran out long ago on the earlier alleged incident. In the 2003 case he said, "The victim urged me in the strongest terms possible that she does not support criminal prosecution of Mr. DeWolf." He went on to acknowledge that she and I maintained a "close social relationship" after the incident. Finally, he said, "This is not the type of case we would prosecute in Lane County. It might not even have been referred to our office if he wasn't a county official."[2]

This felt worse than if charges had been filed. For instance, why would he bring up something from twelve years ago? It felt like nothing I could say about that situation would matter. Friends would support me. Foes wouldn't. I chose to say nothing. Hadn't my reputation been harmed enough? Why go into lurid details? Hadn't the community, not to mention my wife, family, and friends, heard enough already? These thoughts screamed in my head repeatedly. I felt reduced to the salacious things that were said about me in the media rather than the full—though flawed—human that I am.

I submitted my resignation a few days later.

I didn't "get it" until my world exploded in 2005. As much as I considered myself a loving, caring, committed husband, father, grandfather, and contributing member of my community and my profession, I was also occasionally thoughtless and oblivious to the needs of anyone other than me. In other words, sometimes I was part of the problem. As hard as I've fought injustice in my life, I've also contributed to it.

There was no escaping the fact that some people believed I'd committed a crime. At the very least, I was an elected official and had caused harm to an employee. It didn't matter that I considered her a friend and colleague. I lost sight of the fact that she worked for me. I lost sight of the fact that I was a man in a position of power, so we did not have an equal relationship at work.

Other than being on the front page, and being investigated for possible prosecution, the ordeal I faced was fundamentally similar to other times I'd harmed people and been harmed by others. I began to see parallels between myself and others I know who have stolen or lied, or abused another person physically or psychologically, or caused harm in myriad other ways through thoughtless words or actions.

I recognized the irony that *Traces of the Trade* tells the story of powerful and privileged people who rationalized their actions and felt immune from the consequences of their choices.

As I attempted to dig beneath the surface of my own psyche, past simply admitting my responsibility for my actions intellectually, I began to understand things I was either blind to or chose to ignore. This experience, more than any other in my life, helped me more fully understand the suffering of others that results from my blindness to my own privilege. Throughout my adult life I hadn't paid close enough attention. Through the public exposure of my own failings and the subsequent investigation by the district attorney, I was forced to learn what it is like to have no control over what others do to you or say about you. I feared the criminal justice system for the first time in my life. I also learned that living a lie and not getting caught is not the same thing as living the truth.

Long after the headlines disappeared, the embarrassment remained like a millstone I dragged with me wherever I went. The coziness of my life slipped quickly and quietly out the door the night I met with the investigators. It began to feel as though I wouldn't be able to escape my reputation any more than I could my gender or the color of my skin.

Brooding eventually gave way to contemplation. We inherit society's unconscious infrastructure and we perpetuate it. With gender issues, I've been conditioned to believe that young, thin, scantily clad women are the ideal. I believed women enjoyed flirting and pushing the limits of propriety, so long as no one got hurt.

My ordeal became a mirror in which I saw myself more clearly. Sitting in the pitch-black dungeon of Cape Coast Castle, I had imagined what it was like to be an African person. I imagined their suffering, which started me down the path of compassion and connectedness, but I didn't go far enough. The dungeon gave me a glimpse of the pain of others; it didn't show me to myself.

I spent our entire journey through Rhode Island, Ghana, and Cuba distancing myself from people like James and George DeWolf, thinking "I am nothing like those guys." But through my subsequent experiences, when I pondered the fundamental issues of power, privilege, and selfishness, I realized I wasn't quite as different from them as I imagined.

I made choices that harmed people I care deeply about. My privilege and position of power allowed me to get away with it for a while. When I apologized to Heather that next day in 2003, it was over for me. I barely gave it another thought. I should have remembered what Kimberly James said back in Bristol: "It's not over for me."

In Ghana, Eli Jacobs-Fantauzzi said I'd never be able to walk in his shoes. Trying to experience fully what a black person—or any other person—experiences is impossible. However, severe damage to my important relationships opened my eyes to the legacy I inherited and perpetuate as a man.

Eileen once observed that people have parallel experiences, and that's how we connect with what we need to learn. This ordeal was my parallel experience, and through it I learned invaluable lessons.

Eileen's insight was correct. The legacy of slavery was too big, too removed, too distant to fully get my mind around. It was when I experienced utter fear of losing the things I held dear—friends, reputation, freedom—that I began to understand the depth of my inherited legacy in a new way. In my world systemic sexism is the closest parallel to systemic racism. My ordeal helped me understand both more clearly.

CHAPTER 17

Repairing the Breach

I sit in a darkened auditorium with hundreds of others; watching, listening. Credits roll, the screen goes blank, and the lights come up. I've just witnessed, for the first time, a public screening of a rough cut of *Traces of the Trade: A Story from the Deep North*. Katrina, Ledlie, Dain, and I have flown to Columbus, Ohio, to attend the 2006 triennial General Convention of the Episcopal Church of the United States. Also with us is Constance Perry, the African American woman Dain met at church in 1999 and married two months ago. We were invited to show the film at the convention. We're also here to support the Church's unfolding efforts to address the legacy of slavery.

Zena Link, an African American student at the Episcopal Divinity School in Cambridge, has been working with Katrina for the past year. She invites members of the audience to share their own stories in response to what they've just witnessed.

Jay Phillippi, a white man from New York, says, "As the lights came up, there were tears in my eyes. I found myself thinking, how can I not weep? How can I not weep for the people who were torn from Africa? How can I not weep for what was done to the spirit and the souls of the DeWolfs and all the other slavers? How can I not weep for the burden that remains on our country because of what was done? We need to mourn what we did to ourselves; what we did to others. Maybe that's where we need to start, with the tears."

Bettye Jo Harris, an African American woman from Hawaii, says what struck her was hearing that her foremothers were sold for six handkerchiefs. She pauses, clearly disgusted by the image. "June nineteenth is tomorrow. That is our Independence Day. I remember when I wasn't too much older than Katrina in her pretty red-and-white dress. I was jumping around on the Fourth of July and my dad said to me quietly, 'That is not your Independence Day.' A lot of people don't recognize the significance of 'Juneteenth.' The slaves, as we were called in those days, did not know that they had been freed until June Nineteenth [the last of the enslaved to be told they were free were in Texas—they were freed June 19, 1865, two and a half years after the Emancipation Proclamation took effect]. They had us all workin' and diggin' around and gettin' those crops out before they let us go."

Marilyn Smith, a white woman, was born in Bristol, Rhode Island. She watched the Fourth of July parade and grew up in St. Michael's Church. "I know the names DeWolf, Howe, and Perry very well. Wallis Howe was our senior warden for sixty years." To Marilyn, the church didn't look quite the way it did in the movie because the altar rail used to be badly tarnished. Taking matters into her own hands when she was a young girl, Marilyn went to St. Michael's for several days after school with brass polish and rags. She spent an hour every day after school cleaning the brass rail. She didn't know she needed permission to do such things. She cleaned the section of rail where Wallis Howe and his wife, Mary, always knelt for communion.

"All hell broke loose because somebody had removed the sweat of his wife's palms from the railing." A man was commissioned to remove and polish the entire rail before the next Sunday. "I know something about the power of the Howes and the DeWolfs and the Perrys..."

Jean Gordon, an African American woman from Florida, speaks about visiting the slave camps in Africa. "At Goree Island, what was most stunning was coming up those stairs and seeing the church. For months after that it was the hardest thing for me to reconcile going to a church that somehow sanctioned this whole thing. One of the things that helped was that the curator there began by apologizing. He started talking about what Africans had done to Africans. 'It isn't just between you and the white people,' he said, 'it's between you and us and everybody else.' Everybody had a part."

Listening to stories from one person after another makes clear just how personal the wounds from slavery and separation are. Later that evening it becomes even more personal. A glass of wine with my cousins sounds like a peaceful way to finish a long day. Just as we settle into our chairs, Constance says to Ledlie, Dain, and me, "You're here talking all about apology for slavery, but you aren't doing it yourselves. Not one of you has apologized to me."

I look from Constance to Ledlie and Dain. The men remain silent. I have no idea what to say. Constance says she's felt completely invisible to us the whole week we've been here. We've attended committee meeting after committee meeting, trying to be supportive as the church considers resolutions that address its historic role in slavery and racism. Now I sit here with a glass of wine in my hand as Constance says, "I'm proud to be part of this family now but I'm not just your cousin, I'm your *black* cousin!"

When Constance and Dain married in April, most of the Family of Ten attended, including Ledlie and me. For people who live three thousand miles from each other, we've spent a lot of time together. Much of that time is spent dealing, in some form, with issues of racism.

After another moment of awkward silence, I say, "You think I don't know that?" I tell her that three different people approached Zena after the film screening tonight and apologized to her for slavery. Zena didn't like it. She didn't want it. "So what are we supposed to do?" I ask Constance. The conversation stops cold. We sit in complete, heavy silence. Dain soon suggests that he and Constance need to get some sleep. They drive away a short time later.

During our journey five years ago, Katrina, Ledlie, and others talked about how important an apology is before healing can begin. I wasn't convinced. I feel profound sorrow—sadness for the damage caused by the slave trade, the institution of slavery, and the prejudice, racism, and oppression that followed and continue to this day. I'm sorry the slave trade happened, but I continue to be uncertain whether I personally owe African Americans an apology for historic slavery.

Several states and private corporations have made official statements of regret regarding their historic connection to slavery or the slave trade. Some argue about whether or not the various statements are actually apologies. And while such actions tend to make headlines, truly addressing the legacy of slavery is far more complicated. It is one thing to agree that slavery in the 1800s was wrong; it's far more difficult to talk about one's complicity in the effects that remain.

Corporations and other institutions are different from individuals when it comes to dealing with past actions. For instance, the Episcopal Church as an entity has a life that continues beyond the individual lives of its members, and many say the institution itself bears a responsibility historically, and remains accountable, for its actions throughout its existence. Once I'm dead, my ability to make amends ends. The life span of an institution, be it a church, a corporation, a university, or a country, can be never-ending. Its ability to address harm inflicted in its past continues as long as it exists.

At the time of the Revolutionary War, half of all ministers in Connecticut owned slaves.[1] Census records exist for 103 of the 112

Episcopal clergy in Virginia in 1860; 84 of the 103 owned at least one enslaved African.[2] I believe it is appropriate that churches, as institutions, come to terms with their history. Witnessing Episcopalians struggle and take steps to do so in Columbus is a powerful experience.

Attempts made at the last General Convention in 2003 failed. This year, the dedicated efforts of many people produce different results. With the passage of three related resolutions, the church acknowledges and apologizes for its participation in the institution of slavery. They will research the details of the church's complicity in slavery and its aftermath, including the economic benefits derived, and study what actions they can take to "repair the breach" (Isaiah 58:12)—reparations the Church can make to address the legacies of slavery that exist today. There will be a Day of Repentance that will include services across the country, including one at the National Cathedral in Washington, D.C.

I am moved when they adopt the principles of restorative justice as the framework for justice and healing. This was the philosophy adopted by the Deschutes County Juvenile Department shortly before I became a commissioner. Traditional criminal justice asks three questions: What law has been broken? Who broke it? What do they deserve? Restorative justice asks additional questions: Who has been harmed? Why are they hurting? How do we repair the harm? Restorative justice promotes responsibility, repair, and healing for all who are harmed. It focuses on the restoration of victims, offenders, and entire communities to a state of wellness.

Restorative justice isn't simply an alternative to criminal justice. It can, and should be, one of the fundamental principles that guide our lives in all we do. It will help the members of the Episcopal Church through the journey they are now embarking upon. It will help us overcome racism. It's about living a healthier life together with other people, including those I don't understand or those I fear.[3] The Episcopal Church will design a study and dialogue process for congregations with the goal of becoming a church without racism.

Finally, in a move similar to the failed resolution from 2003, they call upon Congress and the American people to support federal legislation initiating study and dialogue about the history and legacy of slavery in the United States, and proposals for reparations to the descendants of the victims of slavery.

I'm surprised that an issue as divisive as reparations for slavery resulted in minimal debate. Only two people testify strongly against the resolutions. Carolyn Jones, an African American woman, is a priest in the diocese of Northern Indiana. She says the resolutions encourage helplessness, victimization, and whining. "Reparations grow from the world of entitlement, but entitlement creates second-class citizens and second-class members of the Episcopal Church. There may be wounds and there may be breaches in the Episcopal Church today, but they are created by twenty-first-century Episcopalians who cannot accept blacks like me for who we are: in my case, a Republican, an Evangelical, a political and fiscal moderate."

I'm surprised to hear this from an African American woman. She's adamant about not wanting to appease some misplaced sense of white guilt. "I do not want your money. I don't want your apology for days gone by. I want your respect. Your respect for me and for all blacks will ensure that the past will not be repeated and I and other blacks will not be treated as second-class citizens or second-class members of the Episcopal Church." The other person who speaks in vigorous opposition to the resolutions is her husband, Bennett Jones, a white man who is also a priest.

Carolyn Jones makes insightful points. If what emerges is some kind of handout to appease white guilt and results in white people buying their way out of racism, the effort won't work. If we can't enter into relationships of mutual respect to do the work of racial reconciliation, then it'll turn into something else, not reconciliation.

Though they don't pass until the last hours of the final day of the convention, the resolutions are approved almost unanimously. The 2006 General Convention has been dominated by controversy surrounding same-sex unions, ordaining gay bishops, and electing the first woman as presiding bishop. Because of the focus on these issues, addressing the church's history with regard to slavery became less of a priority and came close to being put aside for another three years.

Traces of the Trade helped make the issue more accessible during the convention. There's a long history of black Episcopalians, as well as whites, working on issues of racial justice in the church, but many people told us the film helped delegates to participate in the discussion in a way they hadn't before. Perhaps seeing people grapple with these painful issues on a movie screen made it less daunting.[4]

Some may find it ironic—given my longtime anger at the church, which now extends to its complicity with slavery—that I would be in Columbus for the convention. But the New England branch of the family has a long history with the Episcopal Church, so it makes sense to work with them. Moreover, I'm surrounded at the convention by sincere, caring people and I realize that my anger is counterproductive. Conversations about race, privilege, and power can become so contentious that it's important to identify the types of institutions that can create a forum for this kind of discussion. That's what faith communities should be good at.

A few days after the difficult conversation with Constance, I ask Zena why she didn't appreciate the apologies for slavery that were offered to her after the film screening. She says it felt like people got caught up in the moment. Feelings came up and the most important thing to do was to release them. In other words, they haven't worked through anything before moving to apologize. Zena is some-one they'll probably never see again. Why apologize to her and not to their son's schoolteacher, the person who takes care of their chil-dren, or the person at the bank they go to every week?

I tell her about the conversation with Constance and my confu-sion regarding individual apologies for slavery. Zena believes I'm still in the study mode, still processing all this new information about white privilege and the legacy of slavery that I've inherited. She says, "So you did the movie. I mean, please. You know, if you came up to me and started saying, 'Zena, I'm sorry for my role in slavery,' I'd be like, 'Damn. You know, we were getting along so well. Where did this come from?' " She laughs, and then her smile disap-pears. "This didn't happen overnight. We're all broken in our hu-manness. We can't see a film or do a month of antiracism training and change our lives."

I continue to struggle with the concept of apologizing as an in-dividual for the offense of slavery. I didn't commit the act of trad-ing rum for African people. My direct ancestors didn't commit the act. I'm descended from the uncle, the carpenter from Connecticut, remember? I wasn't even alive. I was a child when Jim Crow was eradicated. Yet Constance sincerely desires an apology. Zena wants white people to do the hard work needed to understand just how significant an apology for slavery must be before she would con-sider it sincere. I can see one scenario playing out where I commit to spending the rest of my life listening to individual stories and offering individual apologies to African American people. I ques-tion how productive that would be. Apologies can be perceived as insincere. Real apologies involve concerted self-reflection that leads to understanding and to changes in belief and behavior. Too often apologies are offered for the opposite reason: they may be an attempt to assuage guilt, but avoid the important element of self-evaluation.

In his book *On Apology*, Aaron Lazare points out that if citizens of the United States are going to take pride in accomplishments they took no part in, like victory over the British in the Revolutionary War, the words of the Founding Fathers, or landing men on the moon, then we must also accept the shame—but not the guilt—when our nation doesn't live up to reasonable standards. Lazare cites another powerful reason the United States should apologize for slave trading, even though it wasn't carried out by people living today. We've profited from the land that was taken from indigenous Americans and the slave labor that catapulted the United States into a world power. Though I'm not guilty of slave trading, Lazare suggests I have a moral responsibility to those who continue to suffer as a result of the offense.[5]

Constance and Dain met Lazare when he spoke at their church. After I'd read his book, Constance and I spoke further about apology for slavery. When Constance struggles with something, or has prayed for clarity, the answers often come in the early morning. She says she feels God's presence most at that time of day. She literally sat up in bed one morning with clarity about apologies for slavery.

If someone is sick or a family member or friend has died, you may go to a wake or a funeral. You say, "I'm sorry for your loss." The day after the Rodney King verdict was announced, Constance was standing in line waiting for her morning coffee. Two white women she didn't know were in line. One of them tapped her on the shoulder and said, "I know you don't know me but I'm sorry for what happened." Constance appreciated the gesture. I don't believe Zena would have felt the same way.

Constance's desire is to have white Americans acknowledge the damage and pain caused by slavery. I appreciate her analogy to expressing sorrow at a funeral. Yet the difference between feeling sorry for the death of a loved one and being sorry for slavery is so overwhelmingly mind-boggling. Slavery is millions and millions of people over centuries of time. It's so intimidating for white people because it's like comparing picking up a glass of water to finding yourself in the middle of the ocean and not being able to swim.

It sounds like Constance is making it too simple.

"Tom, it is that simple. It's as simple as Will Hairston's apology at Coming to the Table."

Constance, Dain, Holly, Harold Fields, and I had joined two dozen other people at the Coming to the Table retreat at Eastern Mennonite University in Harrisonburg, Virginia, in January 2006. Descendants of former slaves, slave owners, and slave traders were invited to explore together their unique role in addressing the legacy of slavery.

During that weekend, Will Hairston, a white man, stood in the center of our circle of couches and chairs. He faced descendants of people his ancestors once owned, people Will has known for a decade. I watched the faces of Joe Henry, Ever Lee, Lillie, and Jim as Will said, "I am not sure if you want or need an apology, but I know I need to give one. I am not sure if this will be a blessing to you but I know I need to do this. I apologize and ask your forgiveness for my ancestors' involvement in slavery that deprived your ancestors of their liberty."

He apologized for the emotional, spiritual, economic, and physical pain that has come to them and their family through his family's involvement in slavery, exploitation, and selfish greed. He asked forgiveness for the lingering, damnable racism that has been a curse to all of them through his family's involvement with slavery, and for the barrier it put between them. Will said he couldn't erase the huge injustices from the past, but he offered to do whatever he could to help both sides of their family continue to grow and recover.

Sobs were heard from many of us who sat as witnesses. Will's voice cracked as he concluded through his own tears. "I thank you for letting me come into your life close enough to give this apology. Thank you for coming to the table with me."

Joe Henry Hairston, age eighty-three, then said, "For the part of me that is part of your ancestry, I join in your apology. For the part of me that is not part of your ancestry, I accept your apology."

I was stunned by Joe's words. I sat in awe of that family, black and white, as they embraced each other in front of me. Ever Lee hugged Will and said, "I love you." She later told a reporter from Virginia Foundation for the Humanities Radio, "I was thinking, I've already forgiven him. It isn't necessary. But it's not about me. It's about him. And now the healing process can take place."[6]

I respect Constance's position, but Will Hairston's apology was not comparable to sympathizing with someone's loss at a funeral. If only it were that simple. But simple or not, Constance clearly articulated the key issue for entities like the United States or the Episcopal Church, as well as for individuals like me. Before reconciliation can occur between black and white people, and before the United States can ever truly be considered a nation of liberty and equality, white people must acknowledge the truth of the past and its impact on the present.

CHAPTER 18

SANKOFA

During our final weekend together in 2001 the Family of Ten, joined by dozens of additional extended family members, met with Edward Ball, author of *Slaves in the Family*. He shared what other people have said to him. "My family came to America after the Civil War ... My family suffered ... My family came to Ellis Island. We were Irish potato farmers ... We were Italian peasants under the heels of the padrone ... We were Russian Jews escaping. And my family suffered ... They came here poor. They struggled and they fought for what they have now ... They had nothing to do with slavery. Don't talk to me about that."

Ball acknowledged that the struggles of white families from working-class and peasant backgrounds in Europe are real. Their suffering is genuine and it should be commemorated and respected. "But the minute those people set foot on Ellis Island they entered a society that had two tiers and they set foot on the upper tier. They had access to education that was denied black people who were native-born Americans. They had access to housing, however shabby, that black people could not rent. They had jobs that black people were not allowed to take. These things lifted them into the middle class rapidly. They benefited from the legacy of slavery."

Edward spoke of how anger was a powerful motive for him as he researched and wrote his book. It was during a Ball family reunion that his anger was ignited. They spent thousands of dollars drinking. And in an auditorium where the elder patriarchs of the family came successively to the podium to tell jokes, someone hung a poster-sized photograph of the last "mammy" at one of the plantations.

"And this family is, like all large, extended families, actually a pool of love. That's the bitter, cruel paradox of it. To be in the family is to wade in the pool of love."

What a perfect parallel to the DeWolf family, the Fultons, the Perrys, and so many families. Every time Keila or Holly spoke of their frustration with their family, they finished by saying how much they love them. Most every family swims, to some degree, in a pool of love. I suspect they also do their best to ignore the monsters lurking beneath the surface.

Ball spoke of visiting Cape Coast in Ghana, or southern plantations. "If you are able to see differently, you can get a feeling that one's own family, one's own reality, is built on a pile of corpses. It seems almost as though our own comfort is in inverse relationship to the things that produced it. It's almost like a doppelganger. The sense of place, entitlements, and ease in society that I feel is in direct inverted relationship to the blood and violence that created it. That's an awful contradiction to try to inhabit."

I've never understood the concept of inheriting "the sins of the fathers" so clearly as I do now. Oppressors are damaged by what they perpetrate against others, but it's not just the oppressors and their victims who suffer. Like a stone dropped into a pond, the consequences of oppression ripple out in all directions, impacting everything and everyone.

When I sit with my Family of Ten, or our extended families, we feel, to various degrees, some guilt, some shame, some responsibility, and some accountability for something that happened two hundred years ago. Most of us are proud of the families we grew up in. We think of ourselves as upright, caring, and responsible. It's frightening to consider that our family isn't what we've been taught all our lives.

Once we—all of us in the United States—acknowledge that our ancestors weren't simply a group of sterling characters, we confront the potential for a change in perception about our families and ourselves. This requires more than considering the past. The willingness to explore these questions in the present sets the stage for future perceptions.

I believe men have the biggest challenge in this conversation. We are more invested in our reputations and fear what is at stake. It seems to me that women don't typically need to cling to the patriarchal order. My experience over the past seven years has been that connecting with distant relatives and reconnecting with not-so-distant relatives has been rewarding and invigorating. Confronting uncomfortable secrets has been liberating.

Identifying the different aspects of the legacy of slavery, for our family, and for white people in general, has also been liberating. We've inherited separation, ignorance, and silence. My cousin James calls it a willful silence. We fear losing our privilege, money, and respect, even when those things are unearned or phony. This legacy began with people who have been dead a long time, but it has been perpetuated by our parents, our peers, and by us.

We also had the opportunity to meet with Peggy McIntosh that last weekend in Bristol—the woman who wrote "White Privilege: Unpacking the Invisible Knapsack," the article that had such a powerful impact on me early in our journey. Peggy expanded our thinking by pointing out the unearned privilege certain people have in relation to American Indians, Asian Americans, Hispanics, and others, including the advantages Christians in our society have over Jews. "The most important days are holidays," she said. "For me, that means Christmas, not Hanukkah. And there is no such thing as 'WASP-ing' down the price.

"Males have certain issues they are taught from birth, such as 'win/lose' and 'top/bottom' and 'kill or be killed.' This is taught as the natural order of things. In order to overcome all these burdens, the aim must not be to win, but to mend the fabric. Because if the aim is to win, what doesn't work? Love, sex, family, friendship, and education don't work, to name a few. We need to work for the decent survival of all. Therein lies my own best chance for survival."

McIntosh realized that she can't be blamed for, or feel guilty about or ashamed of, any of this. Having the power of unearned privilege gives her, and all of us who possess it, the ability to decide how to use this power. Peggy got more power from realizing that due to her placement in the system, she's been given more ability to work on changing things than most people have. Her view about how to spend unearned advantage came to this: "I've got a choice about whether to use any unearned power to try to achieve any of those worlds I'd like to live in."

I think of my own life and accomplishments. I've owned my own businesses. I've been elected to local public office. I live in a nice neighborhood in a safe city. Most of what I've accomplished has been done with the help of the connections I have with people in positions of power. What have I earned completely on my own without using the advantages I have had? I earned two college degrees, but how many people never have the privilege of going to college? Everything I've done in my life was built upon an earlier accomplishment. As I sit here, I can't think of anything that didn't come to me as a result of someone else's kindness, a connection, a privilege, a shortcut, or an advantage of some kind. One of the many ironies of my privilege is that I can't get rid of it. Even in fighting racism, my privilege gets me heard. On the flip side, if you're a white person reading these words, your privilege allows, and even encourages, you to ignore them.

The thought of confronting my own privilege, due to having white skin and being male, once frightened me on so many levels. I've spent my life learning to shield myself from being hurt. I've had expert instruction and powerful experiences in self-protection. What I now understand is that I learned to fortify the walls that separate me from people and situations that scare me. I'm afraid the result is that I've succeeded in protecting myself from fully living. The greatest gift I received from this journey is a set of tools with which I can begin to break down those walls.

A bird looks backward while flying forward. It holds an egg in its mouth. The symbol of the Sankofa bird in the Akan tradition teaches that we must go back to our beginning and learn what the past has to teach us in order to achieve our full potential as we move forward. The past will show us how and why we are who we've become. The egg is the future. That which has been lost or stolen can be reclaimed.

I return once more to where our journey began, where I first met my Family of Ten. David Dobbins, the interim rector at St. Michael's in Bristol, has invited Katrina to preach the sermon on Martin Luther King's birthday, January 15, 2006, the day before the holiday. Deborah Howe and I drive in together from Boston.

Today's scripture is from Luke, chapter 6. "But I say to you that listen, love your enemies, do good to those who hate you, bless those who curse you, pray for those who abuse you. If anyone strikes you on the cheek, offer the other also."

When it is time, Katrina walks confidently up the aisle to the pulpit, turns, and faces the congregation. She speaks about our journey, about northern complicity in slavery, how it drove our nation's economy, and how we as white people benefited. She speaks about this beautiful town and its not-so-beautiful history. What has it meant for the Family of Ten to face this history? What will it mean for St. Michael's, for Linden Place, and Bristol to do the same?

"Black Americans try to get white Americans to deal with the legacy of slavery, and as whites we don't like the implication that we're responsible for slavery, or that we're racist, so we resist. Blacks get angrier when they see the defensiveness. We get offended by the anger and everyone is quickly confirmed in their views of each other, and we go round and round in this vicious circle that tends to draw everyone who comes to America into it. For those of us who don't resist the history, and who try to take in all the suffering, we can fall into another trap, which is guilt, feeling terrible about ourselves and our people.

"But I'm here on Martin Luther King's birthday, and he had something to teach. He zeroed right in on the words of Jesus that we heard in the Gospel of Luke this morning. Jesus was saying love the Roman soldier. Love the slave master. King was saying love the white segregationist. Love those who do not love you."

So what's the message for us white folks? Surely no one here thinks of African Americans as their enemy. But many of us undoubtedly resist anger expressed by black people and demands for reparations. Katrina exhorts us to acknowledge the disparity that remains and to show up for the conversation. There is unfinished business that needs tending to.

"As we bring attention to the question of what will create wholeness for people of African descent, we can also ask what will create wholeness for us, as people of European descent. What needs to be healed in us? What are the scars and legacies that we hold? They're different, but they're there."

She describes the healing ceremony at the river in Ghana and how Dain asked the man to perform the ritual for us. The healer suggested we enlist our own elders to play that role. He told us to go home, to look no farther than our own backyard. Do the healing here, with each other.

"So I've come full circle, back to my community, back to the church that my family has attended for generations. I don't know exactly what the ritual or the healing process would look like. But I do know that it should be grounded in the spirit of love for all. I do know that we'll figure it out once we face the history together.

"So let's bring all the stories out into the open. Let's tell all the stories that went into the making of America, without anxiety or dread, but with the trust and hope and faith that are born of love. Amen."

She walks from the pulpit and pauses to bow her head toward the altar, the rector, and deacon, and the stained-glass image I had wondered about the first time I was here, which, as it turns out, depicts St. Michael slaying the devil. She then turns, walks back down the aisle, and sits with Deb and me.

What happens next brings a look of surprise to Katrina's face. David invites anyone in need of healing to come forward. Katrina whispers, "This wasn't planned." She stands and walks up the aisle, as do others. Soon, many members of our Family of Ten stand in line. More and more people walk to the front of the church to kneel at the altar. Most of the congregation leaves their seats to make their way forward. David and the deacon, Janice Grinnell, perform the healing ritual. They lay their hands on the head of each supplicant who kneels before them and they whisper something, a prayer I assume.

I sit with Deb and I watch. As more and more people go forward, she leans over and says, "Are you going?"

"No way," I say. "I don't do things like this."

"You should. It'll be good for you."

"Forget it."

She stares at me with a look that speaks more powerfully than her words. It appears we're the only two people in the whole church who haven't gone forward. I take a deep breath. I look to the front of the church and back at Deb. I sigh and take her hand and we soon stand at the end of the line in the aisle. When we arrive at the front of the sanctuary, a space opens up as two more people finish receiving their blessing. Deb and I step forward and kneel on the cushion before us. I close my eyes, clasp my hands together on the nicely polished brass rail, and begin to breathe long, slow breaths.

The choir softly sings. David places his hands on Deb's head. He prays for her. Within moments, Janice places her hands on my head. Gently and instantly, I am transported. I imagine standing once again at the Donkor Nsuo River in Ghana, where African women, men, and children were cleaned and oiled before being taken to the dungeons in the slave forts. I hear water flow by. I fill my lungs with clear African air. Peace envelops me as branches of leaves are brushed along my body over and over again. Janice speaks clearly and confidently and gently. I barely hear a word she says. I feel more than I can hear. I feel reconciliation and healing and forgiveness and hope. I am a white man kneeling by the river receiving a blessing from my white elder.

The words don't matter. The touch matters. The connection with another human matters. Humbling myself matters. Janice finishes saying whatever she just said, because I hear the word "Amen."

I rise, turn, and look at the faces of people seated before me. I walk back up the aisle, past stained-glass windows and marble plaques dedicated to God in memory of long-dead ancestors. I pass part of my Family of Ten on my right and part on my left. I return to our pew and sit once again between Deb and Katrina.

Holy Eucharist soon follows. Deb says, "Well?" I stare at her without answering. I haven't taken Communion in decades. I envision the church in the open square at Cape Coast Castle, directly above the dungeons. As quickly as my anger appears, it disappears. It isn't Jesus's fault that his followers screwed so many things up. Deb simply smiles. I take another deep breath, and nod.

We walk to the front and I kneel in church for the second time today. David places a wafer in my hand. It soon dissolves in my mouth. Katrina then stands above me and says something about the blood of Christ. I reach up and grasp the bottom of the chalice and guide it to my lips. Katrina's and my eyes meet. I take a sip of wine. She smiles and then moves on. I stand and return to my pew and sit down with Deb.

"This is the most religion I've had in almost thirty years," I say.

"You can find spirituality in religion sometimes." She smiles and winks at me.

For someone who left the church so long ago, I'm sure spending a lot of time in them. I remember that during my three-week program at Harvard, Dr. Ron David revealed that he was preparing for ordination as an Episcopal priest. I can't seem to escape Episcopalians. But the more time I spent with him, the more I understood. He found churches to be places that can help people find ways to move beyond the hurt. Though the church is filled with fault, it is a place where people profess to believe in spiritual things. Within a spiritual community, we can hold each other accountable; we can witness, and can restore and create relationships. Dr. David hasn't given up on science in spite of the evil it has done. He won't give up on the church just because of the evil it has done.

I've come to realize the obvious: churches reflect the people who worship inside. They, me, my ancestors, all of us: we're flawed, damaged people. We seek fulfilling relationships, understanding, and grace. Choices made in the past created our present condition. Choices made in this moment create our future and the legacy we'll pass on to our grandchildren's grandchildren.

It seems so long ago that I stood in front of St. Michael's for the first time, meeting my distant cousins who now feel more like sisters and brothers to me. I imagine standing in Helen's backyard with them once again, our arms around each other. Only now our Family of Ten has grown. We're joined by all the people who have passed through each of our lives, from European, African, and other backgrounds, male and female, from generations past through today. For me, it includes my wife, my parents, my sister, my children and grandchildren, extended family and friends as well as people I haven't gotten along with so well, from Palomares Junior High School to Northwest Christian College, from Bend, Oregon, to Bristol, Rhode Island, and from Ghana to Cuba and back again.

Katrina, standing in our midst, smiles, takes a deep breath, and sighs. Then softly, and gently, she says, "Here we are."

Afterword

Compassion is not a relationship between the healer and the wounded. It's a relationship between equals. Only when we know our own darkness well can we be present with the darkness of others. Compassion becomes real when we recognize our shared humanity.

—Pema Chödrön, *The Places That Scare You*

After our journey retracing the Triangle Trade, and all our probing and research on the legacy of slavery, the Family of Ten continued to grapple with what we could do collectively to address the need for repairing the damage that was caused by the institution of slavery. Each family member focuses on different efforts in our lives and communities, but we agree on one overall direction: we support a national dialogue and education process to lead the people of the United States toward racial reconciliation and the healing of our collective wounds.

I believe the most important activity we can involve ourselves in is furthering and deepening relationships. If Constance had confronted me about apologizing for slavery the day we first met, it would have terrified me. I would've thrown up a barrier. But the fact that she and I have established, and committed to maintain, a relationship that has been growing and maturing, allows me to hear her words clearly because I know and trust her. Because of the seriousness of our conversations, and the activities we've been involved in together, she's one of the people that I think about all the time. We've developed respect for, and commitment to, each other.

Zena feels differently about these issues than Constance does. She doesn't want strangers tapping her on the shoulder to apologize. The only way I can know the difference between these two women is by staying in the conversation with them both. I'm occasionally overwhelmed by Constance's passion. She never lets me forget that she's my black cousin. She's also helped me to understand that I have a luxury she lacks: I can choose not to deal with racism. Most of the time, I want to hear. But it's complicated. Everyone wants to be heard.

Women want to be heard.

Men want to be heard.

Gay people want to be heard.

American Indians want to be heard.

African Americans want to be heard.

I want to be heard.

How do we have these conversations? How do we resolve this stuff?

Inspired by Aaron Lazare's book *On Apology*, I believe there is a logically progressive path—involving four steps—to achieving racial reconciliation. The first step is awareness, which involves active listening, education, sincere self-reflection, and recognition of the inflicted harm. I've watched with interest the outrage expressed in reaction to the racist epithets spewed by certain celebrities in 2006 and 2007. When will we as a nation become as outraged at the gross injustice of poverty, disease, violence, and other byproducts of our damaged society that disproportionately impact people of color? Awareness emerges when we overcome our incapacity, or unwillingness, to see and understand the harm, and recognize our shared responsibility, and our kinship, with one another.

Second, those who caused the harm must apologize. In regard to the legacy of slavery, entities such as churches, businesses, and governments that have existed—or are related, if you will, to entities that existed—since slavery was legal in the United States, and participated in or profited from it, owe an apology. The U.S. government, for instance, cannot claim, "I wasn't there. I didn't commit the act." Unlike its individual citizens, the United States came into existence on July 4, 1776, and continues to this day. Individual white people all benefit to varying degrees from the privileges we enjoy as a result of the legacy of slavery, and, at the least, we owe acknowledgment of the harm that has been, and continues to be, inflicted.

Third, all members of society share an obligation to attempt to repair the damage inflicted due to the legacy of slavery. Failing to address the harm perpetuates it. Wayne Winborne said it best when he told me, "Remember, the choice to do nothing is an expression of power. If you take two years off from this and do nothing, you have perpetuated." This step requires that all parties to a grievance commit to working together to determine what constitutes appropriate repair, and then make it happen.

The final step is for the harmed party to offer forgiveness. We debated this point in Jim's hotel room in Ghana without reaching agreement. But I have now come to believe that without all four of these steps, including forgiveness, reconciliation is not possible.

This process may feel difficult, humiliating, unfair, or even frightening. You never know the outcome in advance. On a personal basis, I've sometimes decided it wasn't worth it to apologize for harm I've caused. Better to leave the damage as it exists in that current or former relationship than to risk making things even worse.

Occasions arise in which the harmed party has no interest in reconciliation. I don't suggest creating additional harm just to ease one's conscience. I believe that in certain situations, doing nothing may be the healthiest option. In facing systemic racism in the United States, however, doing nothing is not a healthy option. Doing nothing increases the damage to all of us, and this wound will never heal until we treat it.

Many have been inspired by South Africa's Truth and Reconciliation Commission (TRC), which was established after the end of apartheid. Public hearings were held in many venues throughout South Africa at which the commission received testimony, from both victims and perpetrators, regarding crimes which violated human rights. Critics objected to the major principle that was included in the TRC process: that amnesty was granted to those who committed abuses, so long as they met the TRC standard. Many victims felt robbed of justice. Though I don't advocate the same model for confronting the legacy of slavery in the United States—in part because most of the individual victims and abusers are long dead —I have been deeply moved by South Africa's commitment to confronting past abuses through national dialogue with a goal of achieving reconciliation.

One powerful opportunity to begin a national dialogue in the United States is with legislation like Representative John Conyers's H.R.40, the "Commission to Study Reparation Proposals for African Americans Act," a bill he has introduced in every Congress since 1989—and which, up through the time I write these words, in June 2007, has never had a hearing. Several Family of Ten members specifically support—and some plan to get involved in—its passage.

As proposed, H.R.40 acknowledges the fundamental injustice and inhumanity of slavery. It would establish a commission to study slavery and subsequent racial and economic discrimination from the end of the Civil War to the present, as well as the impact of those forces on today's living African Americans. The commission would then make recommendations to Congress on appropriate remedies to redress the harm inflicted on living African Americans. Conyers chose the number of the bill to recognize the "forty acres and a mule" that came to symbolize the broken promise of Reconstruction and the abandonment of freed slaves by the U.S. government.[1]

Virginia, once the nation's largest slaveholding state, became the first in the union to apologize for its role in slavery. Four of the first five American presidents were from Virginia; all were slave owners. Virginia's general assembly unanimously passed a resolution in February 2007 expressing "profound regret" for "the involuntary servitude of Africans and the exploitation of Native Americans." Maryland soon became the second state to express its "profound regret" for once trafficking in human flesh, followed by North Carolina and Alabama. As I write these words, other states, including Georgia, Delaware, Texas, Missouri, Massachusetts, Vermont, and New York, are considering similar moves.

Though the Virginia, Maryland, North Carolina, and Alabama resolutions did not propose reparations for their involvement in slavery, this is the logical next step. As a citizen of the United States, I've considered what we face in trying to repair the damage from hundreds of years of atrocities committed against African Americans by our government's participation in, and sanctioning of, the slave trade, slavery, and the legal discrimination of Jim Crow—our own apartheid.

Many complicated questions arise. Who exactly is being apologized to? And who, really, is apologizing? What is appropriate reparation? What if someone is half African American and half European American? What about American Indians and other people of color who have been oppressed in, or by, the United States? We can dance around the various points of contention for the rest of our lives and hand the problem of racism to our grandchildren's children to face. Or we can commit to begin dealing seriously with this.

Much like the U.S. government, the Episcopal Church—and other churches in this country—helped shape, and was shaped by, slavery. What I appreciate about the resolutions passed by the Episcopal Church is, first, that they begin with a commitment to truth telling. Second, the resolutions commit to using the principles of restorative justice as the Church proceeds to study its own role in slavery, and subsequent discrimination and racism, and apologize for it. Third, the Church commits to work to repair the damage. These three steps allow for the possibility of the fourth: forgiveness and genuine reconciliation.

I aspire to the ideals I encounter in our nation's founding documents and pray that someday my nation will finally live up to them. I no longer ignore the fact that although the Constitution was crafted for many noble reasons, it also consciously and willfully protected slavery and white male privilege. Choices made to create our union were made at the expense of black people and others. We must find ways to implement our Founding Fathers' ideals while acknowledging their failings.

Many people believe that such acknowledgement, and exhibiting humility and apologizing, shows weakness. Quite the contrary, when we finally recognize that we're all damaged people, awareness, apology, repair, forgiveness, and the healthy dose of grace that naturally follows require true strength.

Regardless of whether an official apology and reparations are offered by our federal government, individual relationship building across racial lines is imperative. This is the high hope I hold out for the work to which the Episcopal Church, and many other churches and organizations, have committed. In these modern times of political triangulation and governance in response to opinion polls, citizens must lead. Once we do, those in government will follow.

Over the past seven years my views have evolved significantly regarding reparations for slavery. It used to be that when I heard the word "reparations," my brain would freeze. I'd walk away, unable to see that reparations for slavery are about determining how to repair the damage that was caused and continues to impact the lives of people of color, as well as white people, today. I no longer see reparations as an unfair burden or a potential threat to my livelihood or the future prospects of my children. I don't support reparations for slavery and government-sanctioned racial inequality from any sense of guilt. My support comes from my belief in our shared humanity. Appropriate reparations for slavery and Jim Crow meet the highest ideal of democracy: equality and dignity for all.

I embrace Roy L. Brooks's model of repair, outlined in his book *Atonement and Forgiveness: A New Model for Black Reparations.* The debate on reparations for slavery is often about the money, and sometimes about getting even. Brooks shifts the focus to a much broader, "forward-looking" discussion directed toward racial reconciliation. It begins with the United States, through its representative government, atoning for our past and repairing the significant and lingering damage this nation caused and continues to perpetuate. Brooks rejects the concept of lawsuits for reparations in favor of an "atonement model" that focuses on our government willingly entering into a process of apology, reparations, forgiveness, and racial reconciliation. Compared to the enormous material and psychological impact of slavery and the Jim Crow era in this country, meaningful reparations will be a reasonable burden for our nation to bear.[2] While the civil rights movement finally secured the rights to basic legal equality for African Americans that should have come at the end of the Civil War, it did not create a level playing field because of the structural disadvantages still firmly in place.

Harvard law professor Charles Ogletree co-chairs the Reparations Coordinating Committee (RCC), a group of lawyers, academics, and public officials advocating reparations for slavery. In contradistinction to Brooks's proposal, the RCC considers lawsuits a legitimate option in the pursuit of reparations. When Ogletree speaks about the dramatic lack of progress made in terms of black wealth, he references a study by an economist that found that in 1865 when slavery ended, the gross black wealth in the United States was less than 1 percent. By the end of the twentieth century, the gross black wealth in this country still hovered around 1 percent. "That's a staggering figure," he says. "If you think about all that has happened, all that has been accomplished, that tells you something. It's not the inability, or the lack of interest in progress, it's the barriers. It's the impediments, both private and public impediments."

Ogletree's position is that proceeds from reparations should be put into a trust fund to be distributed by a commission focused on the needs of what he calls "the bottom-stuck, those African Americans who are descendants of slaves who have never truly benefited from integration and who have never benefited from affirmative action and other programs designed to help. There are countless people who are living in situations that we would all find despicable and almost inhumane . . .

"And if you think about that," he says, "whatever you think about reparations, if you think about a remedy that solves the problem of the poorest of the poor, that's not a black remedy, that's an American remedy." Ogletree pursues legal remedies "because nothing else seems to work. It's not the choice of first resort; it is indeed the choice of last resort."[3]

After more than three hundred years of slavery and racial oppression, black people found themselves at a distinct disadvantage compared to whites in terms of material assets, education, skills, dignity, and the ability to pursue life, liberty, and happiness. The residual effect today is the persistent overall disparity between the races. Like it or not, we have what Harold Fields calls a "plumbing problem." The basic infrastructure of our society is damaged. We have chosen to keep it buried like a leaking sewer pipe under the house hoping no one will notice, rather than commit to the hard work of repair.

The United States government should fully acknowledge its past harmful actions and state its future intent. It should say something to this effect: Our predecessors supported and codified slavery and the race-based inequities that followed. Certain present-day policies perpetuate social stratification. We are sorry, and we are going to repair the system.

Awareness begins with education. Overcoming the legacy of slavery will involve modifying textbooks and retooling the way history is taught in schools. This will take a commitment to move beyond the tokenism of Black History Month and update curriculums to more accurately portray what went into the creation, expansion, and continued sustenance of our nation. As our Family of Ten discovered, it is far more than the sanitized stories of the few great white men we're all familiar with.

For those who are no longer in school, innumerable opportunities for education are available. A wide variety of books reflecting a broader perspective on U.S. and world history, the legacy of slavery, and the very human impact of privilege, power, and racism have been written in the recent past. White people who haven't already done so can broaden their awareness by partaking of the plethora of works written by black authors. Many powerful films have also been made, from little-known documentary gems to big-budget Hollywood movies.

In 2003, the U.S. government authorized construction of the National Museum of African American History and Culture in Washington, D.C. In January 2006, a prominent site on the National Mall, adjacent to the Washington Memorial, was selected for the museum. I look forward to the day, in my lifetime, when I will enter that museum with my grandchildren and witness with them how our nation has finally, albeit belatedly, chosen to honor the contributions African Americans have made to our country, in the same hallowed ground upon which we honor war veterans, George Washington, Thomas Jefferson, and Abraham Lincoln.

The U.S. National Slavery Museum will be built in Fredericksburg, Virginia, at an estimated cost of $200 million, and is projected to open in late 2008. Major investments in museums like these, which fill in some of the important missing pieces in the public's vision of our nation's history, are long overdue.

When confronted by Juanita in Ghana about whether he had fully overcome his own racism, Dain replied with his concern that racism is part of the human condition. "I don't think it can all ever be shed. What I can do is move how I interact with people beyond where I used to be, and embrace them."

One important step is for white people to examine our own attitudes for remnants of racism. The process will vary depending upon one's background. Opportunities exist for black and white Americans to meet together, closely examine racism as it exists today in the United States—and within each of us individually—and establish, or deepen, relationships. Most of us white folks have a range of other issues to work through that prevent progress: guilt, shame, defensiveness, and fear. Organizations such as Crossroads Ministry, the National Coalition Building Institute, the People's Institute for Survival and Beyond, and many others offer workshops and training throughout the United States in antiracism and racial reconciliation. Schools, churches, foundations, and other community groups can, and should, provide increased opportunities for people to gather together and work toward transformation.

In recounting my journey with nine distant cousins, my intent is to stimulate both reflection and serious conversation. There are no simple answers. But if we don't confront these challenging issues, we will resolve nothing.

We are better than we sometimes imagine, and we are not yet all we are capable of becoming. We can remain mired in the mistrust, avoidance, and the distance inherited from previous generations and pass them on to our descendants—or we can commit ourselves to becoming aware, to listening to each other's stories, embracing the truth, and recognizing and honoring each other's humanity. In doing so, we will finally break through the scars to clean the living wound properly and begin the healing . . . together.

Acknowledgments

When walking through a door for the first time, you never know exactly where crossing that threshold will lead. Such was the case when Lindi and I entered Katrina Browne's apartment in Berkeley in February 2001. I had no idea I would end up so far from where I thought my life was then headed. I am forever grateful to Katrina for her vision and persistence in creating *Traces of the Trade: A Story from the Deep North*, and including me in this powerful journey.

Katrina and I committed ourselves from the beginning to dedicate profits generated from the film and this book to overcoming racism and other forms of systemic inequity that exist in the United States and elsewhere.

My Family of Ten—Katrina, Keila DePoorter, Holly Fulton, Elly Hale, Ledlie Laughlin, Dain Perry, James Perry, Jim Perry, and Elizabeth Sturges Llerena—has truly become my family. We laughed, cried, screamed, pouted, learned, and grew together. Each read an earlier draft of this book and provided valuable insights and suggestions that improved the manuscript greatly.

The support team for our journey couldn't have been better.

While space limitations prevent me from mentioning them all here, I am particularly thankful to those who traveled with us throughout Rhode Island, Ghana, and Cuba: Jude Ray, Liz Dory, Jeff Livesey, and Juanita Brown. Special thanks to Juanita for reading, and offering wise counsel on, my manuscript. Thanks also to Elizabeth Delude-Dix, Lucia Small, Allison Humenuk, Darcie Moore, and Zena Link. I am grateful to Catherine Benedict for her warm friendship, and to Alla Kovgan, Renaissance woman extraordinaire, for too many blessings to mention—other than to say thanks for introducing me to the calming influence of bubble tea.

My knowledge of the slave trade and the legacy of slavery was greatly enhanced by the wisdom shared by the many historians and experts whose names appear throughout the text. Thanks to Peggy McIntosh for granting permission to quote from her article "White Privilege: Unpacking the Invisible Knapsack."

Our journey was enriched by the participation of our international film crews. In Ghana, thanks to Africanus Aveh, Kofi Peprah, Amishadai Sacketey, Ebenezer Quaye, Francis Kpatah, Farouk Amenumey, Joyce Osei Owusu, and Abiko Banchi Eghagha. Thanks to Eric Manu for his continuing friendship and inspiration. In Cuba, thanks to Boris Iván Crespo, Santiago Llapur, Ariam R. Grass, Ricardo Pérez Ramos, Luís Manuel Escuela, Ovideo Gastón, María Teresa "Tete" Ortega, Lisa Maria Cabrera, and Raúl Izquierdo.

In Bristol, Nancy Abercrombie graciously opened her home, and her heart, to me and Ledlie. St. Michael's Episcopal Church welcomed and assisted *Traces of the Trade*. Thanks to interim rector David Dobbins for assistance in my research. Bristol Historical and Preservation Society generously provided us access to documents as well as "headquarters" space.

Thanks to my old youth minister, Dick Wing, for his lifelong friendship and inspiration, and to the members of First Community Church of Columbus Ohio, especially Paula Russell, Kate and Steve

Shaner, Barb and Terry Davis, and Sandy Pfening, for opening your homes to the *Traces* team when we attended the Episcopal Church General Convention in June 2006.

In Bend, Oregon, thank you to Eileen Lock for her wise counsel. Bonnie Baker transcribed dozens of hours of audiotapes, and Kevin Raichl, Jon Ash, Mario Huerta, Susan Ross, and Jean Wood joined me in my home for an extensive conversation on race and oppression during the summer of 2002, only to have it be left on the cutting-room floor of both the film and the book. Our conversation exists between the lines on these pages. Thank you to Myrlie Evers Williams for her friendship, wisdom, and inspiration.

The participants in Coming to the Table (www.comingtothe table.org) provide a constant source of inspiration. My life has been enriched by my inclusion in this powerful group of descendants of slave owners, slave traders, and the enslaved, who trust that by confronting the legacy of slavery, and our connections to it, we will help the healing begin. Howard Zehr was an integral part of our first gathering and continues to inspire me with his deep knowledge of, and commitment to, the principles of restorative justice.

Thanks to Dominic LaRusso, Cornelia Barnhart, Randall Beth Platt, Don Clarkson, and Mike Dooley for support and inspiration and to Marty Linsky for showing me the view from the balcony. Thanks to Jim Bailey for reminding me of the true meaning of ministry.

Two people had a profound influence in leading me to Katrina Browne, and in the writing of this book. My aunt, Wilna Rose De-Wolf Gellert (1917–2004), first told me about the genealogy book *Charles D'Wolf of Guadaloupe* and inspired me to research our family history, which led me fifteen years later to my fifth cousin twice removed, Halsey DeWolf Howe (1921–2007). I love you both, and miss you a great deal.

I owe a debt of gratitude to many others in the writing of this book. Above all, Deborah Howe and Mary Howe devoted tremendous effort and time over several years and drafts—thanks also to Mary for designing the family tree; your father would be proud—leading to a manuscript and book proposal that piqued the interest of my agent and my editor. Several people generously donated their time to read that manuscript. Thank you to Patty Bonner, Hoby Cook, Myrna Cook, Harold Fields, Jan Henrikson, Mwansa Mandela, Constance Perry, Allison Taylor, L. David Taylor, and Debbie Truscott for your valuable input. Thanks to Chuck Collins for his encouragement and assistance with my book proposal. Thanks especially to Lauren Abramo, my agent at Dystel & Goderich Literary Management, for her love of books and her belief that someone would publish this one.

I extend eternal gratitude to Beacon Press for providing the perfect home for my book. My editor, Gayatri Patnaik, made me feel like I was the only author she was working with. Her insight, scrupulous care, and inspiration resulted in the most satisfying and productive experience I could imagine. Thanks to Helene Atwan, Tom Hallock, Pamela MacColl, Leah Riviere, Lisa Sacks, Sarah Gillis, and Tracy Ahlquist for making me feel so welcome at Beacon Press, and for their dedication to its mission. Thanks to my copyeditor, Rosalie Wieder, whose attention to detail is exceptional.

Though not educated as a historian, I've done my best to document facts and present them in a logical and accurate manner. Thanks to Katrina Browne and James Perry for their additional research and fact checking. Any errors that remain are entirely my own. Some names and details have been altered for reasons of privacy or narrative flow.

Finally, to my parents, Giles and Nancy DeWolf, thank you for your love and support. To my children, Shiloh, Emily, Russell, and Jolie, may your grandchildren inherit a healthier, less racist world. And to Lindi, my life's partner and best friend: you stood by me every moment, not only when I participated in the original international journey, but during my subsequent extended trips to New England, and the endless hours I spent alone with my manuscript. My favorite moment each day is when I first open my eyes and see you lying next to me. Here's to our next adventure together.

CHAPTER 1

GROWING UP WHITE

1. Captain John DeWolf, *A Voyage to the North Pacific* (Fairfield, WA: Ye Galleon Press, 1998), introduction, p. G, and preface, pp. iii–iv.

CHAPTER 3

"SO LET ALL THINE ENEMIES PERISH, O LORD!"

1. George Howe, *Mount Hope: A New England Chronicle* (New York: Viking Press, 1959). Historical events not otherwise documented in this chapter come from *Mount Hope*, pp. 20–96.

2. My search for any single acceptable identifying term proved inconclusive, so when not identifying a specific tribe, such as the Wampanoag, I use "American Indian," "Indian," or "indigenous" interchangeably to identify the people who populated North America prior to the arrival of Europeans. Similarly, I use "African American," "black people," and "black folks," as well as "European American," "white people," and "white folks." Labels are sensitive and complicated and I've tried to be consistent and respectful in my use of identifying terms.

3. Nathaniel Philbrick, *Mayflower: A Story of Courage, Community, and War* (New York: Viking, 2006), pp. 48–49.

4. Alan Gallay, *The Indian Slave Trade: The Rise of the English Empire in the American South, 1670–1717* (New Haven, CT: Yale University Press, 2002), pp. 294–99.

5. Dee Brown, *Bury My Heart at Wounded Knee: An Indian History of the American West* (New York: Holt, Rinehart & Winston, 1970), p. 3.

6. Howe, *Mount Hope,* p. 44.

7. Philbrick, *Mayflower,* pp. xv, 332.

8. Howe, *Mount Hope,* p. 55.

9. Ibid., p. 93.

10. Plimoth Plantation website, www.plimoth.org.

CHAPTER 4

THE GREAT FOLKS

1. Peggy McIntosh, "White Privilege: Unpacking the Invisible Knapsack," *Peace and Freedom*, July/August 1989, pp. 10–12. Originally "White Privilege and Male Privilege: A Personal Account of Coming to See Correspondences through Work in Women's Studies," Working Paper No. 124 (Wellesley, MA: Wellesley College Center for Research on Women, 1988).

2. Howe, *Mount Hope*, pp. 70–96.

3. Jay Coughtry, *The Notorious Triangle: Rhode Island and the African Slave Trade 1700–1807* (Philadelphia: Temple University Press, 1981), pp. 6–7, 47–49.

4. Edgar Stanton Maclay, *A History of American Privateers* (New York: Appleton & Co., 1899), pp. 11–14.

5. Howe, *Mount Hope*, p. 168.

6. Charles Rappleye, *Sons of Providence: The Brown Brothers, the Slave Trade, and the American Revolution* (New York: Simon & Schuster, 2006), p. 248.

7. Coughtry, *Notorious Triangle*, p. 235.

8. Howe, *Mount Hope*, p. 124.

9. Reverend Calbraith B. Perry, *Charles D'Wolf of Guadaloupe, his Ancestors and Descendants* (New York: Press of T. A. Wright, 1902), p. 127.

10. Howe, *Mount Hope*, p. 127.

11. Ibid., p. 128.

CHAPTER 5

"I TREMBLE FOR MY COUNTRY ..."

1. Joanne Pope Melish, *Disowning Slavery: Gradual Emancipation and "Race" in New England, 1780–1860* (Ithaca, NY: Cornell University Press, 1998), p. 76.

2. Rappleye, *Sons of Providence*, pp. 253–54, 289.

3. "Declaring Independence: Drafting the Documents," Library of Congress, www.loc.gov/exhibits/declara/ruffdrft.html, Julian P. Boyd, ed.,

The Papers of Thomas Jefferson, Vol. 1, 1760–1776 (Princeton, NJ: Princeton University Press, 1950), pp. 243–47.

4. Howe, *Mount Hope*, pp. 202–205.

5. Ibid., pp. 229–30.

CHAPTER 6

AKWAABA

1. Adam Hochschild, *King Leopold's Ghost: A Story of Greed, Terror, and Heroism in Colonial Africa* (Boston: Houghton Mifflin, 1998), pp. 9–10.

CHAPTER 7

"UNDER A PATCHWORK OF SCARS"

1. David McCullough, *John Adams* (New York: Simon & Schuster, 2001), p. 131.

2. James Pope-Hennessy, *Sins of the Fathers: A Study of the Atlantic Slave Traders 1441–1807* (New York: Barnes & Noble Books, 1998), p. 8.

3. David Eltis, "The Volume and Structure of the Transatlantic Slave Trade: A Reassessment," *William and Mary Quarterly*, 58:1 (2001), p. 1.

CHAPTER 8

THE DOOR OF NO RETURN

1. William St. Clair, *The Door of No Return: The History of Cape Coast Castle and the Atlantic Slave Trade* (New York: Blue Bridge, 2007), p. 1.

2. Roger S. Gocking, *The History of Ghana* (Westport, CT: Greenwood Press, 2005), p. 26.

3. John Reader, *Africa: A Biography of the Continent* (New York: Alfred A. Knopf, 1998), pp. 430–31.

4. Gocking, *History of Ghana*, pp. 30–46.

5. Thomas Pakenham, *The Scramble for Africa: The White Man's*

Conquest of the Dark Continent from 1876 to 1912 (New York: Random House, 1991), pp. 19, 581–82, 670–79.

6. Gocking, *History of Ghana*, pp. 37–41.
7. Ibid., pp. 46–47.
8. Reader, *Africa*, pp. 626–27.
9. Gocking, *History of Ghana*, p. 1.
10. Ibid., pp. 178–79, 189–90, 207–12, 250–54.

CHAPTER 11

THE MIDDLE PASSAGE

1. Robert Harms, *The Diligent: A Voyage Through the Worlds of the Slave Trade* (New York: Basic Books, 2002), p. 303.
2. Coughtry, *Notorious Triangle*, pp. 6–7. (Over seventy-five years of the Rhode Island slave trade, 934 voyages brought approximately 106,000 Africans for an average of 113.)
3. Ibid., p. 6.
4. Eltis, "Volume and Structure," p. 8.
5. Coughtry, *Notorious Triangle*, pp. 146, 154–55.
6. Captain Theodore Canot, *Adventures of an African Slaver* (New York: World Publishing, 1942), p. 107.
7. Harms, *The Diligent*, pp. 249–50.
8. Olaudah Equiano, *The Interesting Narrative of the Life of Olaudah Equiano, or Gustavus Vassa, the African* (London, 1789). Quotes and descriptions from chaps. 1 and 2.
9. Milton Meltzer, *Slavery: A World History*, Vol. 2 (Cambridge, MA: Da Capo Press, 1993), p. 46.
10. Coughtry, *Notorious Triangle*, pp. 145–48.
11. Ibid., pp. 145–46.
12. Ibid., pp. 150–51.

CHAPTER 12

LA HABANA

1. Jaime Suchlicki, *Cuba: From Columbus to Castro and Beyond*, 4th ed. (Washington, DC: Brassey's, 1997), p. 19.
2. Aviva Chomsky, Barry Carr, and Pamela Maria Smorkaloff, eds.,

The Cuba Reader (Durham, NC: Duke University Press, 2003),
pp. 12–13.

3. Eric Williams, From Columbus to Castro: The History of the
   Caribbean, 1492–1969 (New York: Vintage Books, 1970), p. 121.

4. Chomsky, Carr, and Smorkaloff, Cuba Reader, p. 37.

5. Williams, From Columbus to Castro, p. 312.

6. Chomsky, Carr, and Smorkaloff, Cuba Reader, p. 37.

7. Suchlicki, Cuba: From Columbus to Castro, p. 61.

8. Williams, From Columbus to Castro, pp. 361–363.

9. Ibid., pp. 409–10.

10. Suchlicki, Cuba: From Columbus to Castro, p. 48.

11. Ibid., pp. 68–72.

12. Chomsky, Carr, and Smorkaloff, Cuba Reader, p. 122.

13. Suchlicki, Cuba: From Columbus to Castro, p. 80.

14. Williams, From Columbus to Castro, pp. 420–21.

15. Chomsky, Carr, and Smorkaloff, Cuba Reader, pp. 143–45.

16. Suchlicki, Cuba: From Columbus to Castro, pp. 113–20.

17. Williams, From Columbus to Castro, p. 480.

18. "Carnival," Encyclopedia Britannica Online, www.britannica.com/
    eb/article-9020411.

CHAPTER 14
ARCA DE NOÉ

1. Perry, Charles D'Wolf, pp. 38, 136.

2. Joseph Goodwin, Jr., diary, BV Goodwin, reel 20 microfilm (1820–27),
   New York Historical Society.

3. Howe, Mount Hope, pp. 192, 201–206.

4. Ibid., p. 235.

CHAPTER 16
MY HARVARD EDUCATION

1. Chris Barker, "DA says DeWolf groped two women; no charges,"
   The Bulletin (Bend, OR), October 19, 2005, p. 1.

2. Cindy Powers, "Reluctant woman influenced DA's decision,"
   The Bulletin, October 19, 2005, p. 1.

CHAPTER 17

REPAIRING THE BREACH

1. Melish, *Disowning Slavery*, p. 17.

2. Julia E. Randle, "The Economic Benefit of Slavery to the Episcopal Church in Virginia," *Center Aisle*, Issue 2, June 14, 2006 (pub. by Diocese of Virginia), www.centeraisle.net/editorial2-1.html.

3. Howard Zehr, *The Little Book of Restorative Justice* (Intercourse, PA: Good Books, 2002), pp. 3–18.

4. Opinions regarding the reasons the "slavery atonement" resolutions passed at the 2006 General Convention of the Episcopal Church of the United States were provided by Jo Ann B. Jones, co-chair of the Social Justice and Urban Affairs Committee, the Rev. Canon Edward W. Rodman, professor at Episcopal Divinity School, and the Rev. Dr. Ian T. Douglas, chair of deputies of the Diocese of Massachusetts and professor at Episcopal Divinity School.

5. Aaron Lazare, *On Apology* (New York: Oxford University Press, 2004), pp. 41–42.

6. "Descendents Gather to Heal Wounds of Slavery," story by Nancy Marshall Genzer, *News & Notes* (March 1, 2006), NPR, www.npr .org/templates/story/story.php?storyId=5239251.

AFTERWORD

1. "Major Issues: Reparations," Rep. John Conyers's website, www.house.gov/conyers/news_reparations.htm.

2. Roy L. Brooks, *Atonement and Forgiveness: A New Model for Black Reparations* (Berkeley, CA: University of California Press, 2004), preface, pp. x–xi.

3. Katrina Browne, Dain Perry, James Perry, and Jim Perry met with Professor Charles Ogletree in his office at Harvard University during the summer of 2002 for a filmed interview regarding his role with the Reparations Coordinating Committee, his views on reparations for slavery, and other issues related to the legacy of slavery. Portions of the interview appear in Katrina Browne's documentary film of our journey, *Traces of the Trade*.